MURDA', MISOGYNY, AND MAYHEM

Hip-Hop and the Culture of Abnormality in the Urban Community

Zoe Spencer

University Press of America,® Inc.
Lanham · Boulder · New York · Toronto · Plymouth, UK

Copyright © 2011 by
University Press of America,® Inc.
4501 Forbes Boulevard
Suite 200
Lanham, Maryland 20706
UPA Acquisitions Department (301) 459-3366

Estover Road
Plymouth PL6 7PY
United Kingdom

All rights reserved

British Library Cataloging in Publication Information Available

Library of Congress Control Number: 2011924260
ISBN: 978-0-7618-5512-5 (paperback : alk. paper)
eISBN: 978-0-7618-5513-2

*This book is dedicated to my son,
Olando ReChaud Spencer and
Chaquena Bell—my constants.
And to all of my students at
Cheyney University who served as the
inspiration for manifesting this work
and my students at Virginia State
who have reaped the consequences of this work.*

TABLE OF CONTENTS

ACKNOWLEDGMENTS		VII
FOREWORD		IX
PREFACE		XI
INTRODUCTION		XVII
CHAPTER 1	UNDERSTANDING HEGEMONY	1
CHAPTER 2	THE MEDIA AS A HEGEMONIC TOOL	7
CHAPTER 3	THE HISTORY OF AFRICAN AMERICANS IN MAINSTREAM FILM: A SOCIOPOLITICAL AND HISTORIC ANALYSIS	11
CHAPTER 4	THREE DOLLARS AND SIX DIMES 360°	81
CHAPTER 5	CRITIQUING THE GAME: RAPPIN' MURDA, MISOGYNY, AND MAYHEM	99
CHAPTER 6	INTERNALIZING THE LIE: THE PSYCHO-SOCIAL RAMIFICATIONS OF "KEEPING IT REAL"	117
CHAPTER 7	WHAT DOES HIP-HOP HAVE TO DO WITH AMADOU DIALLO AND SEAN BELL?	129
CHAPTER 8	THE ROOTS: BURIED UNDERGROUND AND NEO-SOUL	137
CHAPTER 9	BLACK CONSCIOUSNESS, BLACK POWER	141
CHAPTER 10	CONCLUSION	151
BIBLIOGRAPHY		155

ACKNOWLEDGMENTS

I would like to give due to the Creator first and foremost for the gift of inquiry and verse. Many take for granted the ability to seek knowledge, learn, articulate, write, compose—but we should all remember that the ability to do those things is a gift that should never be minimized or taken for granted. So . . . Thank You God for the gift.

I would like to again thank my students at Cheyney University who served as not only the inspiration for this book, but allowed me to both knowingly and unknowingly use their classes and experiences as the springboard for the sowing and cultivation of the ideas and theories that are *reaped in* this book.

I would like to thank my colleague, Vanessa Brantley, for her continued support and encouragement throughout this process. I would like to thank Alexis Davis for her cover photography and my student models: Chatel Allen, Efuru Ballantyne, and CJ Sivels. You all brought my vision of the struggle and hopefully the contents of this work alive.

I would like to thank my "extended family" in Glen Jean, West Virginia for giving me the space/place that I needed to focus and finally complete this work.

And I would like to thank several of my mentors: Dr. Walda Katz Fishman and Dr. Ralph Gomes for instilling the theory and method in me so deeply that it has become a part of my essence. And my newest mentor, Dr. Molefi Asante for his guidance, support, and encouragement on this work, and especially for his pointed foreword.

To my son, my future daughter in law, my future grandchildren, and the current and future generations of my people, this work is for you—may it contribute to your consciousness—and be an encouragement toward greater levels of self and collective realization, actualization, and resistance to that which contributes to our own destruction.

Foreword

Zoe Spencer announces to us in her new book, *Murda', Misogyny, and Mayhem: Hip-Hop and the Culture of Abnormality in the Urban Community* that we are our own saviors as we have sometimes been our own destroyers. This is a timely work because it speaks directly to the state of the African-American community and goes to the heart of the popular cultural form that is most responsible for the decline in respect, dignity, linguistic propriety, and morality. I know, as does Spencer, that what ails the Black community cannot be resolved by a single vaccine; it will take a vast array of social and cultural medicines to cure the psychic disease that has poisoned so many of our young minds.

We have arrived at a point in our history where the struggles for civil and human rights seem far in the past and our children have forgotten or have never heard the narratives of distress that sent our most courageous young people into the streets seeking justice. Now we are playing catch up in an effort to introduce the descendants of the victorious ones to the reasons for their leisure, their ease, their happy-go-luckiness, their don't give a damn attitudes about the martyrs of the past. This should have never happened inasmuch as there have been no greater heroic battles fought for human dignity than the ones our ancestors led against slavery, segregation, bias, racism, and racial discrimination.

Enter a generation of Hip-Hop artists who have betrayed and who have been betrayed by the society. They are the children of the ones who forgot to teach them the cultural and historical values that made African Americans symbols of freedom and justice for the entire world.

Zoe Spencer might be considered a prophet or a seer because she clearly understands what has happened to our children and she sees more profoundly than most intellectuals the necessity for correction, discipline, and straight talking. For example, she writes that "each song tells the same story as if it is the only story of the community—my community—as if there is just one story, one group of people who are all the same—making us all believe that if we are not what they say we should be, doing what *they* say we should do, then we are not keeping it real—*we* are not from the hood." But as everyone who reads this valuable book knows Dr. Spencer is from Barry Farms Projects and you cannot get any more hood than that. Yet as she writes and as I know from growing up in the various hoods of Georgia and Tennessee everyone in the hood was not walking on the wrong side of ethics, morality and decency. Indeed, at one time it was real to work on the brothers or sisters who would use curse words in front of someone's mother. All these things have changed over the years because we have allowed our youth to teach when in fact they should have been learning from the elders.

The question that Zoe Spencer's work deals with is the content of the teaching. What is it that our children should know and why is it that they are not learning it? The answer is ultimately placed at the feet of the elders because we have not figured out a way to deliver the message of cultural esteem and historical accuracy to a generation that has been lost in the wilderness of individuality, self destruction, misogynist and anti-Black rhetoric. Spencer comes to this subject with the sharp scalpel of a keen observer and a participant in the searches and discoveries of a generation in the throes of forgetfulness. She will not let us forget our historical experiences and she challenges the young African Americans who have been looking for a new way out of the subtle yet numbing culture of personal narcissism.

What is needed at this moment and in this time is an education that roots out the last vestiges of self-hatred, negative images of African people, and the degrading attitudes about Black women. It is not enough to be discontented with the situation; we must all understand and appreciate the intense focus of Spencer's work as she unravels the tangles of nihilism in order to advance a more Afrocentric, that is, agency understanding of our challenge. Africans must rise up and throw off all forms of ridicule, ethical instability, and mental oppression which lead to mentacide and mental illness. We cannot allow our communities and the communities of Africans throughout the world, now that the Internet and satellites have put the media messages of Black America all over the world, to be hampered, hindered, and shut down because of the poor judgment of money makers.

Marcus Garvey was correct when he declared that we could do what we will. The question one asks after reading this insightful book by Zoe Spencer is, "Do we have the will to do what we will?" I have to answer that question in the affirmative because now more than ever I know that there are many readers who share the ideas expressed in this important book. It will become a standard in its field. I am quite pleased to be able to write this foreword to Zoe Spencer's book, *Murda, Misogyny, and Mayhem: Hip-Hop and the Culture of Abnormality in the Urban Community*.

Molefi Kete Asante, author of *The History of Africa*

PREFACE

I must preface this work by stating that this book is not designed to be a Rap or Hip-Hop bashing session. Although, I am sure that it will be interpreted that way. This book has been a labor of love—because I, truly, *used* to love Hip-Hop.

I remember being in gym class in the 8th grade—doing the hustle to the sounds of Sugar Hill Gangs "Rappers Delight." I nurtured the development of my social and political consciousness to the sounds of Public Enemy, KRS One, and The Queen (Latifah). I remember standing in front of the mirror *trying* to mimic Janet Jackson's dance routines, as I empowered myself against the rise in misogynistic lyrics and the sexual objectification of women, as I shouted, "Nasteee boys don't mean a thing. . . . Nastee uhhh . . . Ms. Spencer if you nasty." In essence, I grew up and developed—to Hip-Hop.

I respected the origin, the struggle, the message, and the beat, even when there was no message—*"the Hip-Hop."* You know what I'm talking about. I loved Hip-Hop because it emerged from my people. It was created, developed, and controlled by my people—real people who had a pulse that flowed from the heart of the community—because they flowed from the heart of the community. Not the middle class intelligentsia or academicians who were attempting to make a name for themselves by analyzing the problems in/of an inner city from which they were often far removed, or even far removing themselves from the inner city from where they came. Hip-Hop was the voice of the brothers and sisters who may have otherwise been written off—whose voices may have otherwise never been heard. It was a *true* and *real* reflection of the culture, experiences, and location of a people who created a new and distinct art form, and a venue to tell their stories, or simply—be heard.

When Rap music emerged in the late 1970s with DJ Kool Herc, Afrika Bambaataa, and then Grandmaster Flash, Melle Mel, and Kurtis Blow, it was first ignored and then harshly criticized. The critics argued that "It was just a passing fad with no artistic merit." So the mainstream media did not give it "the time of day." Ask anyone who grew up "in that time," the powers that be, which included the music industry as well as governmental/political forces, never believed that Rap would last beyond a few years, and hoped that it didn't.

It was an era when artists and street promoters were "truly" and literally selling cassette tapes out of the trunks of cars, and off of tables set up at community based shows and block parties. It was an era where outside of those venues, consumers could only purchase Rap music from the neighborhood "Mom and Pop" record stores because it was not being promoted and/or distributed by the major labels and distribution companies, hence, not being sold in major record stores.

But, contrary to the assertions of the critics, Rap didn't die. Hip-Hop didn't die. Instead it grew and quickly became a powerful, profitable, and an "uncontrolled/unregulated" force in the urban community. It was also quickly "seeping" into middle class, suburban communities. Especially in the 1980s, during the harsh Reagan era, when Public Enemy and other socio politically conscious and "rebel" artists, such as N.W.A. began to challenge not only the system, but the consciousness of the masses, with songs like *Fight the Power* and *Fuck the Police*.

Yes, out of the "grass roots" support and energy of the people, the community, Black radio, independent labels, Black owned record stores, and then Black Entertainment Television and other independent "community cable" networks, artists were able to sell thousands, even hundreds of thousands, of records without the support of major labels. And while it may not have been as financially lucrative for the artist, being outside of the control and direction of "the majors" allowed a level of creative and lyrical freedom that kept "the game true"—true to the diversity of the community.

But that "truth" would be short lived because once the major labels recognized how profitable and powerful "Hip-Hop," as a culture, had become on a grass roots level, they realized the large scale financial potential of this new genre—this subculture. And the large-scale potential was that with major financial backing and aggressive promotional campaigns, "Rap or Hip-Hop," as an industry, could be extremely profitable. But more importantly all entities realized that if the majors could harness the Rap industry, they would also ultimately gain control over the collective content and presentation of the craft and the culture.

In essence, by gaining control over the messenger, the label would be able to ultimately control the message, because that *is* what happens when "you sign." "The contract" represents the company's control over and ownership of the entire image—hence, the body, the voice, the content and the creative capacity of the artist. The artist becomes the property of the label, and anything that is created under that contract is done under the direction of the label and remains property of the label—period.

So, like a group of eager pimps, major labels began to court and vie for existing rappers and search for new artists to fill the demand for the new cultural/musical genre, Hip-Hop. And Hip-Hop artists quickly obliged—opting to sell their control over their content, creativity, publishing rights, and higher percentages of record sales, for menial and recoupable advances and quick mass publicity. Consequently, real Hip-Hop was quickly suppressed and buried 6 feet *"underground"* (Nas, Tribe, The Roots, and on and on). And, with a one two punch, gangsta/thug Rap with its consistent themes of murda', misogyny, and mayhem knocked Hip-Hop "the fuck out" and took over the title.

Since the "welcomed" abduction of the artists, the market has quickly become over saturated with a collective of self proclaimed "niggas," "dawgs," "bitches," and "hoes" who really believe that they have control over their content and presentation—a group of people who have chosen to sell their bodies, talent, and souls for the material gain that they brag about (and we so readily consume)—a group of people that have made being from the neighborhood a negative and homogenous experience—a group of people that have made sex, "phat asses," money, drugs, hustling, and murder "normal" and "good"—or even more importantly respected, idolized, and viewed as something that people should aspire to do and be—all in the name of "reppin' da hood," "reppin' the culture."

Now . . . each song tells the exact same story, as if it is the only story of the community—as if there is just one story about one group of people who are all the same—making us all believe that if we are not what they say we should be, doing what *they* say we should do, then we are not keeping it real—*we* are not from the "hood."

But, I am from "da hood," Southeast Washington D.C. to be exact—Barry Farms Projects. I grew up in and around, and remained close to "the hood" all of my life. And I know for a fact that everybody in Barry Farms did not sell drugs when I was growing up there, or when my "church loving, God fearing" grandmother was raising her five children and three grandchildren there—totting them to Bethlehem Baptist every other day. There were (and still are) working class people living in the projects across this nation—who struggled and worked hard to make sure they stayed afloat and provided a safe and decent life for their families.

I never had to come in the house before the street lights came on in the summer for fear of being shot when I was young. The ice cream truck even came around at night and the truck was not a mobile drug distribution site either (at least not that I would ever have known). Yet and still, the fact that most in the neighborhood were *not* involved in criminal activities did not magically change their living arrangements—the "real estate" they were forced to live on. They were *from* the neighborhood.

Think about it, I will bet that few, if any, of these Rap artists mothers even considered dropping it like it's hot at the shakey shake club to provide for them. I will also bet that many were not happy with either the criminal/deviant activities that their sons were involved in, or completely at ease with their celebrations of such in their songs.

The stories of getting ass whoopin's from six people for breaking someone's window because you were throwing rocks when the neighbor told you to stop—communal discipline for simple little kid mischief—did not emerge from/in the middle class neighborhoods. Community parenting and policing emerged in the inner city—in "da hood." Deviance, or being bad, was not favored "in da hood." The Dope dealers, crooks, wife beaters, whores, and fiends weren't respected in the neighborhood, they were labeled and ostracized.

There was even a time, not so long ago, when getting pregnant young and unwed was something to be avoided or embarrassed about "after the fact"—and a time when no girl would ever admit she wasn't a virgin and would lie "on God" before *ever* admitting having performed oral sex (even if she did), much less brag about being able to swallow a coke bottle. These things were never normal and acceptable identities in the neighborhood. There was a time when being called a bitch, a ho or whore, nigger, or dope fiend almost always resulted in conflict because they were all "fighting words" because no one wanted to be perceived, much less stigmatized or labeled in such a manner.

Moral standards, family bonds, love, education, respect, honor, legitimacy, and normalcy were not characteristics that were foreign to those who resided in the inner city, or reserved for middle class Blacks who were "just acting or trying to act White," because morals and values have never been exclusive to other races or classes of people. Most had those characteristics in "da hood." The embrace and promotion of the "culture of abnormality" is only a new phenomenon that emerged in the late 1960s and 1970s with the passage of the Civil Rights Act, the exodus, separation, and ideological assimilation of the Black Middle Class, the subsequent deconstruction of the Black Power Movement through COINTELPRO, the introduction of Blaxploitation films, and the Heroine and LSD trade which then transitioned into the 1980s "crackedemic" which widely promotes the destruction of the family, loss of property and community revenue, accelerated incarceration, and an increase in murder rates in the inner city.

So, contrary to the statement "I'm so hood, I wear my pants below my waist . . . and you ain't hood if ya don't know what I'm talking 'bout . . . " I *am* from the hood and I while I do know what *"you're"* talking about, I do not wear my pants below my waist. I went to school, got decent grades, participated in activities, was scared to curse at or disrespect my teachers, did not use or sell drugs, went to college, was one of the first young ones to walk around pregnant at 19 on Howard University's campus—had my son at 20, worked harder to finish school and raise my son as a single parent, got a Masters and ultimately got a Ph.D.—as many Black folks from the hood have. And nothing but a different frame of reference—a different state of mind—different expectations—and a higher level of consciousness—led me down a legitimate path.

Yet, unlike many who *do* forget, or want to deny where they come from once they "believe" they have arrived because they have successfully assimilated into mainstream society, none of my accomplishments will *ever* change my origin—my alpha—my genesis—my birth and evolution. None of my accomplishments will ever make me detach from the continued struggle of my people. Being from the inner city will *never* be something that I will *ever* minimize, negate, hide, or dismiss as my reality—because it is, in fact, my reality.

So, I also have a right to speak to "my peoples." And I will not let others who *"profess"* that they are from the hood define or dictate what I say. Neither will I let those who "profess" that they are professionals define how I say it. No one can define what *my* reality should be, so I will never internalize someone else's version of it. So, in writing this verse, I will write with clear conscience in my praise and criticism because by embracing where I've been and where I am, no one could ever make me feel guilty or detached, or justify calling me a "sell out" because I knew that being from the inner city did *not* mean that I *had* to conform to criminality, hyper sexuality, dysfunction, or deviance . . . or that being a "professional" meant that I had to deny my cultural roots.

Just like the hustler, I, too, am from the hood, and proud of it! Say it loud! JUST LIKE THE HUSTLER, I TOO AM FROM THE HOOD AND PROUD OF IT! Yet, this version of "hoodstory," has not been told in the verses and hooks that oversaturate the airwaves. And perhaps—it has not been told for a reason.

So sadly, just like a deteriorating relationship, there comes a time when it becomes self destructive to continue to support and nurture something that has become counterproductive, and even detrimental, to one's being. There comes a time when reminiscing on how good it used to be, or declining to ask why it has become so bad, serves no other purpose than to enable and even promote the negativity by encouraging the disillusion that either it doesn't matter or will get better. But it must be addressed because it does matter and it's getting worse. There comes a time when sitting quietly and not challenging the ill becomes just as bad as being the ills soldier—carrying out "ill's will." So the truth must be told.

The reality is that the memories of how things used to be in Hip-Hop have no bearing on what and how it is now. And right now, what they call "Hip-Hop" is a lie. It hates me, abuses me, hates and abuses itself and others. It abuses the concept of brother and sisterhood, Black identity, Black love, true love, real relationships foundations, the Black body, family, Black life and death, Black babies—and the Black community (the place where it was born). It no longer reflects me, but has inevitably become a reflection of me.

Right now, Hip-Hop is not good for me. So, I have to walk—no—run away. But, before I go, I am letting Hip-Hop know why I'm leaving. This book is my letter, my expression, my voice. And I may get a little rowdy at times because it is an emotional and difficult break up for me. I am angry, and in pain. I am angry at those who continue to sell their souls, who continue to allow themselves to be used as "the collective tool of destruction" that is integral to the greater end of the ruling class elite. And I am hurt that many artists fail to either see the destructive nature of their craft, or refuse to buy their souls back (like my hero, Dave Chapelle did when he stopped being the puppet masters buffoon and was thrown from the mainstream—only to be replaced by Flava Flav). So, it may appear that I am bashing. But I assure you that I am not.

Let it be most clearly understood, that this book is a critique of the negative effect that *the new* "Hip-Hop," as a collective entertainment culture, (that includes

Rap, urban rhythm and blues, urban contemporary music videos, urban magazines, and urban feature films), has on the Black community, and not a criticism of any artist, group, or song that may be used as an example. It is a critique of "the relationship," not of those who represent the relationship, are in the relationship. It is a critique of the war of destruction, not the front line soldiers who advance the destruction.

I write this book with due understanding—not respect—but understanding and sympathy for those who, in their unconsciousness, semi consciousness, and/or selfish/narcissistic state have been chosen to represent and promote the ideological and cultural hegemony that is essential to the destruction of the consciousness and movement of the masses, and have consequently become accomplices to the impending genocide of my people. In essence, it can be stated, with tongue in cheek, that I am not "knocking the hustle," just critiquing the game.

INTRODUCTION

It only takes a few moments of exposure to any form of urban media to witness the new face of Hip-Hop. Urban radio will most often over saturate one's auditory senses with heavy beats that are accompanied by unintelligible verses, and clear and repetitive hooks that glorify money, women's behinds, guns, violence, sex, drugs, murder, and even ones own death or brush with death. In the nightclubs across the Nation, new evolutions of songs such as Lil' Wayne's "Every Girl," Trey Songz "I Invented Sex," Jeremih's "Birthday Sex," and Jamie Foxx's "Blame It," and even Beyonce's "Diva," craze the crowd with sexualized lyrics that speak to the disrespect of women, minimization of true intimacy and connection, and the objectification of the "female" body that have become commonplace in Hip-Hop music.

In spite of the misogyny, however, when such songs are played, women rush to the dance floor to gyrate their buttocks' and perform like amateur exotic dancers, often times following the instructions that are being given in the song, protruding their behinds, "droppin' it" like its hot, and pouting their lips while singing the very verses that minimize their sexual being and negate their subjectivity. In concert, they shake their heads in unison as if to agree with the sexualized messages and their own objectification. Men, on the other hand, rush to harness the power and control over the female body, specifically the (butt), that the songs have given them—often posturing women from behind in order to get maximal stimulation and sexual pleasure from the erotic "doggy style" "booty shaking" that is taking place.

Urban videos, magazines, movies, and now awards shows such as the BET Awards will most often over stimulate one's visual senses with the aggressive and hyper-sexual interplay between and among the hegemonic constructs of the Thug Nigga' and the neo-Jezebel that strongly characterize the original stereotypes of Black men and women that freedom fighters and civil rights activists struggled to dispel—the same that were used to promote the notion of the inferiority of the race. Spend 5 minutes watching 106 and Park or any station that features Rap/Urban music, with the volume turned down and the point will clearly be proven.

The videos look like soft strip shows in the daytime and straight pornography on the more "uncensored" shows at night.

Peruse the most popular Hip-Hop magazines such as XXL, King, Vibe, and the Source and the point will be proven. The advertisements reinforce the "hooker" and the "thug" images and promote shoes, liquor, "fake chains," and other materials that are designed to encourage an attachment to materialistic values. Any literary articles are few and far between, and most often of limited substance. Analyze the most popular urban and/or (Hip-Hop) "pre Tyler Perry" blockbusters of 2005, such as Hustle and Flow, Crash, Four Brothers, Beauty Shop, and Get Rich or Die Tryin' and one will see that no matter how creative or entertaining the movie, the same stereotypical constructs are reinforced—the pimp and the ho or the thug and the jezebel.

However, even though history has proven that these images are both deliberate and dangerous, the predominant argument is that "it is just entertainment." It is harmless. It is business. Even those whose images are most drastically exploited are quick to defend the message and the presentation. Misogyny has ceased to be misogynistic and has become an expectation that acts through the objectification of Women of Color who are eager to be chosen for that role. So, in that context, the sexual displays and images are identified and embraced as an example of women "taking agency" over, profiting from, and/or celebrating their bodies and sexuality—by both those who represent the image and those who consume the image. As a result, young girls are encouraged to embrace their own bodies as sexual objects at an early age, and to aspire to be strippers or video hoes above doctors and lawyers.

In addition to the sexualized images, the aggressive, sexually dominant and detached, and materialistic displays of "rappers" become "an example" of men entertaining or relating to the consumer, expressing their experiences, telling it like it is in the neighborhood, being men, or "keeping it real." Consequently, the lyrical and visual content is rationalized and minimized and subsequently becomes a representation of culturally acceptable forms of communication and interaction between and among Black men and Black women in "the real world."

In spite of the arguments and rationalizations though, it is ignorant to assume that the mass presentations of the Black woman as a hyper-sexual object, the Black man as a violent, aggressive and hyper-sexual object, and the Black neighborhood as a culture of crime and deviance have no effect on the social perceptions of the people and communities that the presentations are supposed to represent. Especially since the original presentations were deliberately created and promoted to support the enslavement of a people. It is equally consequential to assume that the language and interplay that the media utilizes to represent the actual interaction between and among Black men and women have no effect on the perception and interaction between and among the same, and the way in which others perceive and interact with them. For it is argued that if internalized and accepted, "media representations" of who and what African-American peoples and urban communities are supposed to be—can, do, and will have an overall effect on the entire race. The media is, after all, the principle tool in the promotion of propaganda that is designed to shape the perceptions and attitudes of the masses.

Therefore, buying into the argument that Hip-Hop is simply entertainment negates the consequences and implications that it has on the community and makes it acceptable to continue to support, promote, internalize, and engage in it. But even more significantly, the argument negates the reality that the media in any form is, and has historically been, utilized as a means to not only convey information about a culture and a people, but a means to dilute the consciousness of the masses in order to promote and ensure conformity. Therefore, it becomes critical to evaluate the media's mass, one dimensional and homogenous presentation of "a people" in order to critique the effects of such on the collective socio political condition and location of those people in the real world.

The questions must be asked. What are the potential consequences of the presentation? What purpose does the presentation serve? Is there an absence of alternative presentations that balance negative/stereotypical ones? Has there been an internalization of these presentations as being real and exclusive identifications of a race and culture? And if so, what are the implications? Where does the variable fit in the path model?

This book will theoretically critique and analyze the impact and influence Hip-Hop has on the Black community by utilizing a socio-political, economic, and a historic approach. Through evaluating the use of the media as a hegemonic tool, the music industry as means of controlling images and "representations," the impact of the use of the "psychology of repetition" on internalization, the deliberate suppression of other forms of Black entertainment, and the detriment of "realizing" the constructions, this book will offer a grounded example of why Hip-Hop is highly significant to the destruction the Black community.

CHAPTER 1

UNDERSTANDING HEGEMONY

The term "hegemony" especially when coupled with preceding terms such as ideological and/or cultural can be quite threatening. It has probably turned many away from a theoretical concept that identifies one of the most powerful means of promoting conformity, productive and reproductive exploitation, oppression, and self destruction. For hegemony is the means by and through which false consciousness is promoted to the masses, with minimal resistance. It is the tool that dominant social forces have historically utilized and continue to utilize to promote the oppressed groups' acceptance and even promotion of its own oppression and destruction without coercion or force.

To put it simply, conformity—that is getting a people to conform to social norms and values so that social, political, and economic agendas can be advanced with minimal resistance is essential to the stability of any society. Conformity is and has been accomplished by two predominant means—through force or through promoting ideological hegemony. Force has proven to be an unstable method, because it produces or keeps constant the possibility of resistance. After all, no one likes to be told what to do. However, if one can get the members of society to "buy in to" an idea, to believe in that idea or that ideology, then he will follow without resistance. This premise is expressed in Carter G. Woodson's quote: "When you control a man's thinking, you don't have to worry about his actions." He will do what you want him to do without even being told. He will internalize the idea/ideology and follow its direction.

In America, there exists a dominant culture that encompasses the ideology, or ideas and interests of those who colonized this land. In short, European colonizers brought with them a set of values, morals, ideas and expectations that shaped the legal, social, political, and economic frame of this colony. The Constitution is the guiding document that makes concrete the patriarchal or male dominated, capitalist, democratic, and supremacist systems that represent those dominant ideologies and world views.

The world view of European supremacy has been the catalyst to the success of European expansion, colonialism, and imperialism worldwide. And it is the continued perpetuation of that idea that ensures the continued power relations that exist today. But more significantly to this work, those world views and ideologies grounded the fallacy of the biological, cultural, and intellectual inferiority of the African continent and people that allowed the institution of slavery to occur with minimal resistance. In essence, if Europe was the dominant and superior continent then Africa was the inferior one. If the White race was the dominant race, than the "Black" African race was the inferior one. With that foundation laid, it was easy to promote the stereotypes of the African and then the African-American and Diasporic race that have yet to be dispelled.

Therefore, as Antonio Gramsci would argue, the State, and the structures of the State, represent and encompass the culture and ideology of the colonizers, land owners, or the ruling class. So, it is the culture, interest, and ideology of the ruling class that is promoted, protected, and enforced by the state—either through force or through the promotion of its ideological and cultural hegemony. In essence, the dominant class can either force conformity to its ideas through force (war) or coercion (the threat of war/violence) or through the promotion of that groups ideas and culture as being supreme, all inclusive, and unchangeable (ideological and cultural hegemony). European dominance/supremacy and later "White supremacy" are the hegemonic ideologies that have provided the frame for expansion, colonialism, imperialism, and ethnocentrism (racism) globally.

Lenin argued that the state "has always been an organ or instrument of violence exercised by one class against another" (Berberoglu 1998:61), one people against another, one nation against another. However, while the use of force and coercion have historically been the predominant and most prevalent means of global expansion, and colonial and imperial domination, promoting ideological and cultural hegemony has been the most essential and the most successful in ensuring the solidification, promotion, and maintenance of conformity to dominant ideologies and the implementation of Western systems (capitalism and "democracy") that have historically been counterproductive, exploitative, and oppressive to Indigenous lands, cultures, and people.

But, what is hegemony? How does one ensure the solidification and continuity of false consciousness/conformity through hegemony? And by/through what means does it operate? In essence, how does the belief in the dominance of one race or culture promote conformity? How does it deter people from embracing and appreciating their own identity, and when they do not how does that do a better job at promoting conformity?

Gramsci argued that violence and the use of coercion was not sufficient in maintaining control over the masses. He contended that it was more important to gain the consensus of the masses, to "convince the oppressed classes of the legitimacy of its rule" (p.62). For it is through the promotion of conformity and acceptance that the likelihood of resistance and rebellion is reduced. So, as he argues in Berberoglu, the state, as an apparatus of the ruling class, represents "the entire complex of practical and theoretical activities with which the ruling class not only justifies and maintains its dominance, but manages to win the active consent of those over whom it rules" (Gramsci in Berberoglu, 1998:62).

Subsequently, through utilizing what Gramsci terms the 'super structural organs' of the state, which includes the media, the ruling class not only promotes the masses conformity to, but even support for, the dominance of ruling class ideologies and interests over their own ideologies, interests, and conditions.. In summation he states:

> With the acceptance of its ideas and the legitimization of its rule, the capitalist class is able to exercise control and dominance of society through its ideological hegemony at the level of the superstructure with the aid and instrumentality of the state. . . . Although the dialectics of the accumulation process, which involves first and foremost the exploitation of labor, ultimately results in class struggle . . . revolution . . . the ideological hegemony of the ruling class, operating through the state itself, prolongs bourgeois class rule and institutionalizes and legitimizes exploitation. . . . The systems real strength does not lie in the violence of the ruling class or the coercive power of its state apparatus, but in the acceptance by the ruled of a conception of the world which belongs to the rulers (Berberoglu 1998:62).

Thus, hegemony involves the successful attempts of the dominant class to use its political, moral, and intellectual leadership (control) to establish its view of the world as all inclusive and universal, and to shape the interests and needs of subordinate groups (Berberoglu 1998:62). This process, he adds, prolongs 'bourgeois class rule' by promoting a false consciousness among the masses that is immersed in the acceptance of not only the institutionalization—but the legitimization of their own exploitation (62).

It is further asserted that as a part of the hegemonic process, once the ideologies of the ruling class are accepted and internalized by the oppressed, they will collectively accept, and even promote, their own oppression by assuming the characteristics *defined by* the ruling class or the characteristics *associated with* the ruling class itself—both of which are antagonistic to their own existence. In essence, it is argued that they will either take on the stereotypical characteristics that have been created and defined by the ruling class to promote their oppression, or assume the characteristics of the oppressor in their effort to remove themselves from their own struggle and the oppression of their people. In either case, they will not be able to see that they are oppressed and will not be able to understand the root of their oppression. They will be devoid of the consciousness that is essential to real social critique, the development of conscious movement, and ultimately social transformation.

Freire elaborated on this condition in his work *Pedagogy of the Oppressed* when He stated:

> But almost always, during the initial stage of the struggle, the oppressed, instead of striving for liberation, tend themselves to become oppressors, or sub-oppressors. The very structure of their thought has been conditioned by the contradictions of the concrete, existential situation by which they were shaped. Their ideal is to be men, but for them, to be men is to be oppressors. This phenomenon derives from the fact that the oppressed, at a certain moment of their existential experience, adopt an attitude of adhesion to the oppressor. . . . Their perception of themselves as oppressed is impaired by their submersion in the reality of oppression. . . . For them the new man is themselves become oppressors. Their new man is individualistic; because of his identification with their oppressor, they have no consciousness of themselves as persons or as members of an oppressed class. . . . The oppressed, having internalized the image of the oppressor and adopted his guidelines, are fearful of freedom. The fear of freedom which afflicts the oppressed, a fear which may equally well lead them to desire the role of oppressor or bind them to the role of oppressor, should be examined (Freire 2002:28).

Thus, ideological and cultural hegemony involve the establishment of a specific race, gender, geographical region, hence, the ideas and systems of such as dominant and superior. That collective then represents the overall "culture" and sociopolitical "ideology" of a people that is promoted throughout the world as dominant, superior, and all inclusive and then utilized to conquer lands and people.

Through global expansion, colonialism, and imperialism, Indigenous lands and people are indoctrinated into the "dominant" social, political, and economic system, and any resistant forces or ideas are suppressed or destroyed. Then, through the use of various systemic or 'structural organs,' such as the media and the educational systems (that are most often established and certainly controlled by the colonizer), the "dominant" culture and ideologies are aggressively promoted. Through intense promotional campaigns, the culture and ideology of the ruling class replaces the indigenous culture and ideology and is ultimately internalized by the oppressed as being their own.

As a result of that internalization, false consciousness is achieved, and the likelihood of true resistance and rebellion is suppressed. For, instead of seeking consciousness and transformation, the oppressed accepts, contributes to, and/or promotes their collective oppression by either remaining apathetic, taking on the negative values that have been assigned them, or striving to assume the characteristics and status of the oppressor which encourages not only a detachment from, but the oppression of, their own collective. This means that when a race/a collective group of people embrace and internalize negative ideas about themselves, they will accept the negative ideas as truth, and either seek to dissociate from who they are, or take on the stereotypical characteristics. Either way they will fail to reach the level of awareness about their conditions and the manner in which they are being exploited, and will consequently fail to seek a transformation or change in their condition—thereby remaining ambivalent and apathetic about their own oppression and exploitations.

Through the promotion of ideological hegemony then, the power structure does not have to actively, directly, or openly promote conformity to the oppression and dominance or enforce acceptance and assimilation through coercion or force which serves many essential purposes. (1) It promotes the acceptance of the status quo as constant and unchangeable. (2) It promotes false consciousness and division among and between the oppressed, which channels the focus away from the system as the point of oppression. But most importantly, it does not antagonize the oppressed, because they take ownership of/in the existing system, and therefore do not view resistance or rebellion as being necessary. In essence, the people become almost oblivious to the reality of their circumstance.

Creating ideological and cultural hegemony allows the State to then utilize the theme of "freedom and democracy" as its expansionist slogan without being confronted with the sociopolitical and economic inequities that are inherent and necessary components of an economic system (capitalism) that is driven by and dependent upon the exploitation of labor, and distributive inequality. Further, it allows the system to blame the oppressed for their conditions because the concept of "democracy" promotes the false notion that every "body" has the ability, freedom, opportunity, and equality to achieve status and power in the existing system. Hence, if they do not, it is not the fault or problem of the system but a flaw in the individual's capacity.

The ideas of democracy and supremacy, then, camouflage the exploitation and oppression that is inherent in capitalism—as a socio political and economic system, and allows the existing system to be maintained and promoted without critique. And even "racism," which was constructed to justify oppression, becomes an excuse for an oppression and exploitation that would exist even outside of the construct and concept of race in a capitalist system. As Malcolm X asserts, as a result of the acceptance of ideological hegemony, the people are "hoodwinked and bamboozled" into not only accepting but promoting their own oppression and exploitation.

What does this have to do with Hip-Hop? Today's Hip-Hop is a direct and undeniable mimic of the historic stereotypes that were developed, promoted, and utilized to promote support for the exploitation and oppression of a people. The early stereotypes and presentations of the Jezebel and the Buck, utilizing first Khoikhoi women and Mandingo men (two African "tribes"), promoted the notions of the biological, sexual, and intellectual inferiority of the African and were utilized to justify the enslavement of a people. Africans were deemed savages, animals, hypersexual, aggressive, violent, lazy, and dumb. Based on that, it was okay to trap, ship, and enslave them. It was okay to rape and/or breed them. It was okay to strip them from their families and sell them like property, treat them like animals—using Black women like "bitches," "mating" them, and then selling their "offspring," using Black men like "studs," breeding them and separating them from not only the "bitch" after intercourse/insemination, but completely detaching them from their "bitches" pregnancy and the delivery, nurturing, guiding, and protecting of their offspring. Sound familiar?

Based on that, it was okay to verbally berate, psychologically abuse, whip, burn, beat, drag, amputate, castrate, and even murder them without consequence, because the race was not human, but animals and property-worse than a dog, or horse, or an ass . The visual presentations were originally *developed* to specifically promote the images of savagery and inhumanity that supported the stereotypes and justified the inhumane treatment of an entire race of people.

After Emancipation, those same stereotypes were used to promote the fear of the Black race in order to support the continued exploitation of the races productive labor and their restraint and exclusion from social, political, and economic access. That is why the media was forced to use White actors in "Black face" to present the Black man and woman in these stereotypical roles. At that point in history, regardless of segregation, no African in America in their right mind would allow him/herself to be used to promote images that were detrimental to gaining inclusion and equality in America. It was only later that those few who were attracted to the popularity and income would succumb to promoting the negative and fallacious stereotypes of "Blackness."

Now, Hip-Hop artists readily assume these same stereotypical roles: "The Thug"—the angry, hostile, violent, hypersexual, ignorant, detached, irresponsible and criminal man, who is now the "nigga" that is keeping it real and reppin' 'da hood.' And then there is the "neo-Jezebel"—the hypersexual, irresponsible, lazy, ignorant "bitch" who is now the sexual object of not the slave master, but the thug. The Queen B (itch) who uses her body to either gain materially from the thug, to play the game of the thug, or to negate the game of the thug by taking on the characteristics of the thug. Either way, the representations are clear cut examples of how the ideologies/ideas of race that were developed to support the agenda of European dominance and White supremacy have now been internalized and are voluntarily being promoted by the oppressed themselves.

CHAPTER 2

THE MEDIA AS A HEGEMONIC TOOL

"As intersubjective communication, discourse is language that encodes cultural conventions. . . . Language is not innocent. It is ideologically and culturally bound, and it both expresses and conceals our realities . . . Language can also shape our realities, and either enslave, by concealing what it might truly express, or liberate, by exposing what might otherwise remain concealed."

– Hassan 1997: 33

In order to negate the rationale that "It is just entertainment," it must clearly be understood that no mass dissemination of information is promoted without purpose. It must also be clearly understood that no matter how it is rationalized, no repetitive promotion of images, information, messages, etc., will fail to have a psychological impact on those who are exposed. As a means of conveying information, presenting ideas, communicating—discourse in any form is not without foundation. From the micro perspective of an individual communicating his ideas/thoughts to another, to the macro perspective of the media communicating system ideas/thoughts to the masses, no communication is without foundation.

As argued by Hassan, language *is* never innocent. It *is* culturally, experientially, and ideologically bound. From the micro perspective of the speaker or writer or producer, to the macro perspective of the state, the presentation and dissemination of information and images via any means of communication is bound to the subjective "reality," or ideology, of the person or entity that controls the voice and vision. In essence, one cannot create what he has not experienced—internalized. One cannot create what he does not know—whether he believes it or not. Everything that "we" manifest/create is a result of what is inside of us. The question then, is how are we programmed?

Before the telephone and internet, the media were the largest and most wide spread means of communication. But more importantly, they are and have always been the predominant means by/through which information is unilaterally distributed on a mass scale. Letters, periodicals, magazines, photography, and later film, radio, television, and cable have all been used to distribute information in mass. And now the internet has made it possible for information to be transmitted globally within a matter of seconds. And, while this efficiency has its privileges, it also has implications.

Arguably, many consumers do not realize that outside of the internet, where information can be (is) passed and posted with minimal intervention and regulation, other forms of media such as the television industry, radio industry, "the news media" industry, the music industry, and the film industry are highly, yet inconspicuously, controlled, regulated, and monitored. The various forms of media are corporate conglomerates that like other "mega-businesses" are owned and operated, and therefore, controlled by the few elite/ruling class individuals and families who have maintained control over these media forms for generations.

Therefore, as Gramsci argues, it is the interests and ideologies of the elite that are served, disseminated, promoted, and protected through the venues that they own. Consequently, no matter how liberal, conservative, or radical the content, presentation, or information, absolutely nothing can, has, will, does, or will ever be disseminated through these mediums without the scrutiny of those who represent the interests of the corporation, the ruling class. This includes the Federal government (FCC) who, under the guise of monitoring these mediums, also serve as the gatekeeper to what "the people" actually receive and how they receive it.

So, while many Patriotic Americans would argue that the "freedom of speech" and the "freedom of the press" are guaranteed, if the major forms of mass media and mass communication are privately owned, a rational man would question whose "freedoms" are really being represented and promoted through these venues. For, if ones ideologies contradict those of the elite, what forms of mass communication/media would he/she be really be able to utilize to promote his/her own individual or collective interests, his/her own freedoms? Would he/she be able to use the Washington Post or New York Times to promote "radical" sociopolitical ideologies that contradict the existing political economy? Would he/she be able to use mainstream mediums to promote the overturn or impeachment of political representatives that have become counterproductive to the people, even though according to the Constitution, the government is supposed to be "By the People, For the People," especially in the wake of the most recent McCarthyist "Patriot Act?" Absolutely not.

What is being suggested is that if the means of promoting the freedoms that are supposed to be guaranteed to "all" Americans are regulated, through private ownership, by the few, then the masses are completely dependent on the few to not only represent but promote their collective interests nationally and globally. For without concrete input, the masses have no power over what is being reported, presented, and promoted. Unlike politics, where the ability to vote at least gives the people the illusion of control, the people have no control over who owns and controls the means of mass communication, hence, no control over what is disseminated—hence, what is received.

Depending on others is only alright if "the others" truly represent the individual or collective interest of the people. However, contradictions arise when those who control "the media" have different ideologies, experiences, interests, and agendas than the people, or certain groups of people. For, like all things, if the goal of business is to control and profit, and the goal of any society is to maintain the status quo through promoting conformity, it would be highly unreasonable to assume that any entity would promote anything that was counterproductive or, worse, destructive to its power, control, and stability. No government would promote an idea, no matter how rational, that would promote civil unrest, resistance, or rebellion.

Given this assertion, the media must be evaluated for what it is, the business of mass communication, the business of conveying information to, influencing, and ultimately controlling the masses. Therefore, everything that the media presents serves a purpose that will impact or effect/affect the masses. Whether the result is a latent or manifest one, the impact—an intentional or unintentional one, the effect negative or positive. Anything that has the potential of reaching and influencing the masses to this extent cannot be minimized.

With that, the question must be asked. How do the media present Black people, the Black community? How has it historically represented Black people, the Black community? Have the "presentations" been accurate representations? Has the media been able to, if not support, then represent the collective interests of Black people? If you are Black, does it represent you? If you are not, do you have other sources of interaction with that group that provides a foundation for your perception? Have you watched the news lately? BET, MTV, VH1? What do you see?

If the images that are portrayed daily on the news were ones only form of interaction with Black people as a collective, what would the major assumptions about "the race" truly be? How would it/does it affect the personal or collective interaction with African-American people? Aside from the Cosby Show, what other mass media representations can you name that have reflected the diverse nature of the Black community and experience? Can you get past your third finger? If so, email me. But do not email any Independent films that no one has ever heard of, or any underground music no one has ever heard of because that is the point.

This work posits that film, video, and music are all subject to the political and intellectual influence and control of the ruling class by way of the economic force that is necessary to produce and distribute these works, and its control of the "gateway" to the masses. So, as the dominant means by which information is conveyed about the Black experience, these systems have historically been and continue to be utilized to promote ideologies and stereotypes that lend support to the continued oppression and exploitation of a people.

This assertion is supported by the fact that not only are most mainstream films written and directed by White males; but by the fact that *all* of the major production and distribution companies in each medium are owned and operated by the White male elite—from Hollywood production houses to mainstream News mediums like the Washington Post and the New York Times. Therefore, it can be surmised that as stated above, what is accepted for production and distribution must meet the criteria and be accepted by those who represent the ideologies and interests of the ruling class. And so, in representing the ideologies of the ruling class, either as a member of that group who has purchased control over this medium, or as a member of the elite class who has accepted the dominant ideology, this group, through its medium, either directly or indirectly perpetuates the interest of the ruling class that is grounded in the hegemonic ideologies of the past.

As a hegemonic tool then, the media serves to legitimize the control, exploitation, and oppression of the Black community by limiting their visual and character presentations to those that support dominant ideologies and stereotypes about the race, culture, and experience. But y'all don't hear me though! As a hegemonic tool—the media—as a collective representation of the interest of the State, hence, the ruling class—serves to legitimize the control, exploitation and oppression, and promote the self-destruction of the Black community, by limiting what all people see and learn to those same presentations that have historically been used to—and successful at—justifying the capture, enslavement, control, oppression, and exploitation of a people.

These media presentations then become an identification of the entire race, with few exceptions, that is internalized by society as a social and cultural representation that negatively effects the sociopolitical and economic condition, location, and experience of Black people as a collective. "Rock Boyz," "Duffle Bag Boy," "So Hood," "Get Money," and "Crank Dat." The simple titles of these songs illustrate the message.

CHAPTER 3

THE HISTORY OF AFRICAN AMERICANS IN MAINSTREAM FILM: A SOCIOPOLITICAL AND HISTORIC ANALYSIS

In order to truly understand the current presentation of African-American men and women in urban mediums, the historical transitions must be deconstructed. It is imperative to lay the historic foundation because it is only through understanding how each of the stereotypical constructs of "Blackness," from the jezebel and buck to the neo-Jezebel and the thug, served political purposes that we can then eliminate the "just entertainment" arguments. It will show that each of the stereotypes were specifically designed and developed to promote support for each point of "laboral" exploitation where always accompanied by a visual presentation. This visual presentation is integral to promoting the imagery, thereby bringing life to the ideology which was necessary in ensuring support for the oppression and exploitation.

This chapter, while rigorous, provides that history by illustrating the key productive transitions that influenced the political and economic landscape of the United States of America during different eras. The cinematic presentation of African Americans in mainstream film during these different era is then placed in the equation in order to show how each directly relates to the way in which the body and labor of the African American was being exploited during that time. This chapter provides context and rationale for each of the stereotypical constructs of the African American-the jezebel and the buck, the mammy and the Uncle Tom, the sapphire and the sambo, the welfare queen and the pimp, and the neo-Jezebel and the thug, and why each was necessary, related, and integral to the promotion of political and economic agendas.

The Historical Development of the Hegemonic Presentation

As Mengara (2001) and Rodney (1994) support, European contact with and penetration of Africa was detrimental to the land and people. Early contact and "exploration" of the continent in the Fifteenth Century made Europe aware of the wealth potential of the continent. As Mengara (2001) argues, "the consequences of the encounter between Europe and Africa very early on left no part of Africa unstirred" (p. 2).

During the initial contact and exploration, Europe was not yet technologically prepared to expropriate and exploit the natural or human resources of the continent for the global economy. However, once Europe had developed the technology that was necessary to implement its strategies for global expansion and exploitation, Africa was a primary target and would prove a valuable commodity to and for its colonialist and imperialist endeavors. For not only would Europe gain control over the country's intellectual resources—knowledge, philosophy, technology, it would also harness its natural resources by utilizing African peoples as a form of collective labor through colonization. But more significant to the African-American experience, Europeans would also extract labor from the continent in order to fuel the agricultural development of other colonized lands, one being the United States of America and the isles of the West Indies and South America.

However, in order to justify the extraction and enslavement of a people, which was in direct contradiction to the principles of freedom, democracy, and Christianity, that Europeans had promoted, what Mengara (2001) terms "a Westernized construct" of Africa that would support the goal and agenda of the colonizer had to be developed. And although much of the literature emphasizes the implication to African/African-American men, this work argues that the Western construction of the African/African-American woman was just as significant in being utilized to more publicly to support the notions of racial, biological, and moral inferiority. This is because not only was she a valuable agricultural producer, who alongside men served as a means of production. But more importantly, she would also become essential as (1) a reproducer of slave labor once the Trans Atlantic Slave Trade was abolished, (2) a means to control and diminish African/African-American men, and (3) a sexual object to White men. And this would require separating her from subjective being, value, and rights as a woman.

Contrary to European assertions though, the people of West Africa, from where most slaves came, once played important roles in African civilization. They were warriors, philosophers, intellects, priests and priestesses, founders of cities, kings, queens, and farmers. But more importantly, they were human beings entitled to the subjective rights that are spiritually afforded—and therefore should be humanly afforded to all humans.

However, the role of human could not be applied to the African if he/she was going to be enslaved. For, in Europe, and later America, the title of "man" carried the notion of power, authority, and dominance, and afforded rights and privileges that could not be attributed to African men if they were going to be broken and enslaved. And the title of "woman" or "lady" carried a gendered notion and tradition of European 'femininity,' that incorporated concepts of frailty, passivity, purity, piousness, and domesticity (Macionis 2002 & Collins 2002), that afforded European women levels of social protection and privilege, that could not be attributed to the African woman if her productive and reproductive labor were going to be maximally exploited: if she were to work as hard and long as a man (alongside him), is she were to be raped, if her sons and daughters were going to be stripped from her and sold—during the Antebellum Era. Therefore, it was important for the visual presentations of the African to correspond with ideologies of difference, hence, inferiority that justified the need to control them through enslavement.

Thus, as the literature posits, the early predominant presentation of the African to European, and later American society, involved the exploitation of the physical characteristics that were different than those of the European. This would serve as the foundation for scientific assertions about the hyper-sexuality, savagery, immorality and animalism that were representations of the false notions of biological inferiority that separated the African peoples from their subjective humanity, and the rights thereof.

In order to promote this 'difference' in the early eras that predated film and video, the spectacle show and the photograph became a means of visual presentation, hence, a means of conveying information about African culture and people. One of the earlier and most infamous examples of the stereotypes of the African body/ Blackness, is the presentation of the Hottentot Venus in the early 1800s. Her visual exploitation was clearly utilized for the purpose of supporting the notion of biological (sexual/anatomic) difference, inferiority, and/or abnormality—hence, the hyper-sexuality of African women. As Collins argues:

> For French and British audiences, Sarah Baartman served as a sign of the difference used to justify the growing belief in the superiority of White civilization and the inferiority of so called primitive peoples necessary for colonialism. . . . She is displayed caged rocking back and forth to emphasize her supposedly wild and dangerous nature. . . . When ordered she leaves her cage and parades before the audience who seems fascinated with what they see as her most intriguing feature, her buttocks (Collins 2004: 50).

Not soon after, the photograph became a powerful and mass means of promoting the ideological hegemony of the ruling class, first in Europe and then in the United States. As Sanders (2002) argues:

> The history of the photographic image of the Black female body in the United States begins in the 1850s, with a model derived from European precedents. During this era, a number of significant developments in Western culture coincided with the invention of photography and further contributed to the way in which Black females were regarded and ultimately visualized. The births of 'popular culture' and modern visual pornography; the development of the

natural sciences and the related disciplines of ethnology and anthropology; and the abolition of slavery both in the colonies and at home were practically simultaneous, and each served to compartmentalize, objectify, and categorize any manifestations of difference from the European ideal (p.3).

Thus, presenting the Black body in ways that exaggerated, or at least emphasized, the characteristics that were different than those of European counterparts was essential to promoting negative and fallacious notions about a people that led to the objectification and commodification of their sexuality, productive and reproductive labor.

The neo-Jezebel and the Thug or the Ho and the Pimp are not new constructs; they are merely recreations of the Jezebel and the Buck/Mandingo—of old. They are stereotypical presentations that preceded the production of the first films in America and corresponded to early European penetration of Africa. They are the result of European misperceptions/misconceptions of African people, rituals, and practices that were initially disseminated through the written correspondence and verbal interpretations of early "explorers," drawings, the photograph, and spectacle shows.

These original "misrepresentations" of Africa provided support for the enslavement of African people during the Trans Atlantic Slave Trade. The original presentation of the Jezebel and Buck rests in misrepresentation of Africa that provided support for the enslavement of African people during the Trans Atlantic Slave Trade when the value of the African as an agricultural producer and a reproducer of the slave—as a form of mass human labor was realized.

Once the British colonized America, its development and ability to compete and prosper in the growing global economy depended on the solidification of a labor supply that could promote its agricultural development. The Indigenous people who were in an active state of resistance and rebellion, and very susceptible to the diseases that were brought to the New World by English settlers—were not an option. Nor were European laborers and indentured servants who not only did not have the agricultural knowledge and numbers to maximize agrarian development and profit in the United States—but could not under the Christian code of "humanity" be enslaved.

Thus, slavery, or the importation of agricultural labor power became the option of the colonizer, and Africans became the target population. This was a feasible solution because, as Mengara (2003) argued, Europeans had prior knowledge of Africa and its culture and knew that Africans were knowledgeable producers. In addition, they would be unfamiliar with the new land and thus would be severely limited in their ability to effectively resist or rebel. So, the notions of White supremacy and the biological inferiority of Indigenous peoples that had already taken form as a justification for Europe's colonialist practices facilitated the transition into the Trans Atlantic slave trade, by negating any argument that the practice/business was inhumane. After all, the African specifically had already been deemed an animal.

Initially slave traders preferred and targeted male slaves due to their physical stamina and dexterity. So, in order to "augment the human capital of the slave owning class" male slaves were, initially, encouraged to marry and reproduce with White women (Staples 1978). However, the consequence this practice (to White supremacy and slavery) was quickly realized as the rate of intermarriage escalated. For White women could not be enslaved; therefore, the status of the offspring was questionable. But, more importantly, the rise of bi-racial offspring was a contradiction to the lineage, and a threat to the race. Consequently a series of laws prohibiting marriages and relationships between slaves and White women and establishing the status of the child as being that of the mother were quickly passed. And then, to quell the established attraction, stereotypes about the Black male rapist were promoted in order to ensure that these unions would not continue and offspring "of this type" would not dilute the race. As a result, the capture and utilization of the African woman became essential to the Trans Atlantic Slave Trade and intensified once the slave trade was abolished in 1804.

Thus, the sexual, productive, and reproductive exploitation of the Black body became not only essential to the continuation of slavery through forced breeding, but a sexual weapon and commodity to traders, overseers, and slave masters. As Staples supports: "During this era of slavery the Black woman's body was forcibly subjected to the carnal desires of any male who took a fancy to her, including the slave master, his overseer, or any male slave" (Staples 1978:12).

Even Gunther (1978) argued that according to the accounts of the Europeans themselves, European men showed a sexual predilection for the African woman from the start. The traders and the staff were able to satisfy this predilection with minimal resistance during the voyage from Africa to the states. As Alexander Falconbridge, a surgeon aboard and English slave trader noted, "the officers are permitted to indulge their passions among them at pleasure, and sometimes are guilty of such brutal excesses, as disgrace human nature" (Gunther 1978:32).

Just as significantly, as their own sexual satisfaction was the utilization of the brutal rape and sexual exploitation of African women as a systematic and frequent means of "breaking" African men by rendering them helpless and unable to protect the African woman, or making an example of those who gave their lives to try. Promoting and asserting dominance and control over African men in this manner served as a concrete form of de-masculinization. For the masculine construct of both European and African cultures define men as the "protectors" and "providers." Therefore, if the man is unable to protect his woman—he is not a man.

Consequently, upon entering the United States as slaves, the African served three purposes: (1) providing the productive labor that fueled agricultural development, hence, the wealth of this nation, (2) providing the reproductive labor that was necessary to sustain slavery, especially after the abolition of the Trans

Atlantic Slave Trade, (3) and providing a body that could be sexually exploited, and forcefully/forcibly bred without cost or repercussion.

As argued above, gaining the acceptance and support for the enslavement of the African and their children, however, required removing the African from his/her status as human being. For under the premise of Christianity that guided the moral code of the colonizers, a human being was afforded, at the least, the basic right of freedom and liberty under God, which was the principle that guided the Europeans migration to the United States and was established and incorporated in The Declaration of Independence. In accordance with their own laws then, the brutal extraction of the African from the homeland, the neglect, degradation and brutality that they endured during the middle passage, and the reproductive and productive exploitation that would be necessary to promote the agricultural economy in the United States, under slavery, could not be justified if they were considered human. Therefore, they had to, not only be objectified, but dehumanized and likened to, as Marx put it, an "animal laboran" in order for the ruling class to be able to justify the forced production, forced breeding and reproduction, sexual assault, and the forced removal of their children without aggressive resistance.

Within the context of this dehumanization and objectification lay notions of immorality, hyper sexuality, inferiority, and savagery that provided the justification for the enslavement, or the need for proprietorship over their bodies and being. And although many studies do not focus on the importance of the visual presentation, it is argued that the visual presentation was essential to the universal acceptance of that dominant ideology. In essence, the visual presentation of the African American provided visual support for the assertions of biological inferiority and deviant sexuality by exploiting the fixation on and creating a binary construction of the external physical characteristics of the Black body that differed from those of the White body, such as the skin, hair texture and build of all Black bodies, but specific to women, the buttocks, hips, thighs and breasts. And Black men—the penis. And in this binary construction, all that was attributed to African Americans would be considered deviant and proof of inferiority, White skin/Black skin, straight hair/ kinky hair, pointy nose/wide nose, thin lips/full lips, little butt/big butt, little penis/big penis.

Therefore, once removed from their subjective selves, the notions about African people provided the justification that was needed to facilitate the sexual abuse, productive and reproductive exploitation of the African (American) that was essential to the growth of the agricultural economy, hence, capitalism, in America.

So, it is argued that in the absence of any significant productive shifts from the Antebellum Era to 1896, the 'Jezebel' and the Buck as the first social identification for the Black woman and man remain the dominant visual presentation during this s era.

The Location and Image of the African American During the Early Industrial Era from 1896 to 1945— The Jezebel and the Buck

Post Reconstruction/Jim Crow 1896 to the 1920s

As industrialism emerged as a predominant productive force in the North in the early 1800s, Northern capitalists became aggressive in their attempts to unify the country under an Industrial economy. While Southern agricultural production was initially essential to industry and trade, transitions in productive forces were allowing for more efficient and larger scale industry and production. However, the South was resistant to any transitions because it was still completely dependent on agriculture as its primary and most profitable source of wealth and accumulation. And, in the decades before this era, and before the invention and large-scale utilization of the cotton gin, the South remained completely dependent on slave labor and then Black labor in the form of sharecropping as its primary form of agricultural production for the world market.

As history shows, the tension between the North and South that emerged out of significant political and ideological differences eventually culminated in the Civil War and later prompted the institution and passage of other laws that were designed to promote the political agenda of Northern industrialist. After the Civil War, while the North was promoting its industrial prosperity, there was a drastic decline in the wealth of the South, as the North, in its attempts to unify America under industrialism, used African Americans to place a political and economic stranglehold on the South (Gomes and Williams 1995). With the abolition of slavery, the prosperity of the 'plantocracy' drastically faded because it had been stripped of its free human labor supply and did not yet have the technology or human labor power to replace it. Thus, faced with economic devastation, Southern Whites became hostile in their attempts to save their prosperity. They subsequently instituted a series of laws, policies, and practices that came to be known as "Jim Crow" that were geared toward relegating the newly freed "Negroes" back to the field.

However, Black people, who were seeking inclusion and equality did not return to the fields in enough force to help the 'plantocracy' to fully recover or return Southern owners to its antebellum prosperity. For as Hines and Thompson (1998) and Clark Lewis (1994) support many Blacks began to migrate to the North and West to take advantage of industrial and educational opportunities. And, in the transition from slavery to sharecropping and other forms of farming and agricultural labor, a vast number of Black women expressed their new found power of resistance and rebellion by refusing to return to the fields as laborers, (Hines and Thompson 1994). This created a labor shortage that negatively affected the agricultural prosperity of the South (Gomes and Williams, 1995).

What was even more significant, is that contrary to the assertions of the infamous Moynihan report, who set the precedent for the argument that Black men have never been present and responsible fathers as a result of enslavement, as Figure 1 supports, the percentage of Black women in the labor force was only 15.70 and 16.90% respectively, which means that over 80% of Black women did not participate in the labor force for the two decades following the abolition of slavery—proving Black men were indeed caring for their families (Spencer, 2005).

After Emancipation, no longer was the former slave a commodity, bought and sold in the market and subject to the control of and dependence on the former master. Emancipation placed Blacks in a wage labor relationship, which posed the threat of significantly decreasing the profit margin of Southern landowners and affecting the condition of working-class Whites who would now have to compete with newly freed slaves as a cheaper labor supply.

Figure 1:1
Black Women and Men in the Labor-force 1880 to 1990.

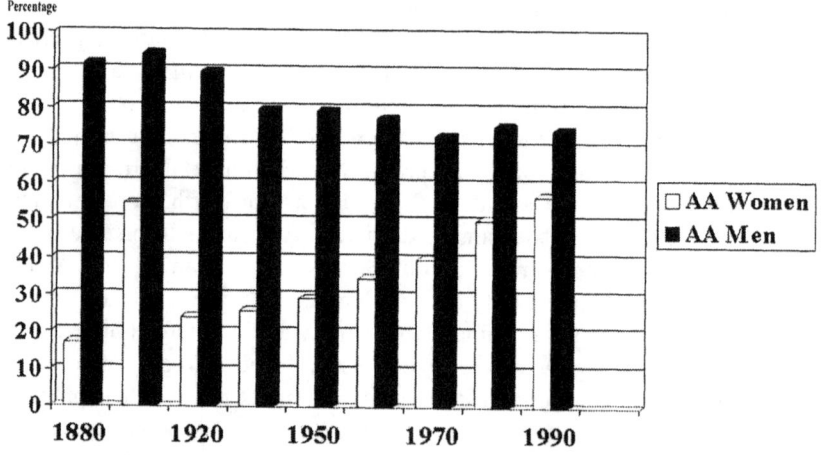

The Census Data was taken from IPUMS EXTRACT www.ipums.ms.edu on January 24, 2005.

The economic plight of the South was further complicated by the informal embargo that the North had instituted to ensure that Southerners did not institute a new form of slavery that would undermine its political agenda. As a part of its political agenda, the Republican government passed the Reconstruction Act of 1867 under which the Fourteenth and Fifteenth Amendments were passed. The Fourteenth Amendment established that African-American men be given the full right, privilege, and status of citizen, which afforded them the same social, political and legal inclusion as White citizens under the law and the Fifteenth Amendment gave African-American men the right to vote. And when the Southern states refused to enforce those amendments, the North placed the South under military rule, wherein Blacks were provided support and protection in order to exercise their newly acquired rights, which allowed the period of Black Reconstruction. As Gomes and Williams argue: "Only the radical faction of the Republican Party supported full political equality for Blacks, primarily as a means of solidifying control over the defeated Southern states and punishing those who had lost the war" (Gomes and Williams 1995:25).

While the Reconstruction Act and the new industrial opportunity gave newly freed Blacks a level of social, political, and economic inclusion, the ease of that inclusion was short lived. As Gomes and Williams (1995) further argued:

> A situation unique in history emerged when the formerly suppressed class of slaves became, for a brief time, politically dominant over their former masters. Reconstruction enabled the military authorities to register over 800,000 Blacks to vote, which exceeded the number of southern Whites then registered.... It is not surprising then that newly emancipated Blacks were treated as pawns in the aftermath of the Civil War. The Black vote was exploited by Republicans who wanted to radicalize and punish the South as well as take advantage of the South's cheap labor, and by Democrats who feared a further loss of power from an alliance between Blacks and poor Whites as represented by the emerging Populist party.... When Reconstruction ended with the withdrawal of federal troops in 1877.... Southern White leaders sought to reestablish dominance over their former slaves through disenfranchisement and the imposition of Jim Crow (p.25).

Consequently, once the North gained the consensus of the South, it retracted the laws that it had instituted under Reconstruction in 1877, and Southern Blacks were relegated to surplus labor status, and once again subject to exclusion, oppression, an the terror of the State. By 1905 most Southern states had passed Jim Crow laws that promoted social segregation, violence against Blacks, and all but annihilated the gains that were made during Reconstruction. (Katz-Fishman and Scott 2002)

However, in spite of the retraction, Blacks had still been integrated into mainstream society, and continued to seek economic inclusion and equality. This new integration created a dilemma for Northern and Southern Whites, as well as European immigrants, who now had to contend with the presence and competition of Blacks for jobs and resources on a large scale for the first time. So, while the Southern states continued to exercise blatant racism that often included violence and terrorism, in its attempts to suppress Blacks, northern states exercised their own forms of segregation, covert discrimination, and exclusion to minimize the competition and integration.

The implementation of Jim Crow in the South drastically prevented and stifled the mobility of all African Americans in the South. The harsh resistance and the Southern region's State support for the exclusion and subjugation of African

Americans all but prevented them from fully integrating into the labor market and society in general. So, in the South, Blacks were still relegated to agricultural labor and low level service positions.

In addition to the lack of mobility, the predominance of terror groups such as the Ku Klux Klan, and the support or reluctance of the State to pursue or punish violence against African-American people, left them subject to beatings, arrest and incarceration without due process, lynching, rape, and murder. These practices would eventually influence the migration of Blacks to the North.

Consequently, while the labor and life opportunity was greater for Blacks in the North due to greater labor demands and a significantly greater level of inclusion than the South, racism and sexism still created labor hierarchies that affected the location of African-American men and women. However, due to the double status of Black and woman, Black women were more adversely affected. Thus, it is argued that through this era, historical notions of inferiority, savagery, immorality, and hyper sexuality continued to predominate in American society in accordance with the movements that attempted to either return Blacks to slavery or keep them subordinated and relegated to the control and dominance of White society.

The predominant constructs of the Jezebel, and the Buck, were the first predominant presentations of the African (American), even before slavery. So, even though film begins in 1896, which is nearly 30 years after the Emancipation Proclamation, in the absence of any significant productive shifts that may have influenced any significant shift in the productive exploitation of Black bodies and labor, these constructs remain steadfast until replaced by that of the Mammy and the Tom when industrial development begins to solidify in the North and South.

This is because, as argued earlier in this chapter, the constructs of the Jezebel and Buck were the predominant and historic hegemonic "presentations" of African men and women—that were geared toward promoting notions of hyper sexuality, savagery, and aggression that were used to justify controlling and exploiting their productive and reproductive labor during the slave trade, and the later colonization of Africa. And because the pre-industrial transition did not promote a significant shift in the way in which the Black labor was being utilized in the South, there was no immediate shift in the dominant presentation. Therefore, the post-bellum visual presentation still coincided with earlier presentations that corresponded to the agricultural era.

This continued visual presentation also represents the sociopolitical resistance to the Emancipation of the slaves and attempts to restore African Americans to their pre Emancipation status. It reflects the ruling class's attempts to maintain control of the labor power of the African American through promoting images of that reinforced the need for such control.

What most importantly must be noted, however, is the reality that the presentation of the African American in the early films is clearly contradictory to the true status and presence of African Americans in the United States during that era.

It is argued that in the Era of post Reconstruction, the early presentations of the African American directly and intentionally related to the ruling class's efforts to restore power relations to those of the Antebellum Era, not as a representation of the real sociopolitical location of Black people at that time. Subsequently, in an effort to regain control over the productive labor power of African Americans and ensure that they remained excluded from the social, political and economic process, Jim Crow, Black Codes and other overt and covert policies and laws were created to ensure that all Blacks remained disenfranchised.

Thus, as Marx argues, the state (and it's apparatus, film), as a tool of the ruling class, was utilized to restore and maintain the prescribed social order and the dialectical power relations that had been established during the Antebellum Era, and would be necessary in order to continue to control and exploit the productive and reproductive labor of African-American men and women. So, in the absence of any new constructs and any significant changes in the mode of production, the visual presentation of Black people in the early films is more related to the pre slavery and antebellum constructs that were designed to promote the hegemony of the ruling class and maximally exploit the productive and reproductive labor power of African Americans. As Hines and Thompson (1998) support:

> White Southerners, of course, believed that Black people should remain slaves in all but name, working in the fields as always and in the kitchens as usual. They even enacted laws, called Black Codes, to try to enforce this condition. . . . Their labor had built the southern agricultural economy and their labor was necessary to maintain it (p.149).

When the people of Africa were extracted from their homeland and forced into slavery, there is no argument that they were also forced to adapt and assimilate to European or Anglo culture. From language to religion, the African was forced to give up the indigenous culture and transform to the norms, values, moral and legal codes of English settlers. After all, "civilizing" the African people, hence, indoctrinating them into Western cultural values, was one of the justifications for their enslavement. However, during slavery, the level of acculturation or indoctrination was severely limited by the ruling classes attempts to maintain control over the being of the slave through the implementation of policies and laws that were devised to keep the slave destabilized, subordinated, and dependent on the master, such as "anti literacy laws," "anti-congregation laws," and laws prohibiting any social and political participation or racial integration.

In the absence of the direct and full control over the Black body after Emancipation, African Americans began to implement and create programs and movements that were designed to empower and reconstruct the race. Subsequently, by the late 1800s, "in the real world," Black society, having to struggle with social, political, and economic exclusion, had fully adapted to the cultural values and practices of the Anglo, and was in full movement to gain validation and equality in American society by proving the collective capacity to successfully adapt Western values and assimilate into mainstream American culture.

As Hines and Thompson (1998) point out, it was the belief of a large majority of Blacks that the way to combat racism and discrimination was "to obey every rule of proper behavior to the letter, to offer no provocation for discrimination" (p.183).

So, in an effort to empower the race and gain social acceptance, literacy programs were created to educate the young and old. Black schools, colleges, and universities were created. The birth rate, although different for Northern and Southern Black women, due to the agricultural versus the industrial lifestyle, had significantly decreased. Black men and women implemented codes to establish themselves as "ladies" and "gentlemen" by negating all of the stereotypes that had been developed to justify their oppression. Black women sought to avoid the sexual exploitation of White men, while Black men adapted practices such as addressing White women without eye contact in order to avoid the repercussion of a perceived or misinterpreted attraction to White women. Through this development, intra racial class and gender lines began to emerge. Hines and Thompson (1998) support this assertion.

> They (Black women) and their husbands wanted certain things for them, certain differences from slavery. First, they wanted never again to be forced out of their homes before dawn, leaving behind children too small to take care of themselves and housework that would never get done. Second, they wanted never again to work under the supervision of White men who might physically and sexually abuse them. Third, they wanted to be seen as women, not workhorses. . . . Both southern landowners and northern reformers considered the desire of Black women to work at home rather than in the fields to be evidence of laziness, and they were outraged by it. Southerners saw it as "acting the lady," since no Black woman could actually be a lady in their eyes (p.153).

This study argues that the presentation of the Black race in the early films directly relates to the ruling classes attempt to restore power relations by promoting the first stereotypical constructs through film.

The Jezebel and the Buck in Film

It was found that many of the early films (1894, 1903) that presented African Americans, such as *the Watermelon Eating Contest* (1894), *Nigger in a Woodpile* (1904), *and Uncle Tom's Cabin (1903)*, more focused on deconstructing the Black male identity through reinforcing stereotypes of infantilism, laziness, ignorance, aggression, subservience, and later hyper sexuality *The Birth of a Nation (1915)*. It is argued that the focus on the deconstruction of the Black male related to the fact that women, in general, would not have been privy to the right to vote and other social, political, and economic rights that were only afforded men during that era, so the Black woman did not pose a significant threat to the racialized perception of "social stability."

Black men, however, served to gain with the passage of any inclusionary laws, and so promoting his disenfranchisement served a greater purpose during this era. For as Hines and Thompson (1998) argue "for the South to be "redeemed" it was first necessary to make sure that Black men could not vote. All else could follow from that" (p.166). It was imperative to obstruct the Black mans political access/power so that it could not be used to gain greater levels of social and economic power.

So, the films of that era focused on either promoting the inferiority of the Black man or promoting the aggression of Black men so as to promote the fear of the Black man in society.

The earliest presentations of the images of Black women were presented in *A Morning Bath* (1896) and *Native Washer Women* (1903). These movies presented Black women semi nude (bare breasted) washing clothes and bathing a child outdoors respectively. It is argued that these images specifically present the Black woman in a like that is more reflective of the indigenous cultural rituals and practices of African women before her extraction and enslavement. Those specific images presented without adequate context perpetuate the misunderstanding and misrepresentation of African culture that European explorers and colonizers originally utilized to establish notions of biological and moral inferiority. Utilizing the presentation of the Black woman nude out of context, and in American media establishes the concept of inferiority, savagery, and sexual deviance. And in an era where the sexual abuse and rape of Black women was a constant threat, this type of hegemonic presentation was clearly harmful.

In 1896, nearly 30 years after the abolition of slavery, and 280 years after the first slaves were brought to America, the images presented in these films do not accurately reflect the true state and location of the African-American—period. No Black man is stealing from the corner store and hiding in a woodpile to avoid capture, and no Black woman is washing clothes by the river without a shirt in the United States of America. Yet, for those that do not have contract with the race, universally presenting those types of images during that time perpetuates the fallacy that the hegemonic presentation reflects the *current* sociopolitical condition and location. And in so doing, reinforces earlier notions about the race that lend support for the need to continue to relegate African Americans to pre emancipatory status in American society.

The Birth of a Nation (1915) which was the most popular film of that era supports that notion. It is the first major motion picture and the most significant testament to the sentiment of White America during that era. It continues to speak to the use of film as a hegemonic tool that was deliberately produced and distributed for the purpose of promoting societal fear of integration. As film historian Lewis Jacobs argued in Mapp (1970):

> This film was a passionate and persuasive avowal of the inferiority of the Negro. . . . The entire portrayal of the reconstruction days showed the Negro, when freed from his White domination, as an ignorant, lustful villain . . . lustfully ogling the White women in the balcony (p.18).

While most analyses of this film (Mapp, 1970; Bogle, 1979; Wallace, 1985) focus on the predominance of the presentation of the Black man's lust for the White woman—most fail to recognize, much less discuss the equally significant, though not as prevalent, presentation of the Black woman's lust for the White man. This presentation, like that of the Black man should not be negated because the concept and presentation of *this* lust has also has its implications both historic and contemporary.

The presentation of the Black man's "lust" for White women was intentionally designed to promote the threat of Black male sexual aggression which was then utilized to justify harassing, and even murdering Black men who were accused of "ogling"—looking at White women in a "sexual" and/or "lustful" manner. This served the purpose of promoting the fear that, if given the opportunity, (not being under the direct control of the White man), Black men would rape White women. This was specifically emphasized in the film, where after "ogling" this White woman for the entire time, the Black man finally seizes the opportunity to rape her. After chasing her through the woods, the White woman jumps off of a cliff, to her death rather than succumb to the hands of a Black man.

Yet, the reality of the times illustrates that rape was not specific to the Black male, it was and had historically been significant to the Black woman. It was common place and something that Black women sought to protect their daughters, nieces, and granddaughters against by teaching them how to passively avoid situations where it might occur. So, the absence of any analyses that focus on the presentation of the Jezebel character in this film is negligent at best.

In this film, it is the mulatto maid who has unrequited affections for the master who rebukes her. In response to his rebuke, she becomes angry and throws herself to the ground ripping off her own clothing. Once her dress is torn, she passionately fondles her breasts and licks her fingers in dramatic lust for her master. This scene in a film made in 1915.

The presentation of the Jezebel in this film was a very significant part of the film because it presented the mulatto in a role where she was literally plotting to receive the intimacy of the White master throughout the film. While the Black man was lusting after the White woman, so was the Black woman lusting after the White man. Thus, her presentation is equally, if not more disturbing than the presentation of the Black man for a very important reason.

In American society during that era, there were serious legal and sociopolitical protections for White women that constrained and restrained the Black man's (imagined) pursuit of her in any capacity. For any advances toward a White woman would certainly result in punishment or more commonly in the South, death.

However, there were no protections for the Black woman against the "pursuit" of the White man—especially house slaves, and later live in domestic workers who were openly exposed and unprotected against the pursuit of those in close quarters to her.

The abuse of the Black woman's body was a part of history and was already ingrained in society as an acceptable practice. Therefore, presenting the Black woman as wanting and lusting after the White man only reinforced the notions that facilitated and justified her sexual and physical abuse and exploitation in the first place and placed her at greater risk for *having* to continue to work in the White man's home.

From slavery through Reconstruction and Jim Crow, White men could rape Black women with impunity. And since a huge majority of employed Black women worked in White households under the authority of and in proximity to White men, they were continually exposed to sexual harassment, abuse, and what would now be considered acquaintance rape. Rape was just another weapon of Southern terrorism, a terrorism that "would make many African Americans decide to leave the South" (Hines and Thompson 1998:171).

Jim Crow/The Great Black Migration/ Domestic Era—The Late 1920s to 1945—The Mammy, The Coon, and the Uncle Tom

There were many productive and sociopolitical factors that led to the migration of Blacks from the South and the transition from agricultural to industrial and domestic labor. The growth of industrial capitalism in America and WWI created a demand for labor that emerged from the decline in European immigration during the early 1900s, (Horowitz et al. 2004). And although there the South had conceded, there was still sociopolitical tension between the North and South, as the North was fully promoting industrial development, while the South was holding on to its traditions and agricultural economy.

Even though the cotton gin had reduced the need for human labor during that time, the tradition of White supremacy and the continued desire to relegate Black people to slavery, and/or keep them oppressed remained the predominant sociopolitical agenda operating through Jim Crow and Black Codes in the South. Any Black person in the South was subject to the violence and terrorism of not only the state, but also racist organizations such as the KKK whose members were, most often members of state and local law enforcement and judicial systems.

The beginning of this era saw the Matewan Massacre (1920), the Ocoee Massacre (1920), the bombing of Black Wall Street (1921), and the Rosewood Massacre (1923) (Horowitz et al. 2004:23,24), just to name a few of the more notable and recorded attacks against Black communities and Black progress. Therefore, the promise of greater opportunity in addition to the escape from terror contributed to the Era of Black migration. (Hines and Thompson 1998)

However, in spite of the promise, labor hierarchies that were supported by discriminatory hiring practices and more covert, yet equally crippling, forms of institutional racism also existed in the North. Before WWI, the United States had already opened its borders to Eastern European immigrants in order to fill the intensifying demand for labor during this era, (Horowitz 2004). However, after WWI, the United States reopened its borders to European immigrants and also sought Puerto Rican immigrants as well.

The ethnic and racial contact, combined with the competition for work that was driven by the Depression fueled racial tension in the North. However, the stereotypes of African Americans that preceded Emancipation did not die with its signing. Instead, it continued to serve as the justification for discriminatory practices in all spheres, leaving African Americans at the bottom of the labor pool. As a result, the hierarchy in the Northern industrial labor market primarily consisted of White American men, White European men, White Eastern European men, and then Black men. On occasion, few White women could be found in the industrial labor market. And where Black women were found, they were relegated to lower level clean up work in the factories.

Consequently, in this transition, the majority of African-American men were relegated to lower level industrial positions, while the majority of African-American women were systematically excluded from participation in the industrial and manufacturing labor markets, and most often relegated to domestic labor—where the large majority of Black working class women would stay until the transition into the electronic era. (Clark-Lewis 1985 and Hill Collins 2002)

The minority who were able to get a college education were able to secure professional and semi professional positions within segregated Black communities—predominantly as teachers, social workers, and nurses. (Hines and Thompson 1998)

In essence, even though Black labor was welcomed and needed, factory work (industrial labor) was still reserved for White men and in menial factory positions, White women. And in those cases the need for domestic labor extended to White working class women, while middle class women sought to utilize domestic labor to assert status, and wealthy and ruling class women continued to use domestic workers in keeping with the tradition.

So, for African-American men, the transition from the agricultural era to the industrial era, led to a transition from slave labor to agricultural labor (farming for wage or in rare cases where Black men were able to purchase or acquire land—farming) or sharecropping, to large scale low level factory labor, specialized and unspecialized skilled labor, and industry service work, such as rail car porters, hotel bellmen, and bus boys. While, the majority of working class African-American women would transition to domestic labor—live in domestics, live out domestics, laundresses, and seamstresses.

The Mammy and the Uncle Tom

The Mammy

This work presupposes that in the same manner that many refused to return to the fields under the same conditions as slavery after emancipation, which caused a labor shortage and created a hardship for White people who were completely dependent on Black labor (Hines and Thompson 1998), there was the fear of the same type of resistance in the domestic sphere. Therefore, the Mammy and Tom constructs were developed to promote continued support for the control and exploitation of Black labor through promoting the acceptance of Black labor in White industries. In essence, the destructive stereotypes that had been designed to promote resistance to integration now had to be dispelled in order to counter the resistance to the, now necessary, integration of African Americans into mainstream labor markets and homes outside of the control of slavery. The visual presentation of the Mammy and Uncle Tom represents the transition in way in which Black productive and reproductive labor had to be utilized and exploited during this shift from an agricultural to an industrial economy.

During slavery, the need to promote the dehumanization of the African was essential to justifying the complete control and exploitation of not only the agricultural labor power, but the reproductive labor power and capacity of Black men and women. Immediately following Emancipation, (during the Pre-Industrial transition), the continued, or even escalated, promotion of the negative stereotypes served the purpose of creating resistance to integration—which allowed the South to continue to exploit African-American people. However, the developing Industrial era created a demand for Black labor in integrated venues. Therefore, earlier presentations needed to be negated in order to promote a level of social acceptance that would allow industries to utilize Black labor without destructive resistance or disruptive violence and/or conflict.

The new presentations (Mammy and Uncle Tom) reflect images that do not pose a threat to the validity of White supremacy, or a threat to the stability of White labor or the White marriage and family. The Mammy and the Uncle Tom negate and replace the original hyper sexual, violent, and aggressive constructs of the Jezebel and the Buck by promoting the "conformed" "submissive" "a sexual" and "a familial" images of Black men and women. They are both images that represent the eager to please, proud to serve beings who enthusiastically and "commitedly" promote the welfare and interests of White people, especially the White family (children) above his/her own or that of his/her absent/nonexistent family.

These constructs represent the images' passive acceptance and appreciation for his/her lower class status of servitude, and establishes commitment, pleasure toward the assigned tasks and privilege at even being allowed to establish a voluntary relationship, however subordinate, with the White family and White people in general. In essence, the dominance of the presentation of these constructs in mainstream film promotes the way in which Black people must be perceived by White society in order to be tolerated in the workplace and especially the homes of middle-class Whites, while simultaneously promoting the hegemony that is necessary to ensure Black conformity to the new form of productive exploitation, and power relations where now all White people—not just the elite—are given authority over the Black being.

Both of these factors are equally important, because although much of the historical literature fails to address the adulterous component of the "masters" sexual exploitation of the slave woman, and later his domestic workers, this had to be a factor and consideration in not only the selection of domestic workers by the mistress, but in the construction of the cinematic image of the Mammy. It is argued that just as the Black woman had previously been subject to the sexual abuse, assault, and harassment and rape by the slave masters, emancipation did not remove the White man's sexual inclination toward Black women. And so, even in her domestic capacity, she was still subject to the same sexual pursuit as much of the literature (Collins 2002 and 2004; hooks 1994; James and Sharpley-Whiting 2001; Hines and Thompson 1998 and Clark Lewis 1984) posits.

In addition to the continued threat of sexual violation and abuse, Clarke Lewis (1984) and Collins (2002) argued that domestic work was very hard and required much time and effort by Black domestics. So even in a voluntary capacity, being relegated to the domestic sphere, the Black body and labor power were still being controlled by the White mistress or master. Therefore, just like slavery, there was no boundaries around the extent to which her labor or body would be exploited in the home of her employer. The only difference is now she was getting paid a wage.

And even though, as Clark Lewis (1985) argues, the North provided an opportunity to "live out" and thereby have an end to the workday no matter how long. In the early part of this era there were still a vast number of 'live in' workers in the North and South that were subject to control over their productive labor 24 hours a day.

The Mammy construct represents the a sexual, unattractive, matronly woman that served as not only the role of laborer but the role of confidante, nurturer, wet nurse, nanny, nurse who readily and happily places the needs of the White family over her own needs and those of her own absent family and social network.

Carby argues in Collins (2002), ." . . the objective of the stereotype is not to reflect or represent a reality but to function as a disguise, or mystification of objective social relations" (p.69). However, this study argues that the construct, no mater how stereotypical the visual presentation, does reflect the sociopolitical reality of the Black woman. There is no doubt, and data supports the fact that during the Mammy era, domestic labor was a predominant part of the working class Black woman's experience, just as deference and subservience was a predominant part of the relationship between the domestic and mistress, Blacks and Whites.

The difference is that the visual presentation in mainstream film does not reflect the familial and physical reality of the Black woman, and hence fails to present the oppressive nature of the relationship accurately. By again removing the Black woman from her own subjectivity and experience as a woman, just as in the previous era, her labor can be exploited without consideration given to her own role as wife, mother, daughter, and community member. In the absence of visual presentations of her husband and children and family and church and community, her labor can, once again, be maximally exploited without conscience or resistance.

In addition, the asexual presentation of the construct creates the notion of the domestic as being a safe addition to the household that does not awaken the issue of the White man's historic infidelity or sexual attraction, disposition, and/ or aggression toward Black women. As Collins (2002) supports:

> The first controlling image applied to U.S. Black women is that of the Mammy, the faithful, obedient domestic servant. Created to justify the economic exploitation of house slaves and sustained to explain Black women's long standing restriction to domestic service, the Mammy image represents the normative yardstick used to evaluate all Black women's behavior (p.72).

So, it is argued that it was not that the Mammy as a domestic laborer did not accurately reflect the condition and location of working class Black women nationally during that era. It is that the image of the domestic worker, and the presentation of her relation to her work was not an accurate representation of real domestic workers or their labor, but rather a presentation of the dominant idea of the domestic worker that represented the visual and attitudinal characteristics that comfortable to White society. A presentation that was necessary to, again, promote the exploitation of the *domestic* labor of the Black woman. Collins supports this assertion in identifying how this relationship "symbolizes the dominant group's perceptions of the ideal Black female relationship to elite White male power" (Collins 2001:72). And it is this representation that is promoted in film by the White men who wrote, produced, and directed films in that era. hooks furthers the contention when she states.

> By Hollywood standards, and this includes films by Black directors, a full figured, plump, Black woman can only play the role of Mammy /matron. She can never be the object of desire. Ever willing to cater to the needs of the marketplace. . . . Black bodies, then, are like clay, there to be shaped so that they become anything that the White man wants them to be. They become the embodiment of his desires. This paradigm mirrors that of colonialism. It offers a romanticized image of the White colonizer moving into Black territory, occupying it, possessing it in a way that affirms his identity (hooks 1994:56).

This passage is profound in that in its way it argues that just as the construct of the Jezebel represents the White male's physical objectification, sexual desire, and lust toward the "eroticism" of the Black body, that White women can not represent, so does the Mammy represent the White male's physical objectification of maternalism and matriarchy that White women can not represent. And so, as Collins states, "The Mammy becomes the public face that Whites expect Black women to assume for them" (Collins 2001:73), a comfortable, trustworthy, and safe being to have around.

In many of the movies (*Pinky, Imitation of Life, Mildred Pierce, Gone With the Wind,* and the later *Guess Who's Coming to Dinner*), the White woman was a heroine of sorts, either single or a single mother. Therefore, there were no White "masters" living in the household where the Mammy worked and very little interaction between the Mammy construct and the White male character in the film.

While all of the films reflect the characteristics of the Mammy, *Imitation of Life* provides one of the clearest reflections of this presentation. In this film, Delilah, The Mammy, accidentally goes to the home of a single mother, Ms. B, struggling to balance raising her daughter with her career, while trying to find another address. Although Delilah is at the wrong house, she voluntarily delves into the household chores of the mistress, cleaning the kitchen and preparing a meal while Ms. B attends to her daughter who has slipped down into the tub of water. When Ms. B returns to Delilah, she is introduced to the daughter who points to her and replies, "Horsey, nice horsey," and they all start to laugh. She begs the mistress to allow her, and her half-White daughter, to remain in the house, making the argument that "I don't eat how I look." Among other issues presented, such as that of Delilah's self-hate and her daughters "passing" (as White), the movie centers on Delilah's faithful servitude to her mistress, and her irrational self-sacrifice.

This is noted when Delilah develops a pancake mix called, ironically, "Aunt Delilah's." And although she could have been rich, she gives up her rights to any of the fortune made from this enterprise to her mistress, who becomes rich off of her pancake mix. She reasons that she doesn't need any money because she just wants to stay with her mistress. When the mistress encourages her to take the money so that she can get her own home, and, in essence, be self sufficient, she replies, "my own house, you gon' send me away, Ms. B. Don't' send me away. Please don't do that. How's I'm gonna take care of you?" Ms. B responds "Oh, Delilah, you're hopeless."

In *Gone With The Wind* (1939), while the Mammy is more loud and aggressive in her presentation, she still presents the devoted Mammy who takes care of the O'Hara family and is absent of any relationship or social interaction with her own family, community, only serving as the "overseer" of the other Black maids in the household. And while some may argue that her assertiveness and verbosity changes the nature of the construct. This work argues that because her presentation is only in relation to "young" Scarlet, and is done in a maternalistic, reprimanding nature, it is not truly an assertion of aggression against the character, but a show of concern and nurturing for the character—as any good "mammy" (mother) would do.

This assertion is made clear when young Scarlet refuses to eat before a date. Concerned about her and how she will present if she is hungry and over eats at the picnic in front of her date, and how it will reflect on the O'Hara family, she scolds young Scarlet O'Hara "If you don't care what folks says bout dis' family, I does!"

This type of presentation is reflective of all of the Mammy presentations. Each movie suggests that the Black woman (Mammy construct) has nothing else to live for but serving her White mistress/master. This is the hegemonic presentation.

This type of presentation promotes the notion of Black women in surplus and service labor positions that are not different from that of the house slave. It promotes the trusting relationship between the Mammy and the mistress of the home in which she works as being more important than her own social and economic stability. And promotes working as a domestic in a highly ideal fashion which, as Clark Lewis (1994) argued in *Living in Living Out*, did not reflect the real experiences of Black domestics who were often mistreated, overworked, and extremely underpaid.

The Uncle Tom

The Uncle Tom is the male version of the Mammy. Like the construct of the Mammy, the Uncle Tom also represents the subservient, eager to please, passive, a sexual and a familial Black man. This construct, as with the Mammy, is necessary to negate the construct of the Buck and the Mandingo—the hypersexual, aggressive, and violent Black man who would rape a White woman if given the opportunity.

As discussed earlier in this chapter, promoting this devotion was is essential to ensuring the continued ability to exploit Black labor during the Industrial era. The North needed the mass labor power and the specialized skills of Black men to promote Industrial development, which meant that integration in the workplace was inevitable. As Collins (2001) argues:

> Black women domestic workers remained poor because they were economically exploited workers in a capitalist political economy. . . . Historically, many White families in both the middle class and working class were able to maintain their class position because they used Black women domestic workers as a source of cheap labor (Rollins 1985; Byerly 1986). The Mammy image was designed to mask this economic exploitation of social class (King 1973) (p.74).

This work also argues that in that same capacity, Black men also served to provide a source of cheap and/or surplus labor and service to White people, White businesses, and White owned industries in their various roles. Therefore, the Uncle Tom construct, like the Mammy, represented the subservient, de-masculinized, a sexual, trustworthy construct of the Black man, that was utilized to deconstruct the threatening image of the Buck.

While the Buck represented all of the reasons why White society should fear, hence, maintain control over the Black man, the Uncle Tom represented all of the reasons why he could be trusted and "worked with." He was harmless and could willingly and easily be controlled by all, even White children—a docile, humble, and soft Black man that neither presented a threat nor warranted fear from White men or White women.

So in presentation, the Uncle Tom is often a middle aged, dark-skinned, bug eyed unattractive, skinny to frail, Black man, the antithesis of the "big, Black Buck." So, not only did he not present or pose a threat to White women, he did not pose a threat to the collective ego of White men by possibly being an "object of desire" for White women.

The Mammy and the Tom were both essential to deconstructing the notions, hence, possible internalizations of the notions of hyper-sexuality that had been the predominant presentation during the Jezebel/Buck Era. For since Slavery, as an institution, had been dismantled, the reproductive labor of Black people was no longer economically necessary, but could no longer be directly controlled by the slave master or the state. Therefore, the Mammy and the Tom constructs served as the antitheses of the Jezebel and the Buck. As it is argued in (Collins 2001 &2004; hooks 1994; and Bogle, 1974), the Mammy and the Tom represent a sexual and undesirable characters that do not interact with Black men or women, her/his own family, or other Blacks in a social setting. Each is dedicated to her/his White mistress and 'master,' and to their children, treating them more like her/his own than her/his own. Each is trustworthy, passive, and highly submissive. So, as it has been argued, the shift in the dominance of the visual presentation from the Jezebel to the Mammy, the Buck to the Tom reflects the hegemonic attempt to: (1) establish and promote the continued use and exploitation of Black people as a surplus labor supply, (2) allow White people to readily exploit the labor without connection to the reality that this labor did take Black men and women away from their own families and lives (4) remove them from their new found subjectivity and keep them relegated to the control and dominance of White society, (5) negate the reality and existence of Black intimacy and sexuality, and (6) to visually remove them from their own familial roles as a latent means of destabilizing the Black family.

The Great Depression/Early Civil Rights Era from the 1920s to 1945

The period of the mechanization of industry that characterizes the late part of this era, was a period of more efficient production, which led to the displacement of factory workers as well as the displacement of domestic workers. With layoffs in the factories caused by the shift to more efficient and specialized forces of production and economic depression, Black men and White women were significantly displaced from the labor force.

As African Americans had traditionally occupied positions of surplus labor, this transition added to the hardship that was created during the Great Depression.

While middle class Blacks were educating themselves and providing services to the segregated Black community in the medical, legal, professoriate, teaching, nursing, and social work professions, and the semi professions of hairdressing, barbers, dress makers, and brick layers (Hines and Thompson 1998), working class Black's were significantly displaced from the labor market.

However, discrimination and institutionalized racism continued to affect African Americans at all levels, and worsened during and after the Great Depression in the 1920s through 1930s; therefore the struggle for equality continued to garner the support of both classes. As Hines and Thompson (1998) state:

> The Great Depression of the 1930s was one of the most catastrophic eras in American history. Americans in all walks of life suffered economic hardships, and African Americans were particularly hard hit. The thousands of Black men and women who had left the South in the 1920s for northern cities and Midwestern communities in search of a better future for themselves and their families now found themselves embroiled in a fierce struggle for jobs, housing, education, and first class citizenship. As their economic status worsened, they also increasingly faced brutal violence, race riots, and blatant racial discrimination and segregation (p.241).

Specifically after WWI, the pressure of the Civil Rights Movement and the overall conditions of race relations in America were points of concern. The devastation that the war had caused in Europe set the foundation for U.S. movement in the global economy. However, in order to solidify its dominance as a world power, it was necessary for the United States to: (1) prepare the infrastructure for larger scale global trade, (2) improve the domestic economy and the condition of the American people, (3) reduce the global *perception* of racism and discrimination within the U.S., and (4) ensure that declining race relations would not lead to another Civil War that would destroy the economic and infra-structural condition of the U.S.

In order to do this, Roosevelt developed the New Deal Act, that comprised of a series of social welfare policies and programs that were designed to build the infrastructure and allow suburban development, such as the Works Progress Administration, and improve the conditions of the American people through providing unemployment insurance, the federal mortgage loan, the Agricultural Adjustment Administration, and Social Security. As Horowitz et al. argue (2004).

> In the first half of the twentieth century, the United States was preparing to assume its leadership in the world economy. The ruling class needed both class peace at home and support of the nation's workers for its imperialist domination of the Third World. The needs of capital coincided with the demands of labor at home. Through the Wagner Act, Social Security, unemployment insurance, and so forth, labor-capital relations were reformed (p. 6).

The Sapphire versus the Sambo Dynamic

The Sapphire construct is the only construct that remains dominant throughout the Early Industrial and Late Industrial eras. However, in the Early Industrial Era the construct is only present in all Black-cast films. So her dominance in Black-cast films exists simultaneous to the Mammy construct in mainstream films. It is argued that Black-cast films rejected the presentation of the Mammy construct as counterproductive to the desire to present "the life of the Black Middle Class." The Sapphire becomes dominant in mainstream film in the Late Industrial Era when mainstream film makers begin to engage main Black characters and majority Black-cast films. It (the construct) remains present, if not dominant, throughout the Electronic Era as well. So the analysis of the relationship of the Sapphire construct to the political economy will transcend the through all three eras.

It is argued that the perpetuation of the Sapphire has three implications. It instigates the intra racial gender and class antagonisms, and perpetuates the deconstruction of both Black female and male gender identity. However, more significant is the utilization of the Sapphire construct or the Black woman as the sexual and/or maternal perpetuator of White male anger and control.

It is argued that Black women, who had forged closer *proximal* relationships to White men, and women alike, through the history of domestic servitude, would assume the responsibility, in presentation, of castrating or antagonizing the Black man. And, in so doing, the White male, as a representative of the state would be removed from the visual role of the degradation, domination, and aggression that the Sapphire represents. Collins (2004) argues:

> Under the new racism, these class specific representations of Black masculinity and Black femininity serve several purposes. They speak to the importance that ideologies of class and culture now have in justifying the persistence of racial inequality. Within the universe of these representations, authentic and respectable Black people become constructed as class opposites, and their different cultures help explain why poor and working class Black people are at the bottom of the economic hierarchy and middle class Black people are not." She furthers. "These class specific images create a Black gender ideology that simultaneously defines Black masculinity and Black femininity in relation to one another and that also positions Black gender ideology as the opposite of normal (White) gender ideology . . . that depicts Black men as being inappropriately weak and Black women as being inappropriately strong (p.182).

Consequently, then, in her quest to de-masculinize/emasculate the Black man, the Sapphire construct represents and perpetuates the de-feminization of the Black woman. And while, it must be clear that this study *is not* presupposing that African-American women needed to strive for, internalize, accept, or have traditional gender roles "bestowed" upon them by White society, or were even consciously rejecting the notions of European patriarchal femininity that she had never been privy too. What *is* being asserted is that the decorum assigned to 'the lady,' and the support and protection provided by 'the man' was always a part of gender relationships between African men and women and was not distinct to the European as has been suggested in much of the Western literature. Breaking this relationship was the focus of "breaking" during slavery. (Mengara 2003)

Therefore, it is argued that mainstream literary and media presentations that promote the Black woman's seemingly inherent aggression toward, and domination over, Black men have no real or significant historical foundation. No literature about African-American women from the antebellum to the early Civil Rights Era (Gibson 1994; Clark Lewis 1985; Hines 1998; and Wallace 1974) supports the presence of the type of anger and hostility toward Black men that the Sapphire construct represents and portrays. And so, as Wallace (1974) argues even though, "It has become a national belief that because the Black woman's master was the slave owner, and not her husband, she became abusive to her husband, overly aggressive, bossy, domineering . . . those who trace such characteristics in the contemporary Black woman back to her slave ancestry . . . find . . . that contrary to the creation and promotion of this construct, Black women remained a 'loyal, faithful, and dutiful' to her brothers" (p.139).

What this work is pointing out is the fact that the Sapphire was more a fictionalized construct of the Black woman than an accurate representation of her relationship with Black men. This construct more represented and perpetuated the projection of the real anger, hate, aggression, and hostility of White America during the Jim Crow Era that had been a prime component of the ruling class's relationship with Black people since slavery.

The assertion that the anger and degradation that the Sapphire represents can be attributed to Black women has no real foundation. Historical accounts do not support those characteristics as being a real component of the Black woman's attitude or interaction with Black men, which may explain why the wrath of the Sapphire is not projected onto White men in mainstream films until it is utilized briefly during the Blaxploitation Era, and has only recently been projected on to White women in film.

It is for this reason that this work argues that while other constructs drive more literary criticism and wrath than The Sapphire, the media Era of the Sapphire versus the Sambo was perhaps the most detrimental for/to African Americans. It marked a transition in the media's perpetuation and presentation of anger, dominance, and hostility from White men to Black women, which, subsequently, led to, or at the least, contributed to, the legitimization of racist stereotypes, the internalization of self hate, and the solidification of class and, especially, gender antagonisms that continue to plague the African-American community today.

This work found that the emergence of the Sapphire versus the Sambo dynamic coincided with the production of (independent) all Black-cast films in the late 1920s, and therefore existed simultaneous to the Mammy and the Tom constructs that were being heavily promoted in mainstream film wherein Black men and women were playing supporting roles. However, the dominance of this construct in all Black-cast films would not occur until the late 1930s, and would not cross interracial lines until the 'Blaxploitation' era in the early 1970s.

The Sapphire construct crosses several important productive and sociopolitical eras. This is why her presentation was so important in the perpetuation of ideological and cultural hegemony. As was discussed in the earlier in the chapter, Emancipation created a great rift between the North and South. The North was dedicated to uniting the country under an industrial economy, but the South was still dependent on its agricultural wealth. In 1865, the cotton gin had not yet replaced human labor; therefore, the Southern 'plantocracy' was still dependent on Blacks for its agricultural development. After Emancipation, as has been argued, many Black women refused to return to the fields and be subject to the control of White overseers (Hines and Thompson, 1998). Therefore, the South faced a crisis.

Early Black films that introduced/presented the Sapphire construct were written, produced, and distributed by White men/companies—later dome were directed by Black men. So the Sapphire versus the Sambo era has a very significant relevance. It is argued that the Sapphire construct emerges in an effort to promote intra racial gender and class antagonisms—a divide and conquer approach. This is argued because the Sapphire construct is specifically designed to 'verbally castrate' the Sambo, hence, the Black man, through promoting the very stereotypes about his laziness, stupidity, irresponsibility, and inferiority that were still predominant during that time. But, now this attitude was not only prevalent to White people, but now to Black women as well. However, the presentation of the Sapphire construct does not reflect the real historic relationship between Black men and women (Hines and Thompson 1998). And as the figure illustrates, neither did it reflect the sociopolitical and economic location of Black men during that time.

In the films where the Sapphire construct is present and/dominant, she was known for her verbal abuse and aggression toward the Sambo who was usually very passive in his reaction to, and dealings with her. The Sambo role presents the Black man as a lazy, ignorant, and uneducated sloth, in relation to the Sapphire construct. The indication is usually that he is unemployed and irresponsible, lying around at home while the woman works in a domestic capacity in order to support the family.

The Framing of the Shrew provides a most profound example of the Sapphire versus the Sambo interplay that was present in all films that met these criteria. In this film, (as will be discussed later in the chapter), the Sapphire construct refers to the Sambo construct as "a low-livered trife. A no-account, lazy scalawag who ain't worth a diddle."

St. Louis Blues also perpetuated this notion. In this movie Bessie Smith plays a blues singer who comes home to find her man with another woman. In this film,

Ms. Smith immediately enters and begins to fight with the young woman. While, very submissive to her boyfriend, Bessie was highly aggressive and volatile with "the other woman." After being knocked to the ground by her boyfriend, Bessie who is assumed to be an alcoholic by her being "familiar" with the bar and getting drunk—sings her song My Man. This is another identification of the Sapphire vs. Sambo construct.

These types of exchanges and interactions are designed to have the Sapphire promote the construct of the Sambo, through having her to reinforce the stereotype and hegemonic ideologies of the Black man. Both of these stereotypes represent the antithesis of the European notion of a man and a woman. The presentation and perpetuation of this type of relationship, as Collins (2004) argued, serves the purpose of promoting the *binary construction* of Black masculinity and femininity that has proven to be destructive to gender relations in the Black community.

It is argued that the sociopolitical goal of deconstructing Black masculinity is to maintain support for the exclusion of the Black man and to relegate him to the control of the White ruling class. This is why the Sapphire construct emerges and becomes visible—if not dominant in this era. This is argued because census data shows that the Sambo is not an accurate reflection of the sociopolitical and economic location of African-American men during that era.

According to Census data, in 1910, 94.40% of Black men were actively participating in the labor force. By 1920, although the rate continued to significantly decline over time, due to the Depression, it was still at 89.5% and 79.9% in 1940. On the converse, the rate of Black women in the work force dropped from 54.4% in 1910 to 24% in 1920 and back up slightly in 1940 to 25.8%, which meant that from 1920 to 1940 less than 25% of Black women were actively participating in the labor market during that time (which does not include those who were working "off of the books" and perhaps being paid cash. Therefore, it can be surmised that in the absence of any social or governmental support, the men in the Black community had to be largely supporting their families.

Therefore, it is argued that the presentation of the Sapphire versus the Sambo antagonism, does not correspond to the real relational dynamics between Black men and Black women. Black women were simply NOT taking care of Black men during that time. The statistics do not support the stereotypical notion that the Black man was lazy and unemployed.

The visual presentation of the Sapphire versus the Sambo interplay represents a highly significant and relevant dynamic. The Sapphire (the Black woman) is now directly utilized to directly support, hence, promote the ideologies about Black men and Black women that were once only promoted by not only the White American ruling class, but vocal and visual White supremacist organizations—namely the Ku Klux Klan. Now, in film, it is the Black woman who oppresses the Black man so that "White figures" no longer need to do so.

As has been discussed throughout this work, the Sapphire construct is centered on her attitude and presentation. She is the physical construct of either the

Jezebel or the Mammy. However, in either of these physical constructs she is loud, verbose, demeaning, and highly aggressive. And her aggression is most often projected toward other Black characters, specifically the Black male.

As mentioned earlier in this chapter, this construct is highly significant for this era as this was the era wherein the United States was attempting to solidify itself as a global power using democracy and freedom as its ideological principle. However, during this era, the conditions of African Americans and the presence of national racism, exclusion, and discrimination gave rise to questions about America's true commitment to the very principles that it was trying to promote. The question was how can America promote freedom and equality abroad, when it did not offer the same to African Americans on its own soil? This made the promotion of overt racism counterproductive to its mission of expansion. Therefore, it was no longer productive and in the national interest for the visual presentation of Black people to include or incorporate any notion of racial subjugation or suppression by the ruling class, the state, or its officers. So, this era marks a very significant transition in the hegemonic presentation of the relationship between Black men and women in film.

The era begins with the transition from the Mammy to the Sapphire construct, the re-emergence of the Jezebel construct, and the shift from films in which Black actors and actresses only played supporting roles in predominantly White films, to all Black-cast films. It is argued that producing all Black-cast films for mainstream consumption not only allowed for the introduction of the Sapphire construct, but facilitated the penetration of hegemonic ideologies into the Black community by filtering them in through the voice of the Black actor. It was understood that limited all Black-cast films would most certainly be welcomed and in demand by Black audiences. Therefore, the concepts, as long as they kept the interest of the audience would be a readily acceptable form of entertainment.

Black-cast films solidified the emergence and dominance of the Sapphire during this era because in the still existing Jim Crow, early Civil Rights Era, the Sapphire construct could have never emerged in relation to White characters in mainstream film. It was rarely a real experience that was not met without severe consequence; therefore, implausible to come to fruition in the minds of mainstream, or even Black writers and producers, which leads to the most important point.

As Gramsci and Freire argue, and this work supports, the real strength lies in the oppressed class's acceptance of the interest of the ruling class as predominant, which is the final premise of this work. It is argued that once the presentations that emerge from the ideologies of the ruling class are accepted and internalized by the oppressed, he will contribute to his own oppression by becoming, or assuming the characteristics defined by the ruling class or the characteristics of the ruling class itself. In each case he will be devoid of the consciousness that allows for his participation in social transformation. In accordance with Gramsci, Freire elaborated on this condition in his work *Pedagogy of the Oppressed* when he stated:

But almost always, during the initial stage of the struggle, the oppressed, striving for liberation, tend themselves to become oppressors, or sub-oppressors. The very structure of their thought has been conditioned by the contradictions of the concrete, existential situation by which they were shaped. Their ideal is to be men, but for them, to be men is to be oppressors. This phenomenon derives from the fact that the oppressed, at a certain moment of their existential experience, adopt an attitude of adhesion to the oppressor . . . Because of their identification with the oppressor, they have no consciousness of themselves as persons or as members of an oppressed class. It is not to become free that they want agrarian reform, but in order to acquire land . . . and thus become bosses over other workers . . . The oppressed, having internalized the image of the oppressor and adopted his guidelines, are fearful of freedom (Freire 1972:28).

The Sapphire construct is essential to the promotion and solidification of intra racial gender and class divisions. For, as has been discussed throughout this chapter, after Emancipation, it was a primary goal of the race to establish itself as deserving of full social, political, and economic exclusion. A large part of that agenda involved dispelling the myths of Black inferiority by educating the people, establishing a "normalized" gender identity—thereby gaining the trust of White society. It was presupposed that shedding the stereotypes that had been imposed upon the race would result in the acceptance of African Americans as equal.

However, during the era of the Sapphire, Black labor was still being exploited and the race was still being oppressed. Therefore, the media presentations still centered on promoting the stereotypes of inferiority. The promotion of this ideology was still necessary in order to maintain the power dynamics and labor hierarchies that discriminatory practices maintained. So, even though, as mentioned earlier in the chapter, America had to dispel the "perception" of inequality and racism, it had not intention of actually promoting equality or negating the racist ideologies that it had developed. It (America) just could not be the face of its own perpetuation—it needed a "face-man" or in this case a "face-woman."

The Sapphire represented the verbose admonition of those who deviated from the norms and values of the ruling class and those who were not favored by the ruling class. So, in order for the Sapphire to be born, all Black-cast films or mainstream films with numerous Black characters had to be present. Black-cast films facilitated the transition of the face of oppression from the White male to the Black woman. And through this transition, the Black woman would serve the purpose of promoting the very stereotypical and hegemonic presentations that the movement was attempting to dispel—which not only removed White males and the state from the forefront, but also validated the stereotypes as being real because they were now "coming from within."

Three of the films that were viewed clearly represent this construct, *Framing of the Shrew, St. Louis Blues*, and *Guess Who's Coming to Dinner*. In *Framing of the Shrew,* the Sapphire is played by a Mammy construct—a large, in this case light-skinned, Black woman with large breasts and buttocks who works as a laundress. In the very beginning of the film, she throws a tirade at her husband who has failed to sort the laundry properly and has caused a mix up in the clothes that she delivered to one of the White mistresses.

She returns home and angrily states to her husband who is on the couch. "I counts on you to sif' laundry and you mix Ms. Richmond and Ms. George. No account lazy scalawag you. You ain't worth the diddle. Low livered trife!"

Her husband is obviously unemployed and speaks in a very lazy-slurred and ignorant voice, preaching why he shouldn't have to do any work. Although his physical characteristics are different than the earlier presentations of the Sambo, his attitudinal and behavioral characteristics are clearly reminiscent of the Sambo construct. This interplay serves no other purpose than to use the Black woman to directly support, and validate dominant ideologies about the Black male by verbally and assertively reinforcing the stereotypes of ignorance, laziness, and apathy.

St. Louis Blues, an all Black-cast short film, also presents the dominant construct of the Sapphire. In this case Bessie Smith, (who is reminiscent of the Mammy construct absent her role as a domestic worker) who is a large, dark-skinned woman with a big buttocks and big breasts, plays a blues singer who is in love with a man who has no regard for her and has been using her for money and support. In the beginning of the film, the man is seen having an intimate encounter with "the Jezebel," construct in the room that he shares with Bessie. She comes home early to find them together. She confronts the woman and beats her up. After the woman leaves, she begins to confront "her man." However, he pushes her to the ground and leaves her begging for him to stay. When he leaves, she begins to sing "My Man." After that she goes to the bar and begins to drink. Her man returns and makes up to her only to steal her money and laugh at her, leaving her heartbroken again.

In this instance, the Sapphire is used again to reinforce notions of Black male sexual aggression, laziness, and immorality.

Carmen Jones also provides a riveting and comprehensive analysis of how the Sapphire construct, also referred to as the tragic mulatto in some literary texts, deconstructs Black male gender identity. In this film, Joe is the most appropriate representation of a traditional male in the dominant sense. He is a respected Army soldier, who is engaged to a woman who represents the traditional Southern lady. It is only through Joe's interaction with Carmen, who uses her sexual and physical beauty and aggression to seduce and then control him. In his quest to "be with" and satisfy Carmen, he makes decisions that ultimately lead to his ruining his life. This process in film, leads to the deconstruction of his traditional male gender identity. He goes AWOL and subsequently becomes paranoid and afraid to move about in society. With no job, no income, and the inability to move freely, he becomes dependent upon Carmen for his livelihood. This dependency emasculates the character—who becomes submissive, emotional, and possessive and ends up a murderer.

The message of the movie depicts a Black man who originally represents the All-American version of man—traditional male gender identity—he is independent, strong, assertive, direct, focused—a provider and protector. He is an officer in the United States Army who is in a steady and pure relationship with a woman who represents "The cult of true womanhood." She is pious, pure, domestic, and submissive. It is through his reluctant interaction, and then relationship with Carmen, that *she* causes his destruction. Through his relationship with her, he is relegated to the original construct of the Sambo, a passive, yet violent, spineless, criminal who when given the opportunity was not able to maintain his "manhood."

And finally, *Guess Who's Coming To Dinner,* which stars Sidney Poitier and Isabel Sanford, is a story about a Black man who is dating a White woman and comes to her home to meet her parents. In the beginning of this film, which was distributed in the '50s when interracial relationships were still very taboo, it was not the woman's family that verbally castrates Poitier's character and presents great disapproval. It is Isabel Sanford's character Tilly—the "Mammy." When he comes to the home and meets her without knowing him, she states "Look here you smooth talking jive-assed nigga, read me boy, I raised her from a baby . . . " She says this to assure him that she will not allow him to date her, because he is not good enough and must be up to something, even though he is a highly respected Doctor. She furthered, "I don't wanna see a member of my own race getting above himself."

All of these examples provide context to the argument presented. By having Black actors to perpetuate the hegemony of the ruling class, it is more easily accepted and internalized by the masses.

Hegemony in Black Film

Oscar Micheaux: Within Our Gates (1919)

As argued above, the hegemonic presentations perpetuated in films written, produced and directed by White people, do no accurately reflect the character of the African-American woman or her relationship to her social environment during that time. During that era, the race was concerned with gaining inclusion into a resistant society. And a principle part of gaining that inclusion involved separating themselves from, and dispelling the stereotypical and hegemonic ideologies about the race, which involved fully assimilating into Western culture and, as Frazier (1957) argued, imitating White society.

Oscar Micheaux's film, *Within Our Gates* (1919), reflects Frazier's contentions about the Black bourgeois. And while this film more accurately reflects the sociopolitical and economic location of the race by presenting characters in their gender specific and middle class roles. This study argues that by attempting to negate the hegemonic presentations of Black characters, this film, as well as others by Micheaux, inadvertently perpetuates intra racial caste and class antagonisms that reflect the internalization of hegemonic ideologies about the race.

This assertion is supported by the fact that in each of Micheaux's films, he solely presents mulatto characters in the roles of middle class "ladies" and "gentlemen," and uses darker-skinned characters, especially men, who have very dark and Afrocentric features, some even utilizing West Indian accents, to play the antagonistic roles of the Jezebel and the villain. He also focuses solely on middle class life.

So, by placing caste preferences on the visual presentations and by solely focusing on middle class life, accurate presentations of the dark-skinned Blacks and working class Blacks are still negated. Therefore, the films become nothing more than intra racial hegemonic presentations of Black life where light-skinned Blacks represent Whites and dark-skinned Blacks represent the stereotypical ideology of Black people.

This film presents the character Ms. Sylvia Landry a pious and pure schoolteacher in the role of lady. Ms. Landry is a mulatto woman who, in a Black and White film, would be mistaken for White if it were not known that the film was an all Black cast. However, Micheaux also presents the Jezebel construct, Alma Pritchard, who is a darker skinned more identifiably African-American woman who is involved in "shady deals" is identifiably jealous of Ms. Landry, and subsequently attempts to sabotage Ms. Landry's relationship and steal her man.

So, while this film is not in the same vein as films like *The Birth of a Nation* (1915), it is argued that while it more accurately reflects middle class life, the film is neglectful in providing an adequate representation of the heterogeneity of caste and class, that this study argues emerges from the internalization of hegemonic ideologies about the Black race.

The analysis of all Black-cast films also yielded another very significant analysis. It was found that while White films were presenting the Mammy and the Uncle Tom as the dominant construct during this era, all Black-cast films were presenting the "lady" and "the gentleman/savior" constructs as the dominant protagonists and the Sapphire in Jezebel form and the Buck/Criminal constructs as the dominant antagonists. And this was true for Black-cast films directed and produced by White and Black men. So contrary to early assumptions presented in this study, the Sapphire construct actually emerges simultaneous to the emergence of Black-cast films.

However, just as in the other works of Micheaux, it is argued that while his film deviates from the hegemonic presentations that are relevant to the exploitation of Black woman's labor. In its attempts to negate the hegemonic presentation, it is argued that this film does continue to present and perpetuate class and caste divisions, and does, in many ways, reflect an internalization of hegemonic ideologies about the race. Black people cannot be good, so the good people must be as close to White as possible. Black people cannot love, so the love interests must be as close to White as possible.

Simply, by using an "all Black cast," Micheaux's films merely use light-skinned Blacks, who symbolically represent mainstream representations of

White characters to portray the love interests and protagonists, and dark-skinned Blacks, who symbolically represent mainstream representations of Black characters to portray the deviants and antagonists in his films. So, while he may be applauded for producing "all Black cast" films, his work merely serves to reconstruct the hegemonic presentations and dynamics in "Black character," thereby reinforcing the notion of White supremacy and European ideals of patriarchy—by promoting what Pat Hill Collins (2004) terms "the binary construction" of not race, but now superior caste and gender within the race.

The Visual Fixation

The Jezebel and the Buck

The first era lays the foundation for the hegemonic presentation of the African American, and presents the most significant "hyper exaggeration" and visual fixation on the characteristics that defined the Black race apart from the White race—namely skin complexion, hair texture, and buttocks (physical features). This era is the most significant in all of the visual presentations in that the early silent films and talkies only cast White actors. Therefore, the presentation of the African-American man, woman, and child in these films is a clear and pure visual interpretation and presentation of the hegemonic ideologies and perceptions about the Black body, Black character, and Black culture.

In each of these films, the Black character is constructed by utilizing "authentic" Black paint to color the skin, a nappy braided wig or scarf to cover the hair, dirty, dingy, or tattered and torn clothing, clothing that would be considered savage or inappropriate for the time, and pads in the buttocks and bust of the woman, depending on the character in order to provide emphasis.

The use of the term "authentic" Black paint is used to give emphasis to the pure Black color, rather than the differing shades of brown that would more accurately represent the spectrum of African-American skin, that is utilized to color the skin of White actors in order to construct the "Black character." This is the reason why the term "Black face" has been used to describe this interpretation and presentation. "Black face" is clearly a hyper exaggeration of the skin complexion of the African American that does not truly reflect the real pigment of African-American skin. Yet "Black face" is utilized to clearly differentiate and establish the race as different by utilizing a technique that was not designed to create a subjective interpretation of the Black body in the absence of Black actors, but to deconstruct the beauty and heterogeneity of and, subsequently make a mockery of African-American skin.

To heighten the hyper exaggeration of the facial features of African Americans, the Black face characters also presented with bright red lipstick that extended way beyond the natural lip line and Black eye liner to exaggerate the "bug eyed" look that the characters maintained.

The common use of braided, or nappy wigs that often bore ribbons also reflects the hyper exaggeration of Black hair texture and style that is constructed and utilized to again make a mockery of Black hair texture and style. The wild styles that are often used create a savage and/or childlike image that reinforces the hegemonic ideologies about not only the Black body, but, Black character and infantilism.

Just as significant is the presentation of the Black woman's body. In all of the films that were viewed as a part of this study, it was found that all White actors who portrayed Black women used padding in the buttocks for the Jezebel construct and the buttocks and breast for the Mammy construct which validates the assertion of this work. And not only was the padding used, but the buttocks and breast became a principal point of camera fixation in each of the silent films by having the characters to engage in activities such as dancing in a gyrating fashion, bending over with legs spread, and even scratching the buttocks or feeling the breast in order allow the camera to fixate on those attributes. Even with the male characters, they would often be filmed jumping into barrels or woodpiles with their buttocks sticking up in the air.

It is clear that not all Black women had big buttocks, and that the buttocks, unlike skin complexion, was not a clear indicator of racial identity. So, what is the relevance of the buttocks as a point of visual fixation?

Skin complexion had already been established as a universal characteristic of the biological inferiority of African-American men and women. After all the definition of race is "a social construct that categorizes a people based on common physical characteristics such as skin complexion, hair texture, facial features and body type" (Macionis 2007). It is a predominant means of categorizing and dividing society into a hierarchical strata. However, skin complexion alone was not enough to remove the Black woman from notions of femininity and womanhood that may have afforded her greater control over, if not her productive, but at least her reproductive self during slavery.

So, it is argued that the hyper exaggeration of the Black woman's buttocks in film is utilized to establish the Black female body, which includes her sexual and reproductive body, as sexually deviant and/or abnormal—hyper sexual. Consequently then, the establishment of the Black body as deviant and abnormal allows the Black woman to be objectified, separated from her subjective womanhood, enslaved and denied the right to control her own sexuality, reproduction and keep her own children.

On the converse, the Big Black Buck or the Mandingo construct is the big, "Black" (dark-skinned), muscular (mesomorph), strong man. Although it would be counterproductive to the masculinity and/or manhood of the European to fixate on and or hyper exaggerate the Black male characters penis, as stereotypes have suggested, the way the Black female characters buttocks is hyper exaggerated, it is clear that the Buck represents the "strapping" man. The unspoken assumption that goes along with the visual presentation of the Black male character, is underscored by his aggressive and/or violent, hypersexual presentation. In essence, he is to be feared—physically and sexually.

In order to promote the objectification and commodification of the African American—specifically the African-American woman, there needed to be a fixation on that which separated them (her), sexually and reproductively, from the Anglo, and could be used as a point of deviance and abnormality, and the buttocks served that purpose. So in the decades before the first film that presented African American was produced, photographs and spectacle shows that exploited the bodies of women who fit the "big ass" and men who fit the "Big Buck" criteria, such as Sarah Bartman and the photos of the Mandingo Warriors, had already been presented to world.

For the Black woman, the buttocks had already been established and utilized for the purpose of deconstructing Black female gender identity historically, so film, merely, provided greater context for that presentation.

The findings of this work support the assertion that the buttocks, as a point of visual fixation, is relevant as the object of racial distinction that has been utilized in, not only, the perpetuation of notions of inferiority; but, in the historical development of the objectification, exploitation, and commodification of Black productive and reproductive labor and the overall objectification and commodification of the Black body and sexuality that will be present throughout transitions in the visual presentation.

It is further argued that both Black and White films fixate on these characteristics. *Topsy and Eva* (1927) presents this fixation by having the character dressed in a dirty and torn dress that resembles a potato sack that is upper thigh length. The camera constantly fixates on the "Black faced" characters buttocks during scenes where the character is either bending over, dancing in a gyrating nature, or scratching her butt in an exaggerated fashion. In one scene Topsy and Eva are in the middle of the woods, and Topsy begins to do a gyrating dance. Eva looks on until Topsy attempts to teach Eve how to do the dance by winding her butt in slow motion and grabbing the hips of Eve in attempt to rotate them for her.

The Birth of a Nation (1915) also represents a significant fixation on the breasts and buttocks of the Black maid. As the presence and dominance of the Jezebel character in this film was directly related to her sexual attraction of the master each scene that involved her expressed this desire. Because the film was a silent film, the movements and expressions of the character were very "large" and exaggerated. So, by having the character dressed in torn clothing that lightly exposes her breasts and having her feel her breasts and be slapped to the ground where her dress is raised to reveal her thigh allows the camera to fixate on the buttocks, thigh and breast in a manner that projects the sexual nature of the character.

The Jezebel Construct in Black Musicals

There was a significant point during the latter part of the Early Industrial Era (1930s) when Black musicals became the prevalent form of Black film. For example, Fats Waller and Duke Ellington both presented musical shorts *Black and Tan* (1929), *Bundle of Blues* (1933), and *The Duke Is Tops* (1938) respectively that were analyzed as a part of this study. Like the films of Micheaux, these films also presented a homogenous group of characters that were all very light or mulatto. However, even more importantly, as dance was an integral part of these films, it was found that there was a very significant fixation on the buttocks and genital area of the dancers at most points.

For example, in *Black and Tan* there were several dance scenes that presented Black women. First, each of the women was light-skinned and appeared to be White. In each of the dance scenes the women were clad in "bras" and skimpy short skirts with midriff and upper thighs showing. In other instances they wore decorated bras and panties or feathered outfits. During the era, "the shimmy," which is a dance focused on winding, gyrating, and shaking the waist, hip, and buttocks, was a very common form of dance. Coupled with the costumes that contained props that emphasized the gyration such as feathers or tassels, and the general camera fixation, the presentation becomes very sexual. In each of these scenes the camera specifically closed in on the gyrating hips, buttocks, and thighs of the dancers. And in one scene in particular, it appeared that the camera had been placed on the floor, where it captured the inner thigh, buttocks and genital area of the dancer when she hopped into a split and bounced on the floor as a part of her routine.

In these Black musicals the animation of Black dance coupled with the very "skimpy" costumes created a sexual presentation. But more relevant was the direct fixation on the buttocks of these women, which created a highly sexual and objective visual presentation of Black women and dance.

This type of presentation is historic, in that as Mengara (2001) argues, the cultural rituals of African people involved dances that involved the hips and buttocks that were presented as examples of sexual deviance and immorality by European interpretations.

The Mammy and the Uncle Tom

"Aunt Jemima" or Aunt anybody, "Mammy," "Mammie," Black and greasy, fat, large breast and buttocks, former wet nurse, nurse, midwife, perhaps even former concubine—but not now, undesirable confidante, asexual, and unattached to her own family and community, submissive, highly domestic, apron wearing scarf totin,' mama, just a big fat mama every Black chile's absent mama and White child's Mammy.

"Uncle Tom," "Uncle Jack," "Uncle Tobey," or even just plain "Uncle," but never anybody's Daddy or Papa. Once the muscular, "Black," strong, tall, strapping man—now reduced to the a sexual, a familial, middle to old age, almost feeble, thin, bug eyed, Black caretaker. Like the mammy, he is the domestic, undesirable, and unattractive confidante who only relates to White children (a la Shirley Temple) or the White man but never establishes a relationship with the mistress (White woman) because that remains taboo. He is every Black child's absent father, but every White child's Uncle. However, unlike the Mammy, his visual fixation is very uneventful. It is almost as if the Uncle Tom character is always "in the background" of the scene—a "backdrop."

Yet, the female constructs remain very prevalent. Even in the transition from the hyper-sexual Jezebel to the asexual Mammy, the exaggerated body specifically the breast and buttocks remain a point of distinction.

> Almost exclusively, Black women were depicted either naked, generally in an ethnographic context; or as laborers, usually domestic, their social status playing a crucial role in the development of visual identity. While the 'neutered' Black female includes representations of the 'Mammy' domestic servant rendered devoid of her sexuality. . . . The relatively large physical size of the Mammy, though not an imperative, is an important element in the representation that recalls the silhouette of the Hottentot, though with an aggressively desexualized component achieved, in part through costume and the particular Puritanism of American culture (Sanders 2002:6).

Although Sanders (2002) argues that the Jezebel re emerges in the twentieth century, as does this study. This study argues that the buttocks—either as a sexualized or de sexualized object—remains a prevalent and dominant point of visual fixation in the identification of the Black woman throughout each productive transition and with each individual construct.

While the Jezebel and the Buck construct represent the physical and sexual objectification of the Black body, the Mammy and the Uncle Tom constructs represent the opposite. As has been argued earlier in the chapter, the productive transition in the American economy created a shift in the sociopolitical and economic location of the African American. The emancipation of the slaves created fear in White society—because promoting support for slavery involved promoting the fear of the African, and then the African-American race.

The fear of the hypersexualized and aggressive Black man that had been created in the imagination of Whites, and fear of the hypersexualized Black woman, who were now free to roam about society, have sex with whomever, and reproduce at will, had to be deconstructed. Because emancipation meant the loss of control, the sexual habits (or the stereotypes of the sexual habits) could no longer be controlled and profited from and because the children would no longer be the property of the ruling class, their sexual or reproductive labor was not only no longer necessary, but now feared. Therefore, the presentation of the Jezebel image and construct was no longer beneficial to development of the capitalist economy.

This sociopolitical shift and the effort to relegate Black people to the control of White landowners resulted in the implementation of Jim Crow, the shift from slave labor to a surplus labor supply, the Black Migration to the North to fuel the industrial labor pool, and the shift from farm and agricultural labor to domestic labor for African-American women and low level industrial and service work for African-American men, made the transition in constructs necessary. It is argued that as the Mammy and Uncle Tom constructs serve to hegemonically promote the exploitation of the domestic labor of Black women, the presentation must establish conformity for the exploitation.

As discussed, these constructs represent the character's willful abandonment of self, family, and community in order to devote him/herself to the needs of the White family. The characters serve as the confidante of the master or mistress, and the surrogate mother/Uncle (father-figure) to the children. In each of the films, the character clearly places more worth on the White family than his/her own and spends much time in the household of the White family. No film that was viewed in this study visually presented either the Mammy or the Uncle Tom construct in her/his own social or familial environment. And the films that did present the children of the Mammy, (none presented the children of the Uncle Tom), they were always bi racial children of the Mammy who were allowed to live in the household of the mistress. Yet in each of those films, no master of the house was present.

While the physical characteristics of the Uncle Tom are very frail, his visual presentation is often uneventful. And for the same reasons that the Mammy construct's characteristics are exaggerated, the Uncle Tom's are minimized. It is argued that the visual presentation of the Mammy, being more profound than that of the Uncle Tom, also exaggerated her physical characteristics in order to promote hegemonic ideologies. However, unlike the Jezebel, it is argued that the hegemonic presentation of the Mammy reflects the presentation of the "type" of image of the Black woman that would make an acceptable confidante and household leader by being non-threatening to the marriage of the mistress. As Collins (2000) posits:

> The Mammy image buttresses the ideology of the cult of true womanhood, one in which sexuality and fertility are severed. 'Good' White mothers are expected to deny their female sexuality. In contrast the Mammy image is one of an asexual woman, a surrogate mother in Black face whose historical devotion to her White family is now giving way to new expectations (P.74).

It is argued that (in real life) as a result of the master's sexual assault of, and relationship with slave women and, later, domestic workers and the bi-racial children that were born from those assaults and relationships, White mistresses made conscious attempts to keep attractive Black women out of the proximity of her husbands. The result was assigning or choosing more matronly, less attractive, older and perhaps post fertile women to the position of head domestic, or Mammy. So even if there were younger women present in the household, the "Mammy" would be responsible for overseeing the "goings on" in the household and keeping and/or ensuring "order." So while it is argued that the hegemonic presentation of the Mammy did not accurately reflect the physical appearance of real domestic workers. It *is* being suggested that the Mammy construct represented the White ideal of the domestic worker, one that did not pose a threat to the cohesion of the White family.

So, while the buttocks and the breasts are visual fixations, they are fixations in a maternal sense. While there are specific camera pans in many instances, in the case of the Mammy, her large size is evident and represents her construct and thus does not need or require close ups or intentional fixations. Casting for the role ensures that this is true. It is no wonder that Hattie McDaniel received the first Oscar for her presentation of the Mammy construct in *Gone With the Wind*. Isabel Sanford, *The Jeffersons*' Mrs. Jefferson, played the role of the Mammy in *Guess Who's Coming to Dinner*, etc.

The Sapphire

Angry, verbose, aggressive, masculine, and abusive is what it means to be a Black woman.

Significant to the transition is the introduction of the Sapphire, who will also minimally appear in the former era (1920s). The Sapphire is the physical construct of either the Jezebel or the Mammy. However, as hooks argues, "No light skin occupies this devalued position" (hooks 1994:69).

Her contribution is to undermine or de-masculinize the Black man through her hypersexual or defeminized attitude. Her verbosity, aggression, violent tendencies and masculine habits, such as drinking and smoking are used to verbally and physically attack the Black man with the purpose of reinforcing dominant ideologies about his worthlessness—while simultaneously reinforcing newly formed dominant ideologies about her own 'masculinization.' However, in her interaction with the White man and woman, she remains passive and submissive until the 'Blaxploitation' era.

It is argued that this construct and presentation serves several important hegemonic functions. It serves to deconstruct the embrace of traditional gender identity by Black people—thereby reinforcing the "abnormalization" of Black men and women. For, if the ideal of 'femininity' or 'feminine tradition' rests in subordination and submissiveness—the binary of aggression and dominance becomes the antithesis of femininity and thus not womanly. On the converse of that binary is the assumption that if assertiveness, dominance, aggression defines the construct of masculinity—to be subject to the control and dominance of the Sapphire would be the antithesis of masculine, and thus is not "manly." Thus, one of the principal components of this construct is to create gender antagonisms within the race.

This construct further serves to antagonize class divisions within the Black community. Because the Sapphire represents the masculinization' of the Black woman, middle class Black women, who are striving for acceptance and legitimization as 'women' (Frazier 1962) will negate this construct as being significant to only working class or 'ghetto' women. Hence, as it was found in all films where that construct is present, the Sapphire will only be represented by a working class or urban woman, and in all Black casts, her actions will be openly chastised by the middle class woman or "the lady."

This construct ultimately serves to deconstruct the Black family, Black love, and Black unity by perpetuating gender, class, and caste antagonisms within the race. As Collins argues: "As controlling images of Black femininity, the bitch, and bad Black mother both present the unassimilated, working class Black woman as unacceptable, primarily because she lacks appropriate female qualities of submissiveness" (Collins 2002:59).

hooks furthers: "To this day, the images of Black female bitchiness, evil temper, and treachery continue to be marked by darker skin. This is the stereotype called 'Sapphire.' We see these images continually in the mass media . . . and in movies made by Black and White directors" (hooks 1994:36).

Consequently, in a time where unity was essential to the power of the Civil Rights movements that were prevalent during that era, the hegemonic perpetuation of the Sapphire construct was useful in undermining Black unity, thereby minimizing or neutralizing the threat of aggressive resistance.

The Location and Image of the African-American woman in the Late Industrial Era from 1946 to 1975

Economic Expansion/The Modern Civil Rights Movement from 1946 to 1973

The next transition represents the productive shift from the early Industrial Era to the late Industrial Era—which corresponds to the social transition from domestic labor to the welfare state, political shift from Jim Crow to the modern Civil Rights Movements, and the economic shift from the Great Depression to economic expansion.

After WWII, Russia and the United States emerged as the two dominant world powers, as most of Europe had been devastated by the war. During that era, the International Monetary Fund was created to provide funding for the rebuilding of Europe after the war. Because of the devastation, the United States was in a position to expand globally. Therefore, it pursued the expansion under the political auspice of the promotion of democracy and freedom. Yet, it was the solidification of global capitalism that was a more accurate reason.

Communism, as an alternative political economy, was the antithesis of democracy and capitalism. Therefore, the United States had to vilify communism or "dictatorship" as "evil" and democracy or "freedom" as "good," and subsequently use the "democratic ideology" while minimizing its capitalist foundation to expand globally. The rise of Russia, hence, communism, posed a direct threat to the prospect for a global capitalist economy and capitalist expansion. Therefore, by presenting a political and economic agenda that was in opposition to that of capitalism—as the two continued to compete for imperial expansion—served to promote National support for the expansion under the familiar guise of "saving the world from tyranny."

Implementing the Cold War of 1948 was essential to the continued progress of the capitalist state and capitalist expansion. In such, Russia, hence, communism, was hegemonically presented as a diabolic, authoritative, and oppressive regime that would suppress and repress the political, social, and economic freedom and progress of the people—all people. So, as Russia was vilified, the United States, hence, democracy was presented as a political system that promoted freedom, equality, and inclusion in the social, political, and economic process—made the hero.

(While not the focus of this work, the utilization of mainstream film was essential in the promotion of this ideological and cultural hegemony about Russia and communism as well. This is reflected in the many spy films, and programs that were very prevalent during that time. James Bond and the many other "spy" films that presented Russia, hence, communism, in a negative light are examples of this.)

In addition, to the ideological warfare, the United States also had the task of boosting the economy of the United States as a whole, the economic condition of the American people, and developing an infrastructure that would be more conducive and efficient for trade and development.

Thus, the New Deal Act that was initially created under Roosevelt was solidified under Wilson. And in such programs such as the Works Progress Administration, the Veterans Administration Loan, the Federal Mortgage Loan, as well as other structural and social welfare programs were instituted in efforts to promote economic stability and consumer spending during the Post WWII and Post Depression Eras. So, while many American people assumed that 'welfare' was created for and specifically addressed the needs of the poor, women, and African Americans, this comprehensive program was one that facilitated the infrastructural development that made technological advancement, suburbanization possible, and trade more efficient. It also boosted the economy by providing benefits to Veterans returning from war, and other working class Americans that allowed them to participate in the market economy at higher levels through being able to secure interest bearing loans.

> Once Blacks gained political resources, the demands and pressures became so great that neglect was no longer a viable option in the context of the nation's economic prosperity in the immediate post WWII Era. As a result, the system responded with a range of available options, including major policy initiatives, symbolic manipulation (as in the manipulation of media images on television), cooptation, and repression (Gomes and Williams 1995:29).

However, in its quest to expand the question became, how the United States can promote freedom and equality, when the conditions of the 'Negro' in America contradicted those very principles. Thus, it became essential that the United States (1) reduce the racial tensions that were resulting in violence in the form of lynchings and race riots in order to avoid any mass internal conflict that could negatively impact progress, and to (2) promote, or at least promote the façade, of inclusion and equality that was not a priority before.

Therefore, as was mentioned earlier in the chapter, it was no longer in the state's best interest to visually present ruling class racial oppression, or White male anger toward Black people. And one of the principle reforms that were made in an effort to promote this shift was the States dismantling of the Ku Klux Klan after assessing a fine of $685,000 for back taxes which caused the organization to loose it's charter in 1944. (Horowitz 2004)

The Sapphire versus the Pimp/Hustler

This study posits that a rise in the dominance of the Sapphire construct and a shift in the presentation and interplay with Black male characters in mainstream film occurs in the second half of this era. While as discussed before, the original Sapphire versus Sambo construct served to visually present the Black woman as the "de-constructor" of Black male identity through her projection White male anger and dominant ideologies about the Black man who stood to gain if given sociopolitical and economic inclusion, this Sapphire becomes the subject of the retaliatory anger of the Black male Hustler character. So, even though the type of tension shifts, it is still argued that the Sapphire construct continues to be used to socially promote the intra racial gender and class antagonisms that have already emerged, and to if not destabilize the Black Power Movement from within, to justify and promote support for governmental intervention in the dismantling of the Black Power Movement.

Cinematically then, in the beginning of this era, especially through the 1950s, while the Mammy and Uncle Tom constructs were still present in mainstream White-cast films, the majority of the all Black-cast films were heavy musicals that may have had a plot, but centered on song and dance. These films included *Carmen Jones and Porgy and Bess*. In these films, the Sapphire construct is merged with the construct of the Jezebel as Dandridge in both films presents a very sexually aggressive, and in *Carmen Jones*, a very savage woman that reflects the Jezebel of old. In each of these films, the Sapphire construct is again utilized to degrade and demean the male suitor; and the Jezebel characterizes the extreme lust that prevents her from being monogamous.

However, it is not until 1970, with the introduction of the Blaxploitation era, that the Sapphire construct becomes fully dominant and crosses interracial lines in the perpetuation of her wrath. It is argued that the force of the Civil Rights Movement and the emergence strength, attraction, and more radical ideologies of the Black Power Movements such as the Black Panther Party, even after the Civil Rights Act was passed in 1964 posed a national threat.

The threat was grounded in two concepts. First, unlike the Civil Rights Movement that was more reformist, hence, focusing on promoting the inclusion, equality, and acceptance of African Americans into mainstream society as it's primary agenda, the Black Power Movements were critical of the system. They understood that while race was the construct that was being utilized to oppress a people, the political and economic system was inherently oppressive. It also understood that because of the nature of the power dynamics that needed to be maintained passive and/or peaceful resistance would not promote adequate change. And, unlike the Civil Rights Movement, the grassroots nature of the Black Power Movement made it attractive to the inner-city youth who were favorable to active and/or aggressive change. Finally, the Black Power Movement was more geared toward promoting the consciousness of the masses, providing education about the systematic flaws that were also causes of the condition of African Americans as an oppressed people. Therefore, like communism, the Black Power Movement became an enemy to the state.

During that era, due to the rising racial tension that resulted in the integration of the cities, declining jobs, and the productive transition that was taking place, in addition to the fact that African Americans had lost patience with the lack of collective progress, race riots had already been occurring, and continued resistance to the integration of Blacks continued to perpetuate the threat of violence. And with the "by any means necessary" mentality that was taking shape, the possibility of massive civil unrest was becoming real. But, any massive civil unrest in the United States would destabilize the economy and the infrastructure, and ultimately destroy the credibility of the perpetuation of "democracy" as the ideology of U.S. expansion—all of the components were essential to the continued solidification of the United States as a World Power.

In order to avoid this, governmental intervention was inevitable. And, it came in two forms. First, the Civil Rights Act was passed in 1965. This strategic move was a formal gesture of extending equal rights to African-American citizens. In essence, the statement that the passage of the Civil Rights Act made was "Here, now you have freedom to pursue wealth and the equality and inclusion to do so." The underscore was the reality that passing a law without providing support, incentive, or consequence to those institutions, businesses, and agencies that continued to discriminate did not solidify true inclusion and opportunity to a people who had been excluded and diminished for so long. It did not change the minds of the masses, and therefore did not really promote any significant change. However, now the responsibility for oppression and discrimination was removed from the state and placed on private entities. So, no longer could the State be held responsible for the inequality that remained prevalent in the United States even after the passage of the Civil Rights Movement.

The second part of the agenda was to dismantle any opposition to the National agenda. The result was the assassination, arrest, and exile of the more prolific leaders of the Civil Rights and Black Power Movement—which included Martin

Luther King, who was beginning to reassess his analysis of race relations and the political system, Malcolm X, Huey Newton, Angela Davis, and Asaata Shakur—to name a few. Although, it will be claimed that this assertion has not been proven, circumstantially, it is in synch with the agenda of the McCarthy Act and the Counter Intelligence Program, also known as COINTELPRO. These acts were carried forth in the name of National security in order to "restore social order" and ensure that there would not be another Civil War or any mass resistance to the political and economic expansion of the United States during this most critical period. After all, it cannot be argued that COINTELPRO was developed to rid the Nation of any person or organization that contradicted the political agenda of the ruling class. This included men and women alike. Therefore, it is not far fetched that the assassinations and attacks on these political figures would be more in line with the mission of this governmental agency than some jealousy or random act.

This work argues that the perpetuation of the Sapphire construct during this era serves to masculinize and "villainize" the Black woman, to present her as a rebellious, resistant radical who did not respect authority, and was fighting against the system—hence, all White people. In promoting this type of image, several things were accomplished. First, once again, the Black woman was removed from her subjectivity as a woman—thereby discouraging sympathy for her abuse or attack. This lack of sympathy was designed to extend past the White community and into the middle class African-American community as well. Through this presentation, the rationale for control over her was established, which reduced the likelihood of resistance once real African-American women, such as Angela Davis and Asaata Shakur who were viewed as deviant and dangerous (without adequate cause) were abused as a part of the COINTELPRO. To those who depended on the media presentations to develop their perception of expressions of resistance, they (Davis and Shakur), like the many other unknown women who were rounded up, assaulted, incarcerated, Black listed, exiled and murdered, were the real manifestations of the Sapphire construct. In reality they like other soldiers were soldiers fighting for a valid and legitimate cause.

The presentation of the Sapphire is identified in films such as *Coffey, Cleopatra*, and *Foxy Brown* all of which represent this assertion. In essence, her aggression not only provokes, but rationalizes "the Thugs" abusive and violent reaction. The masculinzation of the Sapphire gives cause to and justifies her abuse. The message is "If you want to act like a man you can be treated as such." Thus, in many of the films, the Sapphire construct is often physically punched by a man—like a man, pistol whipped by men, and sexually assaulted or aggressively "penetrated" without the emotion that is attached to "love making."

In this exchange then, now not only does the Sapphire promote the aggression, anger, and ideology of the ruling class to the Black man, thereby reinforcing the ideology of Black women. But now, her interaction with the Thug construct reinforces the masculinization of the Black woman by allowing her to receive his violent, aggressive, irresponsible, hypersexual, and criminal tendencies.

To the contrary of earlier presentations of the Sapphire versus the Sambo interplay, the Blaxploitation era re-introduces the Big Black Buck construct. However, this new construct emphasizes either criminality and/or his lack of regard, resistance, and/or blatant rebellion for authority, hence, the state—provoked or unprovoked. He is the original construct, the beginning of "The Thug" (the O.G.—original gangster). Like the original presentation of this dynamic, this new construct emerges in and is directly related to his connection with the Sapphire. He becomes the "new" object of the Sapphires aggression and wrath. However, unlike the Sapphire versus Sambo interplay, wherein the Sapphire de-masculinizes (emasculates) the Black male character, this interaction represents the Black man's retaliation against the wrath, his anger toward her, and provides the rationale for his physically abusing her.

But even more significantly, this new construct represents the "criminalization" of the inner-city Black man, and more specifically, the Black Power Movement. After all, it was the goal of the government to "criminalize" the Black Power Movement as being a violent, communist, and/or anti government organization that was comprised of and run by a group of former criminals who were using the ideology of "justice" to rationalize criminal acts. In the Blaxploitation films such as Shaft, Dolemite, Sweet Sweetback and others, the characters were either drug dealers, pimps, "rebels," or vigilante's who were "bucking" the system and "White folks" in general. In many of the films, he is seen exploiting White women as well as Black women, retaliating or assaulting police and other White authorities, and repeating the common them of "disdain or disregard" for the system.

Like the past construct of the Big Black Buck, this construct too was developed to present a threatening image of the Black man that was designed to promote fear. This new identification of/for the Black man was the result of allowing him to exist and even thrive in society without control. He was now free to exercise his natural tendencies . . . violence, aggression, hyper sexuality, and even murder without fear of the State. But, unlike the slave Buck, this Buck did not have the fear of "the White man" that quelled his inclinations before. Therefore, his violence did not have the boundaries that the terror of White supremacist organizations had previously established. Now the Black man was not scared to rape, assault, or even murder not only "ordinary" White people, but representatives of the State.

Through this constructs constant blaming or bashing of "the system" as the point of oppression, "the cracker" as the agent of that oppression, and then attempting to relate his actions to that, the cinematic figures quickly became erroneous "representations" of those who were involved in the Black Power Movement and more radical Civil Rights Organizations. Consequently, the criminality expressed in the movies became a "representation" of the rationale for resistance and rebellion, thereby negating the true cause and ideology of the real movement.

By vilifying and criminalizing the Black man and woman in this vain, and allowing the cinematic presentation to have each justify the stereotype of the other, the power structure was allowed to remove itself from the presentation. Subsequently, as COINTELPRO began carry out its agenda, the victims that were associated with the more "militant" movements and organizations were not given sympathy because it was believed that the actions of the state were justifiable. Therefore, the State was able to carry out its criminal agenda without resistance or rebellion.

In any event, the White character, in film is completely removed from promoting the visual and reciprocal abuse of one toward another. He is removed from promoting the ideologies, stereotypes, and abuse in the film. Subsequently he is also removed from the presentation in society. But, more importantly because African Americans are now voluntarily playing these roles, reinforcing these ideologies, stereotypes, and notions about Black life, interaction, the community, relationships, etc., it serves the purpose of reinforcing the validity of such

The Initial Stages of Economic Contraction—1973–1975

Many years before, the computer chip was invented. However, it was not until this era that the United States began to utilize the computer chip in production (Horowitz et al. 2004). Although in the early states, this era of the micro chip allowed for the development of more efficient tools of production and communication, hence, trade. These new technological advancements made the possibility of more efficient global trade eminent. However, if corporations were going to maximize global trade, it necessitated the break down of colonial and imperial trade barriers. It also required capital to promote development, which meant that social contracts had to be broken in order to increase profit, production, and trade. Thus, with the institution of the North American Free Trade Agreement, the General Agreement on Tariff and Trade and the creation of the World Trade Organization, first world countries, like the United States, began to transition into the era of neo-liberalism which was paramount to globalization.

Suburbanization and the deconstruction of the center (inner) cities/urban areas had led to the increase in 'ghettoization.' With the shift from the industrial to the Electronic Era almost complete, the types of labor required drastically changed. Factory and manufacture work that required manual labor and minimal knowledge and education was on the decline because as fuel sources changed from coal and oil to electric, and as factories became more mechanized, more specialized forms of labor and knowledge, such as knowledge of electronics became necessary. These factors coupled with the development of agglomerate economies forced a shift that would leave inner-city minorities and the working class poor in a crisis.

On a national level, the rise of the Electronic Era had the promise of allowing for more efficient production with minimal human labor and global trade. Therefore preparations were being made to reallocate national funds in order to promote globalization. This made cuts in social spending and breaking the social contract that was created under the Roosevelt Administration necessary. The increased economic stability and the reduced need for human labor power meant that social welfare was no longer needed to the extent that it was being utilized. Therefore, social welfare policies were continuously reformed with the ultimate goal of phasing social welfare out. However, before shifts in a program that was instrumental in building the national economy could occur, a shift in public perception about the usefulness of social welfare also had to occur. Subsequently, it is argued that a propagandist and hegemonic campaign to redefine who was benefiting from social welfare became necessary. Out of this, the construct of the Welfare Queen was created and perpetuated with minimal resistance from not only White America, but from middle class Blacks many of whom, as Freire and Frazier argued, had adopted the ideologies of mainstream society.

Consequently, once the Civil Rights Act was passed in 1965, the Black Power Movement was systematically dismantled and the media was used as a tool to promote Black conformity and assimilation. This era has a significant hegemonic point in that unlike other eras, the presentation here is not only designed to gain the consensus of the White majority, but it is also designed to influence African Americans, especially the middle class, to internalize the images, and to reject or demonize the group that the images supposedly represent and reflect—the working class poor.

Consequently, in the quest to imitate and gain the acceptance of White society, which Frazier (1962) argues is one of the principle flaws of the Black bourgeois—hence, the Civil Rights Movements driven by the Black middle-class African Americans readily accept the fallacy of the ideological hegemony that guides the construct. And by accepting the dominant ideology about its own kind, the Black middle class further alienates the Black working class, thereby rejecting the continued struggle by accepting blame the victim theories and ideologies—that lend to "divide and conquer."

The Welfare Queen

The perpetuation of the Welfare Queen construct served to directly reinforce the perception of the Black woman as an immoral, hyper-sexual being. Only this time, she was using the 'tax payers' dollars to support her immorality (Collins 2000 and Wallace 1978). It also served to indirectly promote the ideology of the Black man as an unwilling, neglectful, absent and irresponsible father. This is facilitated by the presence of Sapphire-like characteristics in the Welfare Queen in which the Black woman's assertion of dominance and dislike for the Black man makes it easy for him to be absent and for her to not miss—or need—his presence.

This construct identified the Black woman as the primary user/abuser of public welfare—promoting the notion that she chose welfare because now she, like Black men, was lazy, irresponsible, uneducated and unable to assume a decent standard of living due to her own lack of motivation (Collins 2000 and

2004; hooks 1998; and Wallace 1978). This construct also reinforced the hyper sexuality of Black women by depicting them as manipulative baby makers—who were having children to increase the amount of money that the government would pay. The perpetuation of this construct was essential in waging a class war between middle class Blacks and Whites against poor Black women—which took on a paternalistic character. In essence, if welfare was obtained through the State and its tax payer's money, then those on welfare were subject to the control and dominance of the tax payers (Stephens and Phillips). As Collins (2001) argues, the construct of the Welfare Queen allowed society to harness the fertility of the Black woman that was the foundation for her construct during the Slavery Era.

> Controlling Black women's fertility in this political and economic context became important to elite groups. The image of the welfare mother fulfills this function by labeling as unnecessary and even dangerous to the values of the country the fertility of women who are not White and middle class (P.79).

Thus, after the Civil Rights Act and into the late 1970s and early 1980s—during a era of economic contraction, this dynamic further created intra racial class divisions and further alienated the Black poor.

The nature of welfare was inherently destructive to the Black family, because in essence it required, and hence promoted the absence of the Black man in the household. And thus, just like the Black woman subjected the Black man to the same paternalistic perceptions. It promoted the idea that tax payers were paying for the hyper sexuality, irresponsibility, and laziness of poor Black men and women. The development of this construct—then—was instrumental in perpetuating and solidifying the blame the victim perspective of Black economic deprivation (Ryan), that ultimately fueled support for the welfare reforms that began to take place in the early 1980s.

This study found that while the dominance of the Welfare Queen was found in other mediums, the selection of films did not incorporate many films that could support the cinematic dominance of this construct during this era. Therefore, the data did not give adequate enough support to assert and analyze the "dominance" of this construct, although the two films *Claudine* (1973) and *Cornbread, Earl, and Me* (1975) do support the presence of the construct. Even though literature (Stephens and Phillips 2000; Collins 2000 and 2004; hooks 1994) does support the dominance of this construct during this era on television which was growing as the predominant form of visual media during this era, it was not predominant in mainstream film.

Consequently, the construct will be discussed within the context of the preparation for economic contraction and neo-liberalism that this study argues influences the emergence of the Welfare Queen construct, but will provide limited support.

The Welfare Queen construct depends on old notions of hyper-sexuality, immorality, and fertility as a driving force. It is argued that the Welfare Queen actually incorporates the attitudinal characteristics of the Sapphire or the Jezebel while blending in a focus on her unemployment and/or dependence on and manipulation of social welfare, by portraying her as an unmotivated and lazy, yet cunning and manipulative social burden. And in so doing, the perpetuation of the deviance of Black reproduction, Black love, and the Black family is achieved. By presenting an image of the Welfare Queen, those who receive welfare, in real life, become subject to the reproductive control and ridicule of the tax payer, who is led to believe that it is his/her money that is supporting the children.

Consequently then, by presenting and promoting an image of Black women as the overwhelmingly predominant recipients of welfare who intentionally have babies out of wedlock, and negate the moral tradition of family in order to exploit the welfare system, hence, the hard working tax payers of America, the government is able to transition social welfare to 'welfare to work' with full support. And as will be discussed later, welfare to work encompasses sanctions on the number of children that will be covered and health care programs that encourage the use of Depo Provera, the patch, and other forms of birth control. Again, by promoting a blame the victim approach to poverty and inequality, the economic foundation is overlooked and economic and policy shifts occur without question from Whites or middle-class Blacks who have internalized the dominant ideologies about race and class, and hence do not have the consciousness that would lead them to question or resistance.

In perpetuating this construct, focus is taken off of the reality that African-American women have never constituted a statistical majority welfare recipients—period. It also takes focus off of the reality that "public assistance" only constituted a small portion of the National social spending allocation. However, by once again 'villainizing' the Black woman, support is gained for the political agenda of the ruling class—that is now dismantling social welfare.

The late Industrial Era marks the transition from the Mammy who is still present but declining in her dominance from the late 1940s through the 1950s. As discussed, the 1960s marked a significant decline in the presentation of the African-American woman, that this study argues corresponds to (1) the rising use of television as the new media, and (2) the increased racial tension and subsequent uprisings that were occurring in the late 1950s until the passage of the Civil Rights Act of 1964.

The Hegemonic Presentation of the African-American woman in Mainstream Film During the Late Industrial Era from 1945 to 1975

In this section the visual and interactive characteristics of the hegemonic constructs of the African-American woman is analyzed in relation to her sociopolitical and economic location.

The Sapphire

In the latter part of the era, it was found that the presentation of the Sapphire takes a shift. It is argued that the second era of the Sapphire construct serves to again remove the Black woman from her "womanness" and promote the fear of the Black woman in mainstream society as well. This transition in the hegemonic presentation and the prevalence of the construct proved useful in the later part of the era (1960–1970s) and corresponded to the McCarthy Era and the Era of COINTELPRO. During this era, Black women who were members of Black power and more "radical" Civil Rights Movements were targeted and terrorized by the State. And in the quest to dismantle and deconstruct any movement that contradicted the political ideology of America, hence, it's quest to expand and promote global capitalism, the state condemned and assassinated any one who was actively engaged in "treasonous" activities. This included men and women. Therefore, it is argued that by, once again, promoting a dominant presentation that objectifies and "villainizes" the Black woman, those who were involved in the "radical" power movements—and represented the Sapphire construct would not receive the social and political support of the masses, both Black and White, and would consequently not receive due process under the law.

The "Blaxploitation" period represents the transition in the Sapphire construct that was highly prevalent during the second half of this era. In the very films that dominated Black cinema during the 1970s, the Sapphire was an aggressive, sexual, and violent construct. However, unlike the earlier Sapphire construct, this Sapphire not only exerted her verbal wrath against other Black characters, but also exerted her wrath and violence against the system—represented by White police officers and political officials, and in some instances White people in general. So, in an era where racial uprisings and the fear of a Black revolution were not far fetched, these types of presentations validated the need for social control, hence, the abuse and subjugation of the African-American woman in society.

In this era, films that starred Black actresses, especially Pam Grier, dominated the screen. These movies included *Coffy* (1973), *Cleopatra Jones* (1973), and *Foxy Brown*. In each of these films, the Black woman represents the Sapphire construct while, although usually fighting some form of injustice or seeking some form of vengeance exhibits behavior that is violent and aggressive. She uses profanity and often times uses her sexuality to reach her goal

An example of this is *Cleopatra Jones*. In this film, Cleopatra Jones a federal agent who is attempting to rid the world of drugs goes to Turkey and burns the poppy fields of a rich White elite female drug lord. In retaliation, the drug lord calls on the police officers that she has on payroll in the United States, and has Cleopatra's rehabilitation house raided. Her authority as a federal agent allows her to both physically defend herself and, even initiate violence against White police officers without repercussion.

Coffy (1974) also presents an example of this construct of the Sapphire. In this film, Coffy's wrath is not only exerted toward Black characters but to White women and men as well. After having a drink poured on her by a White prostitute, Coffy beats her up, along with several other White women, even ripping their dresses off exposing their breasts. And when the prostitute reaches to pull Coffy's hair she cuts her hands on the razor blades that Coffy strategically placed in her wig. Later in the film, Victor Petrone, a White drug lord bends her hand until she falls to the floor. He spits on her and this dialogue follows.

"Get on the floor where you belong you no good, dirty nigger bitch!" She pleads. "Oh please I know I'm not good enough for you, but please just let me have your precious White body just once." "Let me see you crawl over here you Black trash . . . crawl nigger!" He replies excitedly, even raising up slightly from his seated position to emphasize the word "nigger." She then pulls out a gun and replies. "You want me to crawl, White mother fucker! You wanna spit on me and make me crawl! I'm going to piss on your grave tomorrow." At that point, two men enter and "hits her with a pistol" and she falls to the ground. For the rest of this movie, Grier's character is assaulted by White men, in the same manner as a man would be.

It is argued that this new presentation reinforces the objectification of the Black woman by deconstructing her gender identity. This objectification, once again, allows the character to be physically abused and subjected to the same type of assault that male characters are subject to in mainstream film. Yet, this type of cinematic abuse was not common in White films and did not become so until the 1990s with the emergence of films such as G.I Jane and the Long Kiss Goodnight. It is argued that the perpetuation of this construct that is now being promoted by Black people against Black people encourages the internalization of the objectification of the Black woman and reinforces acceptance for the assault on the Black body in society—not only by the power structure, but by other Blacks as well.

It was found that many of the Blaxploitation films that starred Black male actors and had Black women in secondary roles restore the dominance of the Jezebel construct on a large scale. In many of these films, there is a definite focus on the objectification, sexualizaton, and degradation of the Black woman's body through her sexual and physical exploitation and abuse. This abuse in many of the films, as mentioned above, is perpetuated against her by both Black and White men.

The Sapphire construct in most of these films *Superfly* (1972), *Shaft* (1973), and *Sweet Sweetbacks Badaaaasss Song* (1971), *Cotton Comes to Harlem* (1973), *The Soul of Nigger Charlie* (1972) simply does not exist. And where the construct is present, the presence is not dominant, and/or is her wrath exerted against the Black man, only against the power structure/authority. And where it is exerted against authority, it is done so in defense and/or protection of the Black man.

The Welfare Queen

As mentioned earlier in the chapter, the emergence of the Welfare Queen corresponds to the sociopolitical transition from economic expansion to economic contraction. After World War II, the United States was attempting to establish itself as a dominant world power. In an effort to establish the super structural and infrastructural foundation that was needed to establish economic dominance, Roosevelt implemented the New Deal Act. This Act was designed to restore and build the national economy by facilitating spending, infrastructural development, trade and expansion. The implementation of social welfare programs were a part of this act.

The establishment of the United States as a global power, in addition to the establishment of the computer chip as a more efficient means of production reduced the need for the social welfare programs that had been utilized to rebuild the economy after the war. It is argued that the invention of the computer chip created not only a more efficient means of production that reduced the need for human labor; but, a more effective and efficient means of global communication and trade. The computer chip promoted globalization by eliminating and/or reducing the costs associated with time, travel, and other associated profit barriers.

It is argued that the emergence of the Welfare Queen as a hegemonic presentation, which directly corresponds to this transition, directly relates to that shift and the ruling classes plan to reallocate and shift social spending by implementing neo-liberal policies and retracting social welfare programs. The result was economic contraction. The utilization of the Welfare Queen construct is specifically designed to promote the deconstruction of that social contract.

The Welfare Queen construct utilizes old stereotypes of the Black woman to promote the ideology of the Black woman as the abusers of the welfare system. The physical characteristics of the Welfare Queen consist of a woman who resides in the ghetto and receives services, but apparently does not need them. She often has many material things that are traditionally thought to be "luxury" items and often has many children, is unemployed, and has many of the attitudinal characteristics of the Sapphire. However, unlike the Sapphire construct, the Welfare Queen is also very disrespectful to the system, hence, White people.

This study argues that this construct was specifically designed to promote the hegemonic and fallacious ideology that Black women were (1) the predominant users of public welfare (2) abusing the system by using tax payers dollars to purchase extravagances and luxuries, (3) having large numbers of children in order to increase the amount of public welfare (financial assistance) and were not using the funds for the care of the children, and (4) did not need public welfare but utilized and manipulated the system to promote their unwillingness to get a job. By promoting these hegemonic/stereotypical ideologies, support for the transition from social welfare to welfare to work could be achieved, ultimately facilitating the elimination of social welfare programs altogether.

This construct is specifically designed to promote the notion that Black women were the predominant users and abusers of social welfare. By utilizing and promoting this construct, both in mainstream and Black film venues, but more specifically in television, the presentation was widespread. It is argued that through this hegemonic presentation, acceptance for the dismantling of social welfare under the guise of "welfare reform" was widely unchallenged and accepted by society at large.

"Welfare reform" consisted of "welfare to work" programs that promised society that welfare recipients would be held accountable—trained to work and then transitioned from welfare dependence to work. However, in a productive economy that was becoming less dependent on human labor, the availability of jobs that would pay enough for women to maintain households without assistance were realistically not available. Consequently, poor women were forced off of welfare and into the surplus labor market by being forced to take menial jobs or be free laborers under the guise of training programs.

This presentation promoted a widespread support and consensus for welfare reform. Middle class Americans (Black and White) were convinced through many media campaigns, that were validated by these movies and television shows, that the majority of their "hard earned and given away" tax dollars were being utilized to support irresponsible women who were getting more out of life than them, without having to earn it. Therefore, developing a program that would force "these irresponsible, lazy, fertile women to get up off of their asses and get a job" was more than welcomed. Consequently, under the guise of providing quality training and opportunity, the welfare to work program was successfully implemented and TANF (temporary assistance for needy families) and other social welfare programs were successfully phased out, thereby contributing to the success of neoliberalism and "the race to the bottom" of the next era.

While literature supports the presence and prevalence of this construct, this study found that the presentation of the Welfare Queen construct during this era in mainstream film was not significant or dominant during this era. However, two films, *Claudine* (1974) and *Cornbread, Earl, and Me* (1975) both presented the construct. *Claudine,* although released two years before the Electronic Era and the era of economic contraction, and *Cornbread, Earl, and Me*, which was released one year prior to the Electronic Era both provide the most poignant examples of this construct and the transition from domestic labor to welfare dependence that resulted from the decline in the demand for domestic labor.

Claudine is a single mother who has six children. After struggling to try to make ends meet working as a domestic for a rich White family, she resorts to welfare in order to provide for her family. As a recipient of welfare, she is subject to the subjugation of the system, which includes the "pop up" visits of the welfare/social worker, whose job it is to make spontaneous visits to her home to ensure that (1) there are no Black men present in the home, and (2) that she is not living too extravagantly. In this film, when the social worker knocks on the door,

Claudine must scramble to the clothes and belongings of her boyfriend, and any household appliances that may give the welfare worker the idea her children's father is living in the family home, and that she is abusing the system by using the money to purchase household necessities.

Cornbread, Earl, and Me (1975) also presents the construct of the Welfare Queen in a less conspicuous manner. In this film, Earl's mother, is receiving social service. She is not working due to an illness. The establishing scene occurs when the Black social worker pays a surprise visit and cautions her that should she not show up for her appointments and it is found that she is not ill, her services will stop immediately. The implication of this interaction is to present the fact that she is on welfare and subject to the control of the state. To promote, once again, the middle class Black woman as the keeper of poor Blacks. And to insert a value judgment about the validity of her illness, which leads to the suggestion or implication that even if she may be ill, abuse of the system is so common that these types of admonishments become standard.

It is argued that the limitation in the cinematic presentation of the Welfare Queen construct rests in the fact that after the explosion of the Blaxploitation period that dominated during the first half of the 1970s (1971–1974), the number of mainstream Black films that were being produced drastically declined during the second half of the 1970s and did not significantly increase until Spike Lee began to produce films in the second half of the 1980s. Ironically this decline occurs after the Black Power Movement had been dismantled, and the Civil Rights Movement had been diluted.

It is further suggested that the decline in the production of Black films during that era was also the result of the predominance of television during that era—and the production of television shows that supposedly mimic the struggle of inner-city and working-class Black's such as *Good Times, Sanford and Son, What's Happening*, and the breakthrough middle-class television show, *The Jeffersons*.

What is interesting in all of these shows is the relationship between the Welfare Queen and the "welfare" worker. The welfare worker, who is always portrayed by a Black actor (once again ensuring that the White face is not representing the suppression) represents an agent of the state, who, in her role, exercises the very type of 'paternalistic control' that the State/ruling class have historically represented.

Therefore, just as the previous era set up the Sapphire construct in the management and admonition of Black men by Black women. Once intra-racial class divisions are solidified, films such as this represent the Black middle-class' authority and oppression of the working class and poor in the urban community—wherein the presentation is a direct reflection of the characters internalization of hegemonic ideologies about race and class, or more significantly the characters perpetuation of the ideologies of the writer.

Discussion of Hegemony in Black Film

Mario Van Peebles: *Sweet Sweetback's Badaaaasss Song*

Sweet Sweetback's Badaaaasss Song, which was written, produced, and directed by Mario Van Peebles, was specifically analyzed in order to evaluate differences in the visual presentation of the Black woman by the race of the director.

This film exemplifies a more gross presentation of Black characters than others, which give reason why the film was widely accepted and promoted. In this movie, women (Black and White) are presented strictly for sexual purposes. None of the female characters has any significant role other than objects in sexual scenes. And although there is no violence or aggression presented against the Black woman by either White or Black characters in the film, the film reinforces the hyper-sexualization of the Black woman that is, in this case, presented by a Black director/producer.

This presentation is evident in the first scene. In the opening scene, a dark-skinned woman, who is presumed to be a whore is lying in the bed coaching a somewhat reluctant young boy who appears to be no more than 13 years old to have sex with her. The scene is very sexually explicit with camera angles moving between the legs of the Black woman as the young boy, who is obviously naked climbs on top of her. In the final segment of the scene, the woman cries out "Ooooh you got a sweet, sweet back!"

So, it is argued that while mainstream film perpetuates hegemonic presentations that are designed to deconstruct Black male and female gender identity, Black films are simultaneously doing the same.

The Visual Fixation

The Sapphire and the Era of Blaxploitation

As was argued by Sanders in Chapter II and asserted in this chapter, the Jezebel and the perpetuation of the sexualization of the Black woman in film does not reemerge until after the Mammy Era. And when it emerges, it emerges with strength and dominance particularly during the Blaxploitation Era where Black men now join in the exploitation and abuse of the Black woman's body.

Each of the Blaxploitation films analyzed in this study represents the visual fixation on the Black woman's buttocks and breast for the purpose of objectifying and sexualizing the Black woman's body, the scenes being so explicit that it is surprising that the movies were not rated X.

Foxy Brown (1973) and *Coffy* (1972), which both star Pam Grier, provide support for this assertion. In each of these films, Grier's characters are constantly subjected to physical violence by Black men, White men, and White women. In her quest to infiltrate and or "pay back" the mob, she is constantly subject to the sexual violence of White men and constantly has her breasts exposed as a part of each scene.

In the opening scene, Foxy's brother calls her on the phone and asks her to come and help him. When she gets out of the bed, she is wearing a see through negligee. As she walks to the closet the camera is fixated on her breasts and does not adjust to capture her face. So as she gets her clothes from the closet, the camera stays focused on her breasts. She walks away from the camera and takes of her negligee and the camera still focuses on her body.

After rescuing her brother, the next scene involves her giving oral sex to her boyfriend in the hospital. The rest of this film deals with her physical and sexual abuse by White men who, in one scene, lasso her around the neck with a rope and jerks her to the ground exposing her buttocks with the camera panned between her legs (reminiscent of hanging). The White man replies, "I'm just getting my kicks letting this big jugged jigaboo think she can take a walk." After tying her up and shooting her with heroin, he climbs on top of her and rapes her. Finally, at the end of the movie when Foxy arrives to confront the White madam, she is searched with the White man feeling her crotch and fondling her breasts.

Sweet Sweetbacks Badaaaasss Song, *Carmen Jones*, *Foxy Brown*, and *Cotton Comes to Harlem* also present the Black woman's body as a highly sexualized body that is subject to abuse.

These films represent the re establishment of the hypersexual presentation and objectification of the Black woman's body. But, this marks the beginning of using the visual presentation of the Black woman's body as a commodity in film.

In Disch's book, *Reconstructing Gender: A Multicultural Anthology* (1997), Donnerstein and Linz did a study on the arousing affects that the depiction of sexual aggression and the rape of women had on male viewers. They argued "one of the unique features of these images in their reliance upon "positive victim outcomes," in which rape and other sexual assaults are depicted as pleasurable, sexually arousing, and beneficial to the female victim" (Disch 1997:498). They further argued that the images increased through the 1970s. This study supports this assertion for Black film. Consequently, they furthered that in internalizing these images and the relationship, men may become desensitized to sexual aggression and perpetuate the types of behaviors seen in film in society.

Arguably, the Black woman's body has never been safe from the type of abuse and exploitation that is presented in these films. And it was the fear and "flee" from this terror that encouraged the migration of Black women during Jim Crow, the cultural transmission of ways in which Black women could avoid this type of abuse (Giddings, 2004). However, during that era, and in a time of political struggle, where gender antagonisms had not been solidified, protecting the women from the assault was a primary objective of the race as a whole.

The Blaxploitation Era and the presentation and sexualization of the Black woman in Blaxploitation films reflect a return to the old perception of the Black body as a receptacle for sexual exploitation. However, in these films, it is not only the White male that is privy to the voluntary assault on the Black body, Black men also take on this role. Therefore, this study agrees that in such films, the physical and sexual exploitation and assault of the objectified Black body makes the Black body a commodity—sold to promote the arousal of male and female viewers, Black and White alike. And consequently, the presentation of the acceptance of this assault reflects a separation from the Black political movements, or more importantly the separation from "the struggle" of the race and an internalization of dominant ideologies about the Black woman's body by Black people, and the sentiment that the passage of the Civil Rights Act meant "the struggle" was over.

After this hyper-sexual era, it is found that the emergence of such a dominant and prevalent visual fixation would no longer exist in films that were not rated X and would not re emerge until the neo-Jezebel Era.

The Welfare Queen

It was found that in this era, the data utilized in this study did not provide adequate content for the analysis of the Welfare Queen construct. However, it is argued that the sociopolitical era represented a decline in the presentation of Black films in American society. The decreased number of Black films made during that era, and the lack of literary critiques of films during that era supports this assertion.

The films that did present this construct reflected a significant decline in the level of hyper-sexual presentations of the Black woman that were prevalent during the Blaxploitation Era. It is argued that the more conservative visual presentation was due to economic contraction and the goal of breaking the social contract. It is argued that in an effort to break the social contract, the sexualization of the Welfare Queen was not beneficial to the objective. Yet, it could be argued that without visually fixating on her body and sexuality, her sexual nature was implied by the number of children that she had, and depictions of her relationships with men.

There was no significant visual fixation to be analyzed in this era.

The Electronic Era from 1976 to 2004

In this section the technological forces of production and the sociopolitical and economic location of the African-American woman in the Electronic Era from 1976 to 2004 is discussed. Within this context, the images of the African-American woman and the characteristics of the hegemonic constructs of her in mainstream film are analyzed.

The Location and Image of the African-American woman During the Electronic Era from 1976 to 2004

Neoliberalism and Globalization from 1976 to 1975

Finally, there is the economic productive shift to the era of globalization, which corresponds to the transition from (social expansion to social contraction) or the transition from the welfare state to the prison industrial complex/race to the bottom, and political shift to (neoliberalism, cheap labor, deconstruction).

It is argued that this era completes a cycle and returns Black female characters, as well as characters of color to the first stage of the Jezebel, or what this study terms the "neo-Jezebel" and solidifies the Thug construct of the Black Male, that took form in the Blaxploitation era.

It is argued that in the quest to maximize production and profit, human workers are displaced by technology. Without the ability to earn a wage, individuals are unable to purchase commodities and necessities in the market. In addition, globalization opens other foreign markets for trade and production. Therefore, corporations are now free to, and given incentives to move companies from national to international soils where they can further maximize profits by using a much cheaper labor supply. This transition, it is argued, allows for neoliberalism and is essential to "the race to the bottom."

Without the same level of need for national human labor, the condition of the human no longer needs to be taken into account. Therefore, programs and policies that are designed to break the social contract and reallocate funds to expansionist ventures such as war are made possible. The result is an increase in the poverty, unemployment rate, incarceration, and even the death rate of working class people of all races.

However, specific to this study is the impact of globalization on the sociopolitical condition and location of the African American in society, and how that condition and location relates to her visual presentation in mainstream film.

For the African American who has traditionally been a source of first, free, and then cheap and then surplus labor, especially the working class woman, this transition places (the race) in a state of crisis. Now not only must working class African Americans compete with other races for work, they must now compete with each other. As Fishman and Scott discuss in Gomes and Williams (1994):

> The capitalist political economy is rooted in the necessity to constantly maximize profits, to reduce the cost of production and labor, and to distribute goods and services through the market and wage system. The introduction of electronics has permanently displaced many workers from employment and decreased wages for many more. This undermines the workers abilities to purchase the necessities of life and the ability of the capitalists to sell their commodities. The position of the African-American workers, conditioned by the legacy of slavery, places them at the heart of the United States working class as the most exploited or oppressed section (P.90).

However, it is argued that the role of the African-American woman as not only a surplus labor supply (especially after welfare to work is solidified) but the "reproducer" of surplus labor supply and later a free labor supply that will subsequently be provided by the prison industrial complex, is integral to this analysis. Therefore, like slavery, the agenda is to once again sexualize her and use the sexualization and objectification of her body for two purposes: as a commodity (profit-maker) in and of itself, and simultaneously revert the image back to antebellum status as a surplus and free laborer and the reproducer of a surplus and free labor supply.

The progression of legal and policy reforms that relate to economic contraction and set the stage for neo-liberalism in this era began in the 1970s. However, Ronald Reagan's implementation of his version of the "War on Drugs" (1982), that was originally implemented by Nixon ten years earlier in 1972, creates the foundation for the prison industrial complex. And Clinton's implementation of the Personal Responsibility and Work Opportunity Reconciliation Act (or Welfare to Work) 1996 creates the foundation for the provision of new free and surplus national labor pockets and an increasing poverty rate. These national policy reforms coupled with the implementation of Structural Adjustment Programs and the North American Agreement on Tariff and Trade, sets the "race to the bottom" in motion for all races of people, but has a larger impact on African-American men and women.

As mentioned in the previous section, the perpetuation of the 'Welfare Queen' construct during the era of economic contraction, served the purpose of promoting the belief that Black women were the primary users/abusers of the welfare system, hence, tax payers money while simultaneously promoting the same historic stereotypes of the Black man as being lazy, irresponsible, and hypersexual—coupled with the violent and aggressive (angry) stereotypes that were being presented. In essence, Black women were dependent on the system because Black men were not being "fathers" and taking responsibility (disciplinary, paternal, and financial) for their children. Therefore, society was being placed in a position to take care of the burdens that African Americans in general were placing on them through their character and actions. In response to the concerns of the people, the PRWORA was enacted.

Under the PRWORA (1996) no longer was public welfare an entitlement that required mandatory and somewhat limitless social spending. It was a program that would impose time and familial constraints on all recipients and make eligibility requirements more stringent. With that, the state freed a total of close to 170 billion dollars that could be utilized for other endeavors, specifically its expansionist and global capitalist ventures, that would result in several wars (www.findarticles.com/welfare reform). Under this new reform, time constraints and requirements were placed on cash assistance and other components of the system. Even the title of the benefit changed from Aid to Families with Dependent Children or Aid to Dependent Children to Temporary Assistance for Needy Families. All persons applying needed to register for work programs as a mandatory component and could only receive assistance for up to 5 years which was also limited by a cap. However, there were prohibitions to the receipt of assistance that automatically excluded persons from receiving aid if they had any felony convictions, especially drug convictions. However, even though the program was a welfare to work program, no substantive funding was provided for job training or other education programs that could increase the recipient's employability (Health and Human Service Statistics website: www.hhs.gov/ocr/overview). And no substantive training programs were developed or implemented by social service or other agencies to ensure that the recipients received adequate training.

Ironically, this reform came on the heels of the Ronald Reagan's 'War on Drugs.' Under these new and reformed drug laws mandatory minimums for anything involving the possession, distribution of crack cocaine, a drug that was deemed to be more specific to urban communities, were imposed. These reforms specifically targeted minorities and women and resulted in the escalation in racial profiling and an overall violation of civil liberties—that allowed officers to initiate traffic stops for persons who fit "the profile' of "drug dealers or abusers," and the violation of privacy—wherein bank and other financial records could be obtained by investigators and assets could be seized, which contributed to a sharp increase in the incarceration rate.

According to Drugfacts.org (2004):
1. In 1995 a mandatory five year sentence was imposed for anyone caught with 5 grams of crack. Yet 5 grams of any other drug would constitute simple possession and warrant a maximum one year sentence.
2. In 1986, the federal drug offense sentence for Blacks was 11% higher for Blacks than Whites. By 1992 that rate had increased to 49%.
3. By 1997, the U.S. Sentencing Commission found that nearly 90% of the offenders convicted for distribution of crack cocaine were Black, while the majority of users were White.
4. 80% of the increase in the federal prison population is due to drug convictions.
5. Between 1985 and 1996, the incarceration for female drug offenses increased by 95%.
6. 72% of women are in the federal prison system for drug related offenses while 30.4 are in state.
7. Black females are 2 X more likely than Hispanic women and 5 X more likely than White women to be incarcerated for drug offenses.

These statistics have significance to the condition of working class Black women. First, as a result of drug law reforms, Black women were specifically effected. Consequently, by the time of welfare reform, it can be argued that a significant number of urban women may have been excluded from receiving assistance after their release due to their drug convictions.

With the privatization of the prison system and welfare reform laws, African-American poor women become modern day slaves. In essence, it is argued that in this era, the laws and policy reforms become reminiscent of Jim Crow, Black Codes, and the convict leasing system. Just as Black codes were implemented to try to relegate African Americans back to slavery so have neo-liberal policy reforms done the same in this era. By implementing laws that were specific to the practices of African-American people, and then implementing a system wherein former slave masters could "lease the convicts" in order to provide labor, those who became involved in the system were, in fact, relegated back to slavery. The difference was in that era the laws or Codes were not criminal laws, simply laws such as loitering, vagrancy, that were created to target African Americans, to subject them to state control. However, due to the integration and internalization of the hegemonic and stereotypical values and ideologies about race and the significance of class and wealth, this transition is facilitated and the resulting Prison Industrial Complex comes with little understanding, question, or resistance from the masses.

The Neo-Jezebel and the Thug

Just as the Jezebel and the Buck constructs of the first era represented the ideologies about inferiority and immorality that were designed to subject the Black body back to the direct control of the ruling class, so do the neo-Jezebel and the Thug return them to that original status.

Given the sociopolitical transitions, the development of intra racial caste and class alienation, and the internalization of dominant ideologies—is merely a new version of the hyper-sexual, gyrating, ass fixation, that is the same as her initial representation—wherein, as hooks argues, Black folks who have internalized White supremacist attitudes and values are as much agents of this socialization as their racist non Black counterparts. (hooks 1994).

Of all of the films viewed during this era, 10 of the 18 films specifically presented the Jezebel as the dominant construct perpetuating the visual presentation in the same modern version as the Jezebel in the first era—fixating on her body as a means of conveying sexual and/or hypersexual notions about her, thereby serving to objectify her and utilize the commodification of her body and sexuality in order to promote the film, *She's Gotta Have It (1986), School Daze (1987), Mo Betta Blues (1990), Boys-n-the Hood (1991), Boomerang (1992), Poetic Justice (1993), Baps (1997), Soul Food (1997), Set It Off (1997), Players Club (1998), Jackie Brown (1999), Two Can Play That Game (2002), Austin Powers (2002), Monsters Ball (2003) and She Hate Me (2004).*

The cycle is prophetic as it is argued by Marx. It identifies the significance of the African American's relation to the means of production and productive shifts as indicators of how the ruling class will exploit their labor, hence, present the image in the media. Each productive transition yields a different presentation of constructs that directly relates to the way in which the productive and reproductive labor of the "working class" (mass) African American is being exploited in society. As capitalism transitions, so will the social, political, and economic condition of the people. It is clear and has already been asserted.

Former society, moving in class antagonisms, had need of the state, that is, an organization of the exploiting class at each era for the maintenance of its external conditions of production; that is, therefore, for the forcible holding down of the exploited class in the conditions of oppression (slavery, villeinage or serfdom, wage labor) determined by the existing mode of production. The state was the official representative of society as a whole, its embodiment in a visible corporation; but it was this only in so far as it was the state of that class which itself, in its epoch, represented society as a whole (Marx in Berberoglu 2001:16).

The re emergence of the dominance of the "neo-Jezebel" and the Buck/Thug is reflective of the culmination of the capitalist cycle that has greatly depended on the exploitation of the Black productive and reproductive labor as a very integral part of the growth of capitalism in America.

The Hegemonic Presentation of the African-American woman in Mainstream Film During the Electronic Era from 1976 to 2004

In this section the visual and interactive characteristics of the hegemonic constructs of the African American is analyzed in relation to her sociopolitical and economic location.

The Neo-Jezebel and the Thug

As had been presented above, the era of the neo-Jezebel and the Thug corresponds to the economic era of global capitalism, and the political era of neoliberalism. It is argued that this era reflects the culmination of reforms that ultimately lead to the deconstruction of social welfare and the solidification of globalization. These reforms begin in the 1970s with economic contraction, the deconstruction of social welfare, and the implementation of Structural Adjustment Programs and culminate with the implementation of North American Free Trade Agreement and the construction of the World Trade Organization, which frees global markets for corporate trade and capitalist expansion. This transition was only possible through the invention of the computer chip, and its subsequent use in production which drastically improved the efficiency of communication and trade while significantly and simultaneously displacing humans in the labor market. By displacing human labor and opening global markets, corporations are now able to produce more for less and where human labor is needed they are able to move corporations to third world countries, or, more significant to African Americans, utilize the surplus or free labor that is created from welfare reform and the prison industrial complex respectively.

Where human labor is no longer significant, the condition of the people is no longer a priority. More people of all races join the ranks of surplus labor.

Therefore, conditions are created that force people into more stiff competition for jobs which drives wages down. The rate of poverty is subsequently increased. And the "race to the bottom" is on.

It is argued that the era of globalization creates the condition wherein the productive and reproductive labor of the Black woman can once again be controlled, manipulated, and exploited—in the same manner as slavery. Neoliberalism provides the structure for the creation of excess surplus and free labor supplies in America by privatizing prisons and reforming laws that contribute to higher rates of incarceration for minorities, which reduces the need for corporate migration to Third World countries. By privatizing prisons and reforming laws that encourage the prison population, hence, the prison industrial complex (or the corporatization of the prison system), is created. After all, the 13th Amendment says that slavery shall be abolished *unless a person is duly convicted*.

As it has been argued in Chapter II, the physical characteristics and presentation of the Jezebel construct is not too different from the first era Jezebel. However, it is argued that the motive behind the construct and presentation is different in this era. The original Jezebel construct was specifically designed to promote the ideological and cultural hegemony of the ruling class for the purpose of exploiting the productive and reproductive labor in order to promote agricultural development in the United States. The original presentation did not accurately reflect the sociopolitical and economic location of the Black woman or an accurate representation of the indigenous culture of African people. It was designed to utilize the physical characteristics of the African that were different than those of the European to substantiate claims of biological inferiority, thereby justifying the objectification and commodification of the Black woman's body, and her subsequent enslavement.

Throughout this chapter, the evolution of each construct in relation to productive shifts has been outlined in order to evaluate the relevance of the hegemonic presentation of the Black woman in reference to the way in which her body and labor was being exploited in mainstream society. And through this presentation, the establishment of how the media has been used and useful in promoting and perpetuating intra racial caste, class and gender antagonisms through the internalization of hegemonic ideologies has also been illustrated.

This study argues that the era of the neo-Jezebel reflects the complete internalization of each construct and the revitalization of the Jezebel for profit. It is an era where Black people are full participants in their own objectification and the commodification of their own women. It is also argued that this same era revitalizes the Buck construct and makes the criminal aspect more prevalent in order to encourage the belief in the criminal Black man.

The neo-Jezebel and the Thug interplay is intricately manipulating. The neo-Jezebel is the Sapphire, the Welfare Queen, who now becomes the "gold digger" or "ghetto princess," rolled into a sexualized being. In film, her focus is using her body to gain material or financial support. And in the absence social welfare, she must turn to men for her subsistence and meager accumulation. Her focus is using her body to through objectifying her body, or allowing others to objectify her. And it is the objectification of her body that becomes the commodity for the business. It is her body that is now used as the tool to promote and sell products.

On the converse, the Thug, represents Merton's concept of Innovation. He is supposed to be a man, yet by traditional gender identity standards, a man is supposed to be a "provider" Historically, through all interplays, especially the Sapphire versus the Sambo interplay, the Black man is devoid of/in his ability to provide for his family through legitimate means. Once reliant on his woman, who has now rejected him, he has been given a means to acquire material wealth—hustling "hustling broads" (the pimp) "hustling drugs" the dope dealer—through illegitimate/illegal means. His wealth, being the only attraction, (besides sex) which takes second, is what attracts the woman. And because she is or will only be interested in a man with money, someone that can do for her financially materially, he does not have to and should not become attached to her. This interaction, subsequently gives him the right to at the least remain unattached and at the most abuse her.

She's Gotta Have It is the first film analyzed in this neo-Jezebel/Thug Era. It is a perfect example of the assertions made in this section. *She's Gotta Have It* was the first film produced and directed by Spike Lee. And like many other Black directors, he was hailed in the Black community for this contribution. His films were specifically about the sexual 'habits' of a young lady who was dating three different men without any obvious connections other than the sexual and intimate relationships that they share.

In once scene, Nola Darling, the main character states that she thinks she is "oversexed" and seeks therapy for this apparent addiction. In another scene, one of her suitors who has become insulted and angered by her lack of ability to connect, date rapes her. Snatching her arm tossing her and bending her over while exclaiming, "I guess this is what you want. This must be how you like it. This must be what you want!"

Boomerang provided another example of the neo-Jezebel, Robin Givens, who in this film was a upper class Black woman with a booming career who in spite of her middle class status exhibits very promiscuous, yet masculinized sexual habits. Her whole motivation centers on using her sexuality to manipulate and demean the Black man. And because she has her own money, she only needs him for sex. In the absence of any relational connection that is traditionally identified as a part of relationship dynamics, she is presented as a detached and using her sexuality for no other reason than physical pleasure.

In one scene, she engages in a night of intimacy with the main character Marcus and when he has awakened, she is gone having left money on the nightstand. She embraces the sexual presentation usually reserved for working class Black men.

In this film, Given's character wears short skirt suits and is often shot from the rear switching and shaking her hair to reflect how Eddie Murphy's character Marcus is fantasizing about her.

In the movie *Baps*, Halle Berry plays the lead role. She plays a "ghetto" girl who goes to live with a rich White man in Hollywood after breaking up with her "unemployed" boyfriend. In this film, Berry's character wins the heart of the White male through her lively, "ghettoized," and sexual presentation. Throughout the film, she undergoes a very obvious transition in character and presentation, wherein she becomes more conscious and moral, and more conservative in her appearance. This presentation is dramatically similar to earlier films, such as in *Topsy and Eva* (1927) wherein the plot is centered around the immoral Black woman needing to interact with the White man, or White society in order to develop a her morality.

In the same vein was Halle Berry and Billy Bob Thorton's infamous *Monsters Ball* (2003) for which Berry won an Academy Award. In this role, like her earlier role, Berry's character represented a ghetto woman who was dealing with poverty, the incarceration and execution of her "criminal" boyfriend—who is eventually sentenced to death, and single parenthood. After the death of her boyfriend, Berry's character struggles with trying to make "ends meet" on a waitress salary. Exhausted with life, she turns to Billy Bob Thorton's character, who was the warden on Death Row who cared for Berry's boyfriend until his death, for her salvation. The representation of the neo-Jezebel is projected in the highly present and controversial sex scene in which Berry claws at Thorton's character and begs, "make me feel good . . . make me feel good." While the Thug is evident in Sean Combs' character being on death row from the onset of the movie.

The presentation of these characters reflect the stereotypical constructs and the plots are stereotypical plots that are clearly reminiscent of the original presentations. And like the plots before, the reinforce assertions that slave women and domestics sexually desired and pursued the slave master in order to secure personal gain and that slave men must be controlled in order to suppress his violent and criminal nature.

The final example of the neo-Jezebel versus the Thug interplay is found Ice Cube's film *Players Club* which presents all of the Black women in the film as strippers and all of the men as Thugs (Pimps, Hustlers, Criminals). In this film, even though the main character, Diamond, is trying to finish college as a single parent, she uses her body to make money in the meantime. The show reflects the Thugs criminality and his objectification of the Black woman's body as his primary concern. And ultimately the assertion is reinforced by the infamous phrase, "Make that money; don't let it make you."

In *Austin Powers* (2002), Beyonce Knowles plays a Foxy Cleopatra, who is supposed to be a replication of the Blaxploitation "heroines" discussed above, Foxy Brown and Cleopatra Jones. In this supporting role, Foxy's role is to support Austin Powers. Each of her costumes expose midriff from breast to lower hip. And other than her visual accentuation, her role serves no other purpose.

Although much of the literature argues that these types of films represent the Black woman's control over her sexuality and relationships, her visual presentation, primarily, and then the relationships that she engages in and how her character utilizes her body and sexuality in the film is clearly reflective of the objectification of the body and sexuality of the character. That the woman actively engages in this presentation as an actor or character does not change the nature of the objectification. That she receives compensation for the role does not change the nature of the objectification or commodification of her body and sexuality in film. The same can be said of the Thug.

While it may be thought by the mainstream that the characters presented in these movies reflect the story of the neighborhood, and are therefore cannot be questioned. The fact that the presentation reflects a one-dimensional story is questionable. Many of the actors are not "telling their own stories." They are seasoned actors who come from middle class upbringings and have had the privilege of getting an education that allows them to read their scripts and negotiate their money, and even training in the field/profession of acting. Therefore, they are not taking agency of their own experiences, they are being used to tell a story that is not reflective of their own.

It must, most clearly be understood, that in order to have true control over the ones body and sexuality, one must have control over the way in which the body and sexuality are presented in that medium. Each of these films were written, directed and produced by men. In many instances these men were African American (Spike Lee, John Singleton, Ice Cube). However, each was distributed by a mainstream production company owned by White men, and most often produced and funded in conjunction with White corporate owners. Therefore, without true control over the production of the film, the notion of the actor's control of his presentation is superficial at best. The only control that can be asserted is the control over whether to accept the role or not. Each actor has the option of participating in their own exploitation or not, that is the extent of the control. Once they become active participants in the exploitation, they are subject to the complete control of the writer, director, and producer of the film.

This is significant because what is being suggested and shown in this entire chapter is how the images of Black people have continuously and purposely been manipulated in order to promote the image of the race that would justify how the race was being exploited during each era. So, like the eras before, it is being argued that these presentations also serve the same purpose of promoting the internalization of the ideological hegemony of the ruling class.

With the solidification of globalization, neoliberalism, and the prison industrial complex, perpetuating the interplay of the hyper-sexuality of the neo-Jezebel and the Thug serves to continue to deconstruct Black love, the Black family, and the Black community. It also serves to once again utilize the African American as the producer of a surplus labor supply by 'single parenting' illegitimate children that are presupposed to become a source of free labor through their continued legacy of criminality; thus, incarceration which is promoted through the legal reforms that were designed to increase the minority incarceration rate.

The Visual Fixation

Although not in the same vain as the Blaxploitation Era or the original Era of the Jezebel, the Era of the neo-Jezebel marks a return to the visual fixation on the Black woman's buttocks for the purpose of once again "sexualizing" the Black woman's body.

In this era, especially the latter part of the '90s and into the new millennium, the shift involved casting women who had larger butts, hips and thighs in the role of leading lady—with the presupposition that these women represented the urban Black body which was now being claimed as beautiful. In this manner, it was no longer necessary to be so explicit in the camera shots of the Black body, it would present itself. Therefore, in casting, attention would be paid to those actors who had the physical characteristics that were easily identifiable.

This study found that in many of the films viewed during this era, the "ass" was present and prevalent. Tracy Camilla Johns (*She's Gotta Have It*, 1986), Tichina Arnold (*School Daze*, 1989), Tisha Campbell (*School Daze*, 1989), Lisa Raye *(Players Club, 1998)*, Beyonce *(Austin Powers, 2002)*, Janet Jackson *(Poetic Justice, 1993)* and Halle Berry *(Baps, 1997)*, *(Monsters Ball, 2003)*, Jennifer Lopez *(Maid in Manhattan, 2005)* all represent the visual presentation of the "urban ass."

In dance, gesture, walk, sex scenes, and camera fixation the presentation begins to link the construct to her physical characteristics. For, example, instead of the hand on the waist in discussion or reprimand that was prevalent during the Mammy Era, it is now hand on the hip or buttocks. And clothing, such as tight jeans, hip huggers, cut off shirts, and other types of clothing that accentuate and reveal the Black woman's body become associated with urban wear, and thus presented in film.

However, this new presentation of the Black buttocks and the manner in which it is fixated upon is now redirected. Black women that are selected for the roles have Black bodies that accurately represent the hegemonic ideal of Black sexuality, which negates the need for props and/or a deliberate camera fixation. And now instead of being marginalized, the Black body and the fixation upon it is celebrated as an identification of Blackness, just as the Afro in the 1960s and 1970s. And as Collins (2004) argues "the ubiquity" of the presentation creates the perception of normality and acceptance for the fixation.

Now, in this era, individuals are specifically cast in certain roles because their bodies reflect the hegemonic and historic notion of the Black body—just as McDaniel reflected the hegemonic idea of the Mammy. There is no longer a need to hyper exaggerate through costume or camera fixation those characteristics that defines "Blackness." Be it the Black woman's buttocks or the Black mans muscular body, "tatted up" neck, arms, back, torso, or even face, his dark skin, and his angry urban look—an actor (now rappers are being used as actors to get 'the look'), there are now voluntary participants for the hegemonic presentation.

However, unlike assertions by actors, rappers, etc. the voluntary participation or the extent of compensation for these presentations do not dismiss the current visual presentation as a perpetuation of the Black body as "other" or sexually deviant. The historical foundation that has been established has never been retracted. The people have never been debriefed. The rule has not changed. Yet, this new fixation is often interpreted as sexually liberating or as Black people taking agency over their sexuality and sexual presentation or even their presentation in general.

School Daze (1987), a modern day musical, presents the fixation in the most clear fashion. In this film, there is a party scene where there is a dance off. The dance is called "da butt" which originates from the title of the theme song "Doin da Butt" a percussion-heavy Go-Go song. In this scene, women must wildly shake their butts in a circular motion while placing their hands or having hands placed on their butts. In this scene, the camera specifically fixates on the buttocks of all partygoers. But, more importantly, 'da butt,' or the fixation on the buttocks, becomes a deliberate identification for Black woman and urban culture. Collins (2004) discusses this film in her work. "In Lee's party sequence, being able to shake the booty is a sign of authentic Blackness, with the Black woman who is shaking the biggest butt being the most authentic Black woman" (p.129).

It must be added, that his film, by Spike Lee is also a film that explores the intra racial caste system that exists on college campuses—referring to light-skinned characters as "wannabes" and darker-skinned characters as "jigaboos." And so in the presentation of the butt, Lee presents the more Afro centric women with the biggest butts which again reflects the hegemonic ideologies about race, through presenting "Europeanized" versions of racial hierarchical constructions.

Players Club (1998), written and directed by rapper Ice Cube, presented another example of the visual fixation on the Black woman's buttocks. This film was specifically about the life of a stripper, Diamond, who dances to support herself and her son while she is a student in broadcast journalism at a local University. The plot of the story centers on the life of strippers who work at a local club, the conflict between them, the dilemma between dancing and having sex with clients, and rape. So, the plot allows for an open, visual, and relevant presentation of the Black woman's buttocks as a part of her frequent dance routines and interaction with clients. Each woman in the film has a relevantly large buttock. And so like most other films, this all Black-cast film adapts to a caste system that define and stratify the women in the movie.

The protagonist, Diamond, played by actor Lisa Raye, is a very attractive light-skinned girl, while the protagonist and the 'Jezebel among Jezebels' is the brown-skinned bi-sexual or gay rival stripper and the dark-skinned cousin who eventually sleeps with Diamond's boyfriend in her house and is ultimately raped after disregarding warnings and going to a private party.

Monsters Ball, presents one of the most highly sexualized interracial sex scenes in an R-rated film. In this scene, Berry exposes her entire body as she engages in a very aggressive sex scene where she begs for the White man's sexual penetration. She cries out, "Make me feel good; make me feel good," as she pulls him on top of her. The sex scene escalates into a highly charged one that no where near represents a passionate sexual exchange. But, conversely, reflects a highly emotional, aggressive, and animalistic exchange that is even spattered with quick periodic pulses of a woman rattling a small cage with her hand. In this part of the film, while only a small segment of the overall plot, the explosive sex scene serves to undermine the developing relationship by presenting a sex scene that represents White male dominance over the Black woman's body and sexuality, only this time it is not only done with her verbal or passive consent but with her begging to, "Throw it on him."

This era represents the internalization of hegemonic ideologies by both Black men and Black women, that this study argues, leads to their voluntary participation in their own objectification and exploitation and that of others for personal gain. The voluntary presentation of this construct by the race then validates the "truthfulness" of the presentation. Then, when internalized it leads to the perpetuation of the stereotypical constructs in "the real world" which leads to fulfilling the ultimate agenda of the ruling class.

It has been found that the fixation on and hyper exaggeration of the physical characteristics of the African American is a very significant part of the visual presentation in film that is both present and prevalent and remains so throughout each of the eras and transitions. It has also been found that once the physical characteristics of each construct has been established, the visual presentation of the construct does not change even when the construct is no longer the dominant one. For example, the original construct of the Mammy, that was not present in all Black-cast films or films by Black directors, re-emerges in contemporary films, like *Big Momma's House*, all of Tyler Perry's movies with Madea, *The Klumps*, and even *Soul Food*, to name a few. And as has been argued, the "ass" as a point of visual fixation and exaggeration as established in the first era, is desexualized but is still present as a dominant fixation during the second era, and is revitalized in the third and fourth era.

Finally, it is found that there is no significant difference in the way the African-American woman's body is fixated upon in films produced and directed by Blacks and Whites after the first era, which results from the internalization of the hegemonic presentations by unconscious Black filmmakers, and has served as the foundation for the predominance of these stereotypical images in urban media.

CHAPTER 4

THREE DOLLARS AND SIX DIMES 360°

Where does it come from? How is it grounded? What are the social and political forces that fuel the condition and location of African-American people?

The historic and socio-political foundation of the presentation of Blacks in the media is integral to understanding and providing foundation for the critique of "the game." In the absence of a theoretical explanation of the way in which images of "Blackness" have systematically and purposefully been manipulated and exploited in the media, it becomes easy to dismiss the *current* images and presentations as "entertainment"—to just "believe the hype." But, when the historic foundation is laid, it provides a greater rationale for understanding that just as images have been manipulated to promote the economic interest of the ruling class in the past, so are they now. The question can then be asked, what social, political, and/or economic agendas do the current images promote?

This chapter is designed to more clearly illustrate how the sociopolitical and economic direction of the United States has dictated the ever-changing conditions of African-American people. It will further hypothesize that as the United States, once again, engages in corporate (global) agricultural production (as a source of environmentally friendly fuel) so is it, once again, laying the (same) foundation for the legalized re-enslavement of African-American peoples through the Prison Industrial Complex. This chapter will show that just as the historic constructs of the Jezebel and the Buck were developed to justify the enslavement of African people in the 1600s, the contemporary presentations of the neo-Jezebel and the Thug are being utilized to promote the incarceration, hence, the legitimized *re-enslavement* of African-American people today—thus, representing, as Erykah Badu sings, ."... three dollars and six dimes" (three hundred and sixty degrees).

Deconstructing the Myth

Many, through mainstream conformist schooling/education, specifically in the areas of history and social studies that are both required and repetitive components of the public and private school curricula—are taught, through "miseducation" or omission, to believe that the enslavement of African people was just "something that occurred and existed." The curriculum does not analyze the institution and purpose of slavery. Consequently, students are not given a sociopolitical and/or economic explanation about the institution, and hence do not have an adequate foundation for understanding the oppressive and exploitive necessity of the institution or the essentiality of the institution to the economic development of the United States.

In many instances, the literature, specifically primary and secondary school history texts, posits that slavery provided the opportunity for savage Africans to be socialized and civilized, and allowed them an opportunity that they would not have had, had they remained in "primitive" Africa. For most, including Africans in America, the myth of the biological inferiority and savagery of the African still serves as the unspoken explanation for why Africans were enslaved.

The myth of the animalistic African was a necessary fallacy—a stereotype that was devised to justify and garner support for the enslavement of a people. For European colonizers, who were predominantly Christian, enslavement went against the most essential religious principle from which the concept of "democracy" was borne and is based—"All men are entitled to the basic right to freedom, and the pursuit of happiness." Therefore, to remove a human from his/her right to freedom in order to exploit his/her productive and reproductive labor for wealth accumulation would be an abomination. So, if slavery were to be accepted with good conscience and minimal resistance from "the people," constructing an animalistic identification for the race became essential.

The stereotypical constructions were created in order to remove Africans from their rights as human beings by distorting the cultural rituals, destroying and omitting the history of African people in the literature, and creating and promoting the notion of the biological inferiority, innate criminality, and violent nature of the African and then the African American. Through constructing and promoting these ideas, the world was led to believe that Africans were, in fact, animals or at the least "sub-humans" with animalistic tendencies, who needed to be confined, controlled, trained, and even "saved," which gave "European Americans" the right to enslave them and treat them as such.

Consequently, like animals, Africans could be hunted, captured, and stripped from the Motherland against their will. They could be chained, caged, and confined, bought and sold in the market, and forced to conform to Western ideologies and religious principles. They could be put to work under the most severe conditions (that most others would not have survived) without regard to the mental, physiological, or spiritual limitations of the human mind, body, and soul. They could be denied the right to their subjective and natural roles as "men" and "women," such as being a wife or husband, mother or father, son or daughter, sister or brother. And in such, they could be denied the ability to connect and establish meaningful relationships, marriages, and family bonds. They could be raped, forcibly bred/mated—like animals against their will, denied the right to keep, nurture, control, protect, and raise their own children—and ultimately whipped, castrated, beaten, burned, dragged, and hanged/murdered without question or consequence. They were nothing more than the property of the slave master, who could do with them as he pleased.

These brutal practices were normal and essential during the Antebellum era—that Americans have since become desensitized to. They are the practices that are omitted, minimized, and even negated or denied in the literature and discussion about enslavement. Yet, these are the practices that African Americans would have to endure for centuries. But, the question remains, why was slavery really necessary? What were the real political and economic implications of the institution?

England experienced an Industrial transition in the 1700s. This transition to industry required labor and the production of natural resources that could be transformed into commodities. The United States was colonized for the purpose of utilizing the land to produce natural resources for the European Industrial market—specifically the textile industry. As Feagin (2000) argues:

> From the early 1700s to the mid 1800s much of the surplus capital and wealth of North America came directly, or by means of economic multiplier effects, from the slave trade and slave plantations. With the growing demand for textiles, U.S. cotton production expanded greatly between the 1790s and the beginning of the Civil War. Cotton was shipped to British and New England textile mills, greatly spurring the wheels of British, U.S., and international commerce.

So, contrary to traditional teachings and discourse about slavery, that minimize, negate and/or exclude the economic reality of the institution, slavery was essential to the success of the colony because agricultural production was the foundation of its wealth accumulation. Therefore, this relationship (institution) *must* be placed in political and economic context in order to truly understand the rationale for slavery and deconstruct the myth of the inferiority of the African.

It must be clearly noted that contrary to dominant assertions and stereotypes about the savagery of African people, slavery *was not* an institution that was developed in order to "save the savage African." It was designed to promote global capitalism in an industrial economy by providing an essential labor supply that would be essential to agricultural production, hence, global trade and wealth accumulation in the United States and Europe. Feagin (2000) summarizes this point when he argues:

> It is unlikely that the American colonies and, later the United States would have seen dramatic agricultural and industrial development in the eighteenth and nineteenth centuries without the blood and sweat of those enslaved. Much of the wealth generated between the early 1700s and the 1860s came from the slave trade and the labor of enslaved men, women, and children on plantations

and in other profit making enterprises . . . Slave grown cotton became ever more central to the U.S. economy and accounted for about half of all exports, and thus for a large share of the profits generated by exports . . . In the North the profits from the cotton economy and from the sale of products to slave plantations stimulated the growth of investment in financial and insurance enterprises, other service industries, and various types of manufacturing concerns, as well as, by means of taxes, investment in government infrastructure projects . . . Their agricultural production undergirded national economic development. . . . British and New England manufacturers' demand for cotton fueled the demand for more enslaved workers and for more Native American land. . . . Labor was perhaps one of the most critical factors in American economic production, so any scarcity in workers slowed development. . . . Slave labor not only removed this scarcity, but also made possible the development of the industry that spurred economic growth. . . . In the decade before the Civil War the dollar value of those enslaved was estimated by one leading planter to be 2 billion—a figure then exceeding the total value of *all* northern factories (Feagin 2000:52-53).

This is the real cause and need for the institution of slavery. For contrary to the assertions that were designed to promote this institution, Africa as the "Motherland" or the birthplace of all humanity, civilization, and order (Leakey, Wilson and Cann, Asante) was also the birthplace of not only agricultural production—which led to the development of the first calendar that the Greeks would later adopt, change, and claim—but technology, writing, religion, architecture, medicine, anatomy/physiology, astronomy, philosophy, and mathematics—just to name a few of the contemporary "sciences/disciplines" that were born (have foundation) in Africa—therefore developed by the African. As Asante (2007) asserts.

> The first books of mathematics are Kemetic books. No books on mathematics existed in the world before the African books produced in the Nile Valley and what is now called the Rhind Papyrus . . . Imhotep was the first philosopher to deal with the question of volume, time, the nature of illness, physical and mental disease, and immorality. He was the first philosopher in human history. He lived around 2700 B.C.E. The earliest form of architecture was developed in Kemet, where the first masonry construction was the Saqqara Pyramid build by Imhotep for Per-aa Zoser in the Third Dynasty. . . . It is believed that writing was invented around 3400 B.C.E. in Kemet, about 300 years before we see a cuneiform system of writing was done on almost any type of surface, but the favorite was papyrus, a reed that grew in the Nile, now found far south of Egypt in Sudan. Immediately writing served three purposes: recording historical events, communication between the king, priests, and scribes, and literary and instructional writing (Asante 2007:31-38).

Yet, this is the story that is never told in mainstream institutions because it is contrary to the hegemonic ideologies that have been presented as fact for centuries—the same ideologies that remain essential to the preservation of the ideology of White/European supremacy, hence, the power dynamics that exist today.

Western ideology, hence, Westernized education, would have the world continue to believe that all that is good, civil, and progressive emerged in Europe in order to preserve the ideology that has lended to non confrontational expansion, colonialism, and imperialism and established a global power structure that has now solidified itself as a reality. Therefore, all who choose a Western education will be taught Western ideologies, Westernized constructions of "the truth." From philosophy courses that give credit to Greek Philosophers, such as Plato, Socrates, and Aristotle for the origin of a "science," "practice," and "thought" that existed in Kemet long before there was even a civilization in Greece, to the promotion of notions that the first civilizations or at the least the first structured societies emerged in Europe, the fallacies continue to support an ideology that is designed to maintain the existing power relations—while, the truth about Africa continues to be omitted or denied.

In such, slavery becomes the beginning of the African-American story, as if Africans in America had no "story," no connection, no culture, and no existence of value before their "tenure" as slaves. The American "presentation" of Africa as being a savage place then encourages a cultural detachment or feeling of disconnectedness and even superiority among African Americans who have been "trained" again to believe that the race "was saved" when the ancestors were bought to this country. In such, they have no collective desire to research, study, understand, or embrace any pre-American history or connection and must consequently rely on European ideas and cultural values to evaluate and develop an identity of "collective self."

While slavery does mark the beginning of the African experience in America—it does not mark the beginning of the African experience, and therefore, should not be constructed as the genesis of the race in the minds and consciousness of the people that the truth serves to save and empower. The deliberate purpose for promoting the "disconnect" must be understood so that the connection can be rebuilt. The truth about the heritage of a people must be studied so that the collective esteem and consciousness of the race can be rebuilt.

By removing 'a people' from the reality of their heritage—their origin, the dominant class has secured its ability to shape and manipulate the collective psyche of the race without complication or resistance. Erasing the legacy of a people, and then disconnecting those in the Diaspora from the legacy, culture, and people in the mother land, facilitates domination through the "divide and conquer" tool. Creating and promoting the story of inferiority to the European but superiority to the African—that will be culturally transmitted and then internalized "as the reality" of each group in the different parts of the Diaspora from the United States to Jamaica—facilitates European control, exploitation, and dominance over the continent with minimal resistance from those in the Diaspora. These processes have been deliberate and essential.

This is why the mental and cultural breaking process—which involved forbidding Africans from speaking their indigenous language, practicing their indigenous cultural rituals, reading and writing in their indigenous language, communicating and congregating in groups, marriage, establishing and maintaining family and community bonds, etc., and even learning to read and write in the English language—was so fundamental to the institution. All of these slave codes where designed to remove "a people" from their history and connection so that they could be indoctrinated, "re-programmed," conditioned-taught/coerced and/or forced to internalize hegemonic ideologies that undermined their true identity and the true power that the people enjoyed before the European penetration of Africa—thus, ensuring their almost certain dependence on the European for validation and survival.

360°

As mentioned in the previous chapter, each transition in the constructs or presentations of the African American in the media corresponded to transitions in the means of production, hence, transitions in the way in which the labor of African Americans was being utilized/exploited during those eras. America underwent five key productive transitions/shifts, The Agricultural Era, the Pre-Industrial transition period, The Industrial Era, The Electronic Era, and the Era of High Technology and Globalization. Each era determined the socio political location and condition of African-American people.

As just mentioned, the agricultural era was the first era. The mean of production during that time was human labor, the source of that human labor, was the slave. The constructs that were utilized to justify the exploitation of the race, the Jezebel and the Buck—the hypersexual, immoral/a moral, aggressive, and violent animal that needed to be controlled image.

The second transition was the Pre-Industrial Era, which was the United States preparation for Industrial trade and a shift from an agricultural to and Industrial economy. Contrary to assertions that the Civil War was about abolition and humanity, wherein the North represented the hero to "the cause" and the South represented "the antagonist," the Civil War was no more about humanity than the Civil Rights Act or any other acts would be. The Civil War was about productive and economic transition, and what the North deemed progress. The "slaves," hence, African-American people, were just pawns.

As Weber would argue, the Civil War was a war between tradition and rationality, status quo and progress. It was no different than any other War or revolution. The Civil War was the result of the conflict between the traditional South, who were dependent upon, and had gained their wealth from agricultural production—hence, slavery, and Northern Industrialist who were seeking to transition into an Industrial economy and accelerate Industrial production and trade.

Emancipation was a tactic that was utilized by the North to "drain" the South's labor supply hence, the profit from agricultural production in an attempt to coerce the South to concede to Northern demands.

During that era, because the goal was not to promote the humanity and/or inclusion of the African American, and because the industrial economy had not yet been solidified the constructs of the Jezebel and the Buck were still being promoted as the dominant constructs of African-American men and women that continued to support societal fear and resistance to integration.

Once the South conceded, the move to solidify the economic and productive shift was aggressive. And just like the agricultural era, the industrial economy also necessitated the need for mass labor. In keeping with capitalism, again, the wealth accumulation of the country was dependent upon a labor supply that would fuel industrial production and development. White American labor was not sufficient enough to propel maximum production. While Eastern Europeans has already entered the United States, the number of immigrants that were being allowed into the country was not sufficient enough to promote the development that Northern industrialists were seeking. Therefore, once again, Black labor was depended upon to fuel this development.

In order to gain support for "workplace" integration, then, the stereotypes that had been developed to promote the fear of integration had to subsequently be negated. But, they could not be negated in a manner that would undo the power dynamics and bring question to the discrimination and oppression that African Americans had been, and would continue to be subjected to. The truth about the race could not be told. Instead, new fallacies had to be created in order to promote workplace integration with minimal resistance or violence, while still giving White America power and agency over the Black body and Black labor. This made the constructs of the Uncle Tom and the Mammy critical.

Promoting constructs whose characteristics were the antithesis of those of the Jezebel and the Mammy proved successful. By developing a character of the African-American man and woman as being docile, infantile, un-knowledgeable, submissive, trustworthy, weak, and a sexual, society would feel more at ease working with, near, or around the African American, and/or allowing the African American to be the societies servant. The Mammy and the Uncle Tom proved successful at negating the presentation that African Americans were to be feared, could not be trusted, would not work, and should not be allowed to integrate—while still promoting a clear and recognizable level of "inferiority" that would justify relegating those who were "given the opportunity to work in mainstream industries" to the lower echelons of the labor pool, in controlled and/or restricted duties and with limited or no mobility. In such, the African-American working class who were hired to work in the integrated industrial settings (for which their labor was needed) would be relegated to service level work regardless of their experience and expertise, while African-American professionals/elite would be relegated to working in segregated sectors.

The transition from the Industrial era to the Electronic era was another significant transition that greatly affected the sociopolitical location of African Americans. It was an era where the harnessing and distribution of electricity through the development of the electric grid, and the invention of electric domestic tools such as the electric oven, washer, dryer, vacuum, dishwasher, etc., as well as the mechanization of factory machinery would lead to the displacement of human beings in the labor market. Consequently as African Americans occupied the lower levels of industry, and the non specialized manual labor positions, and the domestic positions, they would be most adversely affected.

This era further corresponded with the passage of Brown versus the Board of Education (1954) and the Civil Rights Act (1965), wherein African Americans were given the "legal" right to "equal" and "fair" treatment in housing, employment, loans, education, which although meaningful to the Black Middle Class who were able to take advantage of the new opportunities, was instrumental in the deconstruction of the economic foundation and condition of the inner city, and the unity of the race. The Fair Housing Act and suburbanization coupled with the Equal Employment Opportunity, allowed middle class African Americans to (1) move out of the segregated areas of the inner city in which they were once confined, and (2) work in integrated workplaces—(although not in great force initially) Black Doctors and nurses could now work in mainstream hospitals, lawyers in courts and mainstream law firms, and other mid-level workers in governmental agencies such as the Post Office, printing offices, etc. More significantly African-American children were now able, and in some instances forced, to attend mainstream schools, and then able to go to mainstream institutions of higher education—instead of being "relegated" to Historically Black Colleges and Universities.

The movement of the race after the passage of the Civil Rights Act reflected what Frazier (1935) and Freire (1972) argued was the detriment of the African-American middle class because it reflected their collective internalization of notions of White supremacy and the dominance and superiority of the White race. It reflected the lack of consciousness that either guided the movement or was lost as the struggle progressed. The exodus of the middle class from the community, as soon as *they* were given the chance, reflected the collective quest to be accepted by and integrate into "White society" above promoting the continued development of Black communities or concern for the majority who would be left behind. The continued bragging about being "the first Black" to live in the White community, work in the White, join the White, be invited to the White . . . is reflective of the internalization of supremacist ideals.

Not to undermine the Civil Rights Movement and/or its accomplishments; but, this work must critique the detriment of either its "misguided" agenda or its misguided response to the passage of the Civil Rights Act. This work must critique how it could appear that the middle class "used" the working class to promote its own agenda and achieve goals that were only specific to that class of African Americans and then not only "abandoned" but in some instances became "sub-oppressors" to the working class and poor. And finally, this work must critique how this movement was either directly and/or indirectly manipulated in order to not only quell racial tension but to promote conformity to and for dominant ideologies and the continued dominance of the ruling class by implementing reforms that provided very limited positive change in/to the condition of African Americans. Let's examine.

The first of these "accomplishments" was the passage of Brown versus the Board of Education which preceded the passage of the Civil Rights Act by a decade. The original purpose of the Civil Rights Movement was to provide an education for African Americans so that they could ultimately be able to participate in the social, political and economic spheres of society in general—so that the race could survive. The undertone was to dispel the myth and stereotype of a people that had been, and continued to be detrimental to its survival and progress. Ultimately the goal was the acceptance and integration of "the race" into dominant society where they would be given an equal opportunity to achieve.

However, it was not only "teaching" the masses the basic skills-reading, writing, and arithmetic that were essential to the movement; it was developing the consciousness of the masses by teaching them the truths about racism, oppression, and the condition of the people. So, while the movement was seeking integration, it was the autonomy and independence provided in segregation that was most essential to the development and solidification of consciousness, hence, the progress of the movement. After all, the movements were led by men and women who went to "all Black" schools, colleges/universities, and were nurtured, supported and protected in "all Black" communities where the truth about the legacy of a people was told, stereotypes negated, and the mental, intellectual, and even spiritual being was nurtured by the teachers and professors, community members, pastors, and friends who had a vested interest in the development of each student.

It cannot be denied that segregated schools represented an uncensored, unregulated venue for students to receive the most important gift—education. The teachers and administrators were African-American teachers and administrators who were not limited in/by any racist ideologies or beliefs about the intellectual inferiority of the race that would undermine their ability to reach, teach, and nurture the potential of the student. So segregation had a concrete benefit. However, it was the argument of the movement that African Americans were not receiving an "equal" or even a "quality" education simply because they were not privy to attending White schools.

Just as it had been argued under Plessy versus Ferguson (1896), Brown v. Board argued that African-American institutions (facilities, etc.) were separate, but not equal to those of mainstream (White) institutions. Again, because Blacks were not permitted to attend White institutions and facilities, it was argued that they were not being provided "equal" (to White), hence, "better" (than Black) services, treatment, education, opportunity, etc.

But even a critique of Plessy v. Ferguson reveals that the suit did not argue that there was disparity in the cars reserved for Blacks, or the services, or lack thereof. Plessy, simply wanted to be able to exercise the right to sit in the same rail car as White folks. One of the principle premises of the case was the question of whether the 1/8^{ths} drop of "Black blood" in Plessy, or any other Black that "could pass" should be cause for removing him (them) from "White privilege." Thus, Plessy, as argued by some, was more a case that challenged the "social definition of race" and the subsequent social assignment of persons to an oppressed or privileged class than any representation or claim of "separate but equal."

Not that the challenge to exclusionary, discriminatory and racist practices are being criticized or the need for such negated; what is being criticized is the mentality, agenda, purpose, and goal for/of the challenge. The cases represent the desire to be accepted by Whites and the envy of "White things" above respecting and understanding the true gift of the social and economic independence, self sufficiency, and potential power of the race.

Certainly, African-American schools and institutions remained infrastructurally less developed than mainstream schools—did not have the quality of *material things* that mainstream schools had such as facilities, books, equipment, etc. But the first question is what prevented the race from investing in the development of its own? And more importantly, what did the race truly give up in order to gain access to the "material quality" that it apparently envied? In order to analyze the implications, education as an institution must be evaluated.

In his work, *Pedagogy of the Oppressed,* Freire states:

> The oppressed, who have been shaped by the death affirming climate of oppression, must find through their struggle the way to life-affirming humanization, which does not lie simply in having more to eat. . . . The oppressed have been destroyed precisely because their situation has reduced them to things. In order to regain their humanity they must cease to be things and fight as men (Freire 1972).

This was the original premise of "the movement" to restore African Americans to their status as men (and women) by negating the stereotypes and oppressive status that America had imposed upon them. This was to be done by developing the consciousness of the masses so that they could be prepared to undo the stereotypes and oppressive status derived there from, and engage in the struggle. Therefore, African-American men and women sought to gain knowledge and consciousness, and those who were fortunate enough to do so, came back and offered their gifts to the masses—for the purpose of uplifting the masses. This was essential. Freire (1972) furthers:

> The only effective instrument is a humanizing pedagogy in which the revolutionary leadership establishes a permanent relationship of dialogue with the

oppressed. In a humanizing pedagogy the method ceases to be an instrument by which the teachers (in this case revolutionary leadership) can manipulate the students (in this instance, the oppressed) because it expresses the consciousness of the students themselves (P. 56).

What Freire underscores is the fundamental necessity of allowing those who are engaged in the struggle to teach the masses. For as mentioned above, the oppressor and those who have been shaped by oppressive ideologies cannot reach the oppressed. It would be completely counterproductive to the maintenance of the status quo, hence, the power dynamics, for the oppressor (the ruling class) to undo the ideologies that were created for establishing the power dynamic. More significantly, those who receive a Western education, will not have the knowledge and consciousness to teach "the truth" in a manner that will uplift or promote the consciousness and well being of the oppressed. Therefore, integration must be questioned. So, what did Brown versus the Board of Education really do for the race?

By "getting to go to White schools," African Americans "got to get" a Western education, wherein they would once again receive the same "information" that the movement was trying to undo. Especially in the early stages, African-American students attending integrated schools were subjected to not only the content of a White education—that was designed to promote the "well being" of White people, but to being taught by those who held and upheld oppressive and racist ideologies—and in many instances hated, and wished ill upon those they were forced to "teach." Now, just like White students, African Americans were subjected to the constant repetition of, exposure and reconditioning to the very same ideologies that supported their oppression and now served to promote their own self hate, while now being under the control of a power structure that would neutralize the ability to continue to promote consciousness, activism, resistance, and rebellion.

> Oppression-overwhelming control-is necrophilic; it is nourished by love of death, not life. The banking concept of education, which serves the interests of oppression, is also necrophilic. Based on a mechanistic, static, naturalistic, spatialized view of consciousness, it transforms students into receiving objects. It attempts to control thinking and action, leads men to adjust to the world, and inhibits their creative power (Freire 1972:64).

During an era where the Civil Rights and Black Power Movements were at a critical peak, the passage and subsequent acceptance of Brown versus the Board of Education was not only a means to "give the dog a bone." But more importantly, it was the most clever means by/through which the education of the African American could not only be regulated, but where the minds of the African American could be trained to accept and conform to its own oppression.

Because the goal of the movement did not include truly reaffirming the value of "self approval" and subsequently seeking independence and power first, and then inclusion, and acceptance "as is," it unconsciously defined its "self" by its success in conforming to White ideals (dominant cultural values) and it defined its acceptance as its ability to force White society to "let the race" or at least "some of 'them'" into their world.

Consequently, the mass departure of the Black middle class from the inner city would exacerbate the condition of the masses of working class and poor African Americans who would be largely affected by the productive shift. The departure of the middle class resulted in the removal of not only an income and tax base that ensured the thriving of the inner city, but it also resulted in the removal of the communal sharing that often ensured the survival of the less advantaged in "troubled times."

When the neighborhood Doctor moved to the suburban area and closed his practice in the inner city to work at a mainstream hospital, when the neighborhood lawyer moved to the suburbs, the neighborhood grocer closed the shop to take a job with the Post office, etc., no longer would Ms. Mary be able to receive free care, Nathan get free legal representation, and the community get food necessities on credit, when they "didn't have it at the time." Therefore, when the unemployment rate increased as a result of the displacement of African-American workers, the mobility created by the passage of the Civil Rights Act, created a crisis for the inner city. And because the exodus also broke the connection that the middle class had with the community, it could no longer depend on its own for assistance.

Middle class "privilege" did not come without a cost either. Extending the right to inclusion and "equality" was not done out of the acceptance of the humanity of the African American, it was done to appease and continue to control and manipulate the race. The price that the middle class would have to pay was not to threaten their inclusion by "being" or acting ungratefully. "False charity constrains the fearful and subdued, the 'rejects of life,' to extend their trembling hands" (Freire, 1972). The Civil Rights Act made passive the few that had truly benefited from the act and removed them from the continued struggle of the masses. It made them reluctant to continue to fight for true equality and true justice, by making them fearful that if they "made waves" they would lose the gains that "they" had received.

Consequently then, as the economic state of the working class and poor African Americans (and others), that resulted from the industrial shift, necessitated the need for governmental assistance, (welfare), the Black middle class adopted the blame the victim ideology of mainstream society and accepted the validity of the welfare queen and thug constructs, did not "give back," failed to challenge and/or fight the for more comprehensive "welfare reform" laws when Clinton introduced them, and lent their support to the continued systematic oppression of the masses.

This important shift was extremely consequential to the inner city, and arguably the ultimate goal and function of the power structure. For it laid the foundation for anomie, and the solidification of the 360° return to the slave state—through providing the foundation for mental colonialism (That will later be discussed.), gentrification, and the ultimate solidification of the prison industrial complex.

While movies such as *American Gangster* almost laud those who profited from the drug trade, both heroine (1970s) and crack (cocaine) (1980s–present), the rise in the distribution and use of these types of "hard" drugs (and the derivatives thereof) in the inner city would serve as the ultimate catalyst for its deconstruction. Even though drugs have always been present, not only in the inner city, but in the world, the extensive supply and concentration of two of the most highly addictive drugs that most often render the abuser dysfunctional and unable to fulfill social, familial, financial responsibilities—proved detrimental.

Yet, while the "system" may have introduced and promoted this phenomenon in the inner city, it was the peoples "buy in" to the drug trade that facilitated a crisis that would justify the implementation of the "neo-Black codes" disguised as the War on Drugs. These laws and policies breached search and seizure policies established in the U.S. Constitution by allowing officers to not only utilize racial profiling as a justification for traffic stops, but to utilize the traffic stop as a grounds to search the vehicle. However, unconstitutional, the searches resulted in an escalated number of arrests that eventually encouraged police departments to implement harsher arrest practices, and legislators to impose harsher penalties (charging and sentencing)—which included imposing mandatory felonies with minimum prison sentences for "crack cocaine" related offenses. The drastic increase in the incarceration rate that resulted from the trade and the implementation of the War on Drugs would fuel the Prison Industrial Complex.

As has been constantly surmised in this work, no social, political, or economic move is carried forth without foundation. While there may be, what Durkheim terms, latent functions that result from some of the strategic moves, most moves are implemented to bring about very calculated results. That is why it is always important to understand and evaluate history, to uncover and recognize patterns in the transitions that occur within a society, and to analyze not only the relevance of the transitions, but by/through what means the transitions are solidified. That way one can more effectively, if not predict or foresee, then at least hypothesize about possible connections/correlations and directions of the future.

As mentioned before, the Thirteenth Amendment asserts that slavery shall be abolished unless the individual has been convicted. Specifically, the Thirteenth Amendment to the United States Constitution states: "Neither slavery nor involuntary servitude, *except as a punishment for crime where of the party shall have been duly convicted*, shall exist within the United States, or any place subject to their jurisdiction."

Yet, it appears that people do not understand the reality and ramification of this amendment and its exception. The "exception" serves as the "out clause" to the amendment. Slavery shall be abolished, unless the individual is convicted of a crime. And so, just as historical analyses reveal that Black Codes were deliberately implemented to promote the incarceration of African Americans during the "Post Bellum" period, and the Convict Leasing System, subsequently implemented to allow former slave owners to "re-enslave" Black people after Emancipation, this contemporary phenomenon must also be analyzed and placed in context.

In evaluating the "War on Drugs," one will find that "the war" was a never a comprehensive and global war on drugs. It was a war on the inner-city drug trade and the "street level hustler." It consisted of a limited set of laws that imposed harsher and more concentrated profiling, arrest, charging, conviction, and sentencing practices and laws on the possession and distribution of "crack cocaine" and any practices that related to the "crack cocaine" trade. Notwithstanding, the fact that "crack" is a derivative of a larger (global drug) cocaine, is mainly prevalent in the inner city, and is common/popular among urban and lower status dealers and users, the set of laws made the war a war on "crack cocaine," hence, a "war" on the inner city.

In essence, subjectively targeting drugs that are more prevalent in the inner city allows the inner city and its occupants to become the targets. So, it can easily be argued that as statistics reflect, the "war on drugs" represented a set of contemporary Black Codes, (as does gun legislation that does not target all guns and all possession, but that which is common in the inner city) that are, again, designed to promote the accelerated incarceration rate of African Americans.

Again, as delineated in the previous chapter, according to Drugfacts.org (2004).

1. In 1995, a mandatory five year sentence was imposed for anyone caught with 5 grams of crack. Yet 5 grams of any other drug would constitute simple possession and warrant a maximum one year sentence.
2. In 1986, the federal drug offense sentence for Blacks was 11% higher for Blacks than Whites. By 1992 that rate had increased to 49%.
3. By 1997, the U.S. Sentencing Commission found that nearly 90% of the offenders convicted for distribution of crack cocaine were Black, while the majority of users were White.
4. 80% of the increase in the federal prison population is due to drug convictions.
5. Between 1985 and 1996, the incarceration for female drug offenses increased by 95%.
6. 72% of women are in the federal prison system for drug related offenses, while 30.4% are in state.
7. Black females are 2 times more likely than Hispanic women and 5 times more likely than White women to be incarcerated for drug offenses.

These statistics reflect the specificity of the "war on drugs" on/to the African-American community. It reflects the subjectivity and disparity of the application of the law in the processing and conviction rates of African-American men and women relative to those of other races. More specifically, the "war on drugs" reflects the means by which the Prison Industrial Complex's labor supply is being fueled.

For it would be far more logical to conclude that if the goal of the "war" was to diminish the distribution and use of illegal substances (as asserted by governmental officials and legislators), the war would be waged against—at the least—national, if not global production and distribution—*a la* Afghanistan, China, Burma, and Vietnam, etc. Yet legislation associated with the "war on drugs" specifically targets distribution and possession of "crack cocaine" the cheapest and most diluted form of cocaine, in the inner city—which is undeniably the lowest level of the trade. It targets the lowest level of distribution (the inner city), and imposes harsher penalties for distribution and possession of a "derivative," a diluted form (crack) of cocaine. Does this really make sense? Is it a logical approach to the "verbalized" agenda of the legislation?

Statistics show that the implementation of this "race specific" legislation directly related to a very sharp increase in the arrest and conviction rate of African Americans—specifically African-American women. The disparity in the arrest and conviction rates also reflect the subjective targeting of African Americans for arrest and "stiffer" sentencing that is achieved under the guise of this legislation. Currently, the Bureau of Justice Statistics (2006) reports that "At year end 2006, there were 3,042 Black male sentenced prison inmates per 100,000 Black males in the United States, compared to 1,261 Hispanic male inmates per 100,000 and 487 White male inmates per 100,000 White males" (BJS Summary, 2006).

And while many would argue that this statistic validates the assumption that Black males commit more crimes, this statistic only reflects, that even today, African Americans are sentenced and imprisoned at a rate that is nearly 3 times more than Hispanic men, and more than 7 times higher than White men—a rate that results from the concentrated efforts of "the war." African Americans have, under these laws, become "casualties of war." So, without argument about the "deliberacy" of the laws, it cannot be argued that this legislation certainly mimics and serves the same purpose as, the "race specific" Black Codes of the past.

Given these sets of laws, the thirteenth amendment must be revisited. Slavery will be abolished unless a person is convicted and imprisoned, which means that the relationship of laws and the prison system can most certainly be used as a modern day legalized "slave trade." And it can be produced in the same manner as history has illustrated. Race specific laws can be implemented in order to target and accelerate the incarceration rate of a given population. And in the same, yet more efficient, manner as the slaver trade and the convict leasing system, wherein the slave master was able to buy the slave from the trader or prison and use him as a source of free labor, so can he now.

No one can argue the point that prisoners have always served as a valuable source of free labor. What is not discussed is the extent to which that labor is utilized. Historically, as with colonialism and imperialism, prisons were operated/owned by state and federal governments. Therefore, the prisoners were literally "property of the state." Only the state could utilize and/or negotiate the labor of the prisoners, any others who wished to utilize that labor had to go through the government/state. Subsequently, the labor of prisoners was predominantly utilized to satisfy governmental needs and then governmental contracts. However, just as globalization opened world markets for corporate global trade—hence, capitalist expansion, so did the privatization/"corporatization" of the prisons.

Through allowing corporations to build their own prisons, slave complexes (plantations) are formed. Who ever, be it the state, feds, or private corporations, owns the prison/penitentiary owns and controls the labor of the prisoners (slaves). Thus, as the Thirteenth Amendment states, the prisoners can be used as a source of free labor without limitation—re-enslaved, thereby allowing the State or corporation to once again derive maximum production by being able to circumvent the limitations imposed by U.S. labor laws and being able to remain the U.S. to do so. They are also able to maximize profit, even beyond using third world labor, by reducing the most costly expenditure—wages and benefits.

The Prison Industrial Complex (PIC) represents the exploitation of prison (free) labor in order to maximize corporate profit. Just like slavery, prisoners are collectively and minimally housed, fed and given basic health care in order to ensure their ability to function and participate in the labor pool. Like slaves they are subjected to the complete control and dominance of the prison guards (overseers), hence, those who control the prison—the state, the corporation, the ruling class (plantation owners).

However, even better than the antebellum era, it is not the ruling class (the plantocracy) that pays for the slave and his/her existence, it is the government, by way of the tax payer—or even the prisoner him/herself who often must pay rent for his bunk, who pays for the "slave." Unlike having to go to the slave auction and use personal resources to purchase the slave, hence, his labor and then use personal resources to house and feed and care for the slave, in this PIC, the corporation builds the prison, the prisoner ensures his own incarceration (enslavement) and then the tax payer pays for his stay in prison (on the plantation). The corporation or state gets the profit from his labor and production. How sweet is that deal?! Without having to adhere to labor laws, minimum wage laws, health care benefit policies, or having to move businesses overseas to circumvent these laws, the prison provides a convenient and otherwise impossible source of labor.

Shlosser (1998) argued: "The prison industrial complex is not only a set of interest groups and institutions; it is also a state of mind. The lure of big money is corrupting the nation's criminal justice system, replacing notions of safety and public services with a drive for higher profits. The eagerness of elected officials to pass tough on crime legislation—combined with their unwillingness to disclose the external and social costs of these laws—has encouraged all sorts of financial improprieties."

Davis (1999) adds:

> The Prison Industrial Complex is a complicated system situated at the intersection of governmental and private interests that uses prisons as a solution to social, political, and economic problems. The PIC depends on the oppressive systems of racism, classism, sexism, and homophobia. It includes human rights violations, death penalty, industry and labor issues, policing, courts, media, community powerlessness, the imprisonment of political prisoners, and the elimination of dissent.

Therefore, the prison industrial complex represents the predominant relegation of African Americans back to the institution of slavery through the promotion of race specific laws that are systematically developed and subjectively applied to promote the incarceration of African Americans, wherein they become slaves—which leads to the projection that represents the solidification of the 360°.

As illustrated in the previous chapter, there has been a return in the visual presentation of the African American to that of the neo-jezebel and the thug, which represent contemporary versions of the jezebel and the buck construct of the past. The original presentations reflected the hypersexual, aggressive, violent, ignorant stereotypes of "Blackness" that promoted support for slavery, which was essential to agricultural development. The contemporary version of these constructs only adds the component of criminality to the constructs. Both images serve to justify the control over the Black body that was essential to the exploitation of the productive and reproductive labor of African-American people during the antebellum period, the agricultural era.

This work argues that Global warming is a critical piece to this puzzle. Global warming is the term that is used to illustrate the increase in surface temperature that results from the depletion in the ozone layer that allows more harmful and intense rays from the sun to penetrate and effect the climate and environmental condition of the Earth. The depletion of the ozone layer results primarily and predominantly from the emission of "greenhouse gasses," such as carbon dioxide, methane, nitrous oxide, and fluorinated gasses, such as hydroflourocarbons "that result from industrial processes" (EPA 2007).

In order to reduce the effects of global warming, and in essence, save the planet, Industries (which are the primary contributors to this problem) must find ways to reduce the level of harmful gasses that are being emitted into the atmosphere. One of the predominant sources of the problem is automobile emission. Therefore, one goal is to begin to utilize "cleaner" sources of energy and fuel to replace oil. Thus, the United States and other world powers have already begun utilizing ethanol in conjunction with gasoline as a source of fuel. The use of Ethanol—a fuel that uses natural resources such as corn, wheat, sugar cane, and grain, but predominantly corn in the United States, reduces the rate of automobile emissions, and is therefore more "environmentally friendly."

According to reports at present, "10% of the U.S. corn crop is dedicated to ethanol production." And while, at present, ethanol blends range from 10 to 30%, automakers are producing cars that are capable of using an 85% blend as a fuel alternative, (Western New York Energy 2007). Thus, if ethanol were to replace oil as the predominant source of fuel, it would necessitate agricultural (corn and wheat) production. Accordingly, agricultural production would again surface to the forefront of the United States economy.

While mechanization has facilitated agricultural production, it is still an industry that requires human labor. If the United States were to engage, once again, in agricultural production for world trade, it would require mass human labor. But, who wants to farm? Farming is considered a "primitive" form of labor by most Americans. And in spite of the mechanization that has made agricultural production more efficient, it is still an extremely laborious task.

In spite of the assertions and sentiments about farming, "supermarketization" has desensitized most from the reality that farming (agricultural production) has never ceased to being essential to the survival of humanity. Someone is producing the food that consumers so easily and readily find at the local supermarket. Yet, in spite of the importance of it, most shun the possibility of having to work on a farm—especially if it is not their own. So, it is imaginable that if the U.S. were to transition to an agriculturally based fuel, that the amount of labor that would be necessary would be excessive. This is because agricultural production for food must occur simultaneously. (Has anyone noticed the price of cereal *these days*?)

So one must ask, how will enough labor be secured to produce enough to supply fuel and food globally? More significantly, if the United States, as a capitalist economy, is going to participate, much less maximize profit from the production of agricultural resources for global distribution, how, from where, will it secure a labor supply large enough to meet demands?

"Neither slavery or involuntary servitude, *except as a punishment for a crime where of the party shall have been duly convicted*, shall exist in the United States, or any place subject to their jurisdiction" (U.S. Constitution). The Prison Industrial Complex . . . serves as a contemporary source of mass slave labor. By being duly convicted, the individual becomes the "property of the state," the corporation, the ruling class, and is subsequently subjected to enslavement and/or involuntary servitude, which would not preclude his/her labor from being utilized in agricultural production, just as it was during the Antebellum Era. Just a hypothesis that reflects . . . THREE HUNDRED AND SIXTY DEGREES . . .

CHAPTER 5

CRITIQUING THE GAME: RAPPIN' MURDA, MISOGYNY, AND MAYHEM

> "Many people have identified the demon in the past and have accepted the irreversibility of the mental slavery. We definitely wanted to give credibility to the reality of mental slavery. We did not want to suggest that it was irreversible neither because of its origin in the past nor because of its collective form. We wanted to help people know where the ghost came from but we wanted to destroy the ghost, not give safe refuge to it."
>
> – Excerpts taken from Dr. Naim Akbar in *Breaking the Chains of Psychological Slavery*

From Lil' Wayne to, yes, even Beyonce, the celebration of murder, misogyny, and mayhem is ever so prevalent in the lyrical content. The argument about the sexual content, degradation, violence, substance abuse, and the blatant objectification and disrespect of women is clear. Not only does it exist, but it exists in abundance—from *I Wish I Could F' Every Girl in the World* to *I'm So Hood,* from *Rock Boyz* to *Diva,* from every new "Rap star" or Hip-Hop artist, as The Roots put it, contemporary artists *Ain't Sayin' Nuthin' New.* So, instead of simply 'bouncin' to the beat and singing the hook, *read the lyrics of your favorite Rap song, watch a video with the volume turned down, and analyze what you see*—only then will light be shed on the reality of this counterfeit "Hip-Hop."

In order to change the African consciousness we must change the information that is in the African mind. We cannot equate awareness with information though information is the road map to awareness and it is a critical part of the process (Akbar, 2006).

The songs chosen to "critique the game" were the songs that were most commonly and repetitively being given air play at the time this book was written, and/or those that topped the Billboard charts for Rap/Hip-Hop during the time in which this book was being written, not the result of any deliberate selection or "calling out" of any specific artist. Although during the time that this work was being developed, Alicia Keys, Mary J. Blige, Trey Songz, J. Holiday, and Keisha Coles topped the charts, because Billboard combines Rhythm and Blues with Hip-Hop. The songs selected for critique represented the top Rap/Hip-Hop songs for January, 2008.

Given the socio-political and economic foundation of slavery, and the subsequent exclusion and oppression of African Americans, as well as the identification of the hegemonic tools that have all been meticulously analyzed and discussed not only in this work, but in the works of Akbar (2006), Asante(2005), Feagin (2001), Collins (2004), Davis (1995), Rodney (1997), and hooks (1994) just to name a few)—it is clear that the "counterfeit Hip-Hop" reflects the replication of the original stereotypical constructions of race that served to provide support for the exploitation and oppression of African-American people. It represents a concrete deviation from the original Hip-Hop that cannot be denied. But most significantly, the new Hip-Hop reflects 'ruling class' domination over, and exploitation of, *the once* "real" presence of Hip-Hop as an accurate reflection of the heterogenous cultural experiences of the urban community. It represents the manipulation of the voices of the people that Hip-Hop is supposed to represent—a domination and manipulation that, again, most artists fail to "inner-stand" much less acknowledge.

Hip-Hop has now become the predominant venue by/through which the "unchallenged" dissemination and subsequent validation of historic stereotypes and contemporary fallacies of universal racial inferiority and criminality are being promoted. And it is detrimental because it reflects not only the voluntary replication and presentation of the historic stereotypes of hyper-sexuality, violence, aggression, immorality, and irresponsibility. But, it represents the artist's conscious and arrogant ownership of the constructs as identifications and representations of not only his or her self and/or experience, but as a universal identification and representation of the experience of the race and the inner city.

So now, far more significantly is the reality that the counterfeit Hip-Hop represents the systematic undoing of the humanity, subjectivity, and heterogeneity of the race that the "movements" struggled to establish. No longer do the elite need to put White actors in "Blackface" to present the stereotypical images, now African-American artists/actors voluntarily present the image and represent it as a real construction of their lives and experiences. And in order to promote and maintain the perceived integrity of the "new authentication" of ruling class ideas of "Blackness," the industry selects and chooses to promote those who have either lived the experiences, or most closely resemble the stereotypical constructs of those who have lived the experiences.

Subsequently, those who have lived the experiences of criminality (and survived) become icons that consumers are conditioned to "respect" and "emulate." It is the "street cred" rather than the "lyrical credibility" of the artist that becomes a gauge of whether or not he will be promoted by the label and accepted by or even "forced upon" the public. The more closely related each artist is to the stereotypical constructions of criminality or the "inner-city experience," the more popular (more highly promoted) and profitable they become as a commodity to the label. The more closely the female artist is to European ideals of facial beauty, yet the ideals of the "exoticism" of African bodies (booties), the more sexualized her image becomes, and the more widely promoted and profitable *she* becomes as a commodity to the label. Prime examples of this assertion are 50 (Cent) and even Beyonce Knowles, aka Sasha Fierce.

MURDA'

"Today in African American communities around America, we carry the mark of the strong-armed stud from slavery. He occurs as the modern day pimp or the man who delights in leaving neglected babies dispersed around town. He is the man who feels that he is a man only by his physical, violent, or sexual exploits"

– Akbar, 2006 – Relate the quote to 50 Cent's *Baby By Me*

For 50 Cent, arguably it was not his "purported" life as a hustler that garnered him acclaim and respect before he began rapping, or even in the beginning stages of his career. He was no Rayful Edmonds when he was "supposedly" in "the game" and no Biggie Smalls when he first entered the Rap game. It was his brush with death, after being shot several (reportedly 9) times that validated/"authenticated" him. And it is my assertion that it was that tragedy that made the labels more interested in promoting him.

His introduction to the market was marked by the promotion of the fact that he had been shot, and presented as his celebration and ownership that fact. But, it was not a celebration of being given a chance to continue living, and using that experience to re-evaluate his self, past, or future, to find some kind of spiritual connection, or to use that experience to focus his gift and perhaps promote change—life. The fact was promoted in order to validate the idea of "Black manhood and masculinity," "soldier" status, "street credibility," and even "superiority" over others in the hood who have either never been shot, or the many who did not live to tell the story. 50 represented the immortal man—the exception to the rule that one can engage in violence and not succumb to it.

Being shot served as proof and validation of his criminal involvement and street prowess. But more importantly his survival represented *his* ability to avoid the worst consequence of his purported lifestyle—death, where mortal men do not. *That* gave the label an angle from which he could be promoted. That gave him an "up" that other Rap artists simply did not have. 50 truly represented the hegemonic idea of "hood life" and "Black life" that the industry was aiming to promote. And it is argued that because of "this" 50 not only became a representative for "street cred," but was elevated to icon status which allowed, and continues to allow him to "spit" accepted stories about his experiences with "flipping kilos," making G's, shootin' and murderin' niggaz, and pimpin' hoes, in the hood—true or not.

MISOGYNY

> "The African American woman was valued primarily as a breeder or sexual receptacle capable of having many healthy children. . . . Her work as a human being was reduced to the particular financial value or personal pleasure she could hold for the master. She was usually expected to be receptive to the sexual exploitation of the slave master, his relatives, or friends. . . . Even today, we find too many frustrated young African American women choosing to become breeders in their search for identity."
>
> – Akbar, 2006

Misogyny takes on two forms. It takes on the manner in which male "artists" present women of color in their songs and videos. Whereas violence, criminality, and substance abuse in its many forms are predominant, no song or video in the Rap/Hip-Hop genre is promoted without the lyrical or visual sexploitation of women of color. Lil' Wayne, who has been voted the preeminent rapper extraordinaire has a catalog that is filled with songs that epitomize misogyny.

Beyonce Knowles, an undeniably attractive woman, is another example of the assertions of this chapter. And in evaluating the presentation, she must be contrasted with equally talented artists like India Arie, Chrisette Michele, Jill Scott, Corrine Bailey Rae, and even Erykah Badu. The difference is the image—the genre/selection of material and approach.

If one were to analyze historic presentations of similar artists, predominantly the original "crossover artists," it would be noted that Beyonce is the epiphany of Josephine Baker. Her performances, dance routines, image, costume, and presentation are all reminiscent of that of Josephine Baker. And despite her talent, like Baker, Beyonce's publicity centers not around her natural beauty or vocal ability, but it centers around her body—more specifically her hips, thighs, and buttocks. . . . "It's not ya beauty, it's ya booty."

In the literary, photographic, and video presentation, her "bootyliciousness" is most often the focus and photographic frame of reference. In her videos and performances, there are only a few, less notable instances, where Beyonce can be seen performing without shaking her booty, or having fans blow her dress up exposing her hips and thighs where they are not already. The camera loves it (her booty). The acclaimed and awarded *Single Ladies* video is a prime example of this fact.

Her body (booty) represents the European ideal of the "Black body." She is more curvaceous than the average European entertainers. Hence, she is labeled as an exotic/erotic beauty. However, she is not the urban ideal of "thick" because for mainstream—the "Southern booty" as represented in the video's of Southern artists such as Nelly, Outkast, and even the earlier works of artist such as Luke and Trick Daddy, would be too big for European/White audiences to relate to and embrace as erotic and not pornographic and consequently would not be suitable for cross over appeal. Yet it is Beyonce's facial features that lend greatly to her popularity and crossover appeal, just like artists/actresses like Alicia Keys, Halle Berry, Vanessa Williams, and J. Lo (reconstructed). Her more than fair skin, slender nose, delicately full lips, almond eyes and her bleached blond long weaves make her the epitome of the European ideal of an exotic beauty. Her image allows her to be accepted as an ethnic beauty without being locked into the "urban" category. Although it can be noted that in the corporate "crossover" promotional campaigns such as cover girl, Beyonce's skin is lightened, featured slimmed, to the point where in some of her photos, she even appears White. She represents the construct of the erotic mulatto and can thereby be accepted as beautiful by the mainstream, while simultaneously being objectified and sexualized as a Black woman.

This point is proven in analyzing and critiquing Beyonce's most widely promoted, hence, her most successful songs. Most of them, especially those from the Destiny's Child era, B Day, and then those in which she created "Sasha Fierce," which is easily characterized as a "Hip-Hop" album (that deviates from the RnB Pop feel of *Dangerously In Love*), represent the idealization and promotion of her own body (booty) and encouraging others to promote and use their bodies. And now, even more significantly is the marketing genius creation of her "alter ego" Sasha Fierce who allows Beyonce to align with the hypersexual and gangster images and appeal of urban culture while still maintaining a mainstream marketability that allows her to endorse mainstream products. In essence, through creating the alter ego, Beyonce is able to brilliantly detach herself from the "ghetto" persona that Sasha Fierce is supposed to represent—creating two entities of her 'self' that allows her to keep both feet planted in urban and mainstream media.

One can easily review her video for *Single Ladies*, which ironically won Video of the Year on MTV's 2009 Video Awards, or evaluate the lyrics to "Diva," where although more subtly than other artists like Lil' Kim and Trina, Beyonce celebrates being a "female version of a hustler" by embracing and promoting mayhem in "Diva" and hypersexuality in the dance routine and video angles in *Single Ladies*.

MAYHEM

> *"Such leadership, too, has continued into our day and it goes from bad to worse. The very service which this racial toady renders hardens him to the extent that he loses his soul. He becomes equal to any task the oppressor may impose upon him, and at the same time he becomes artful enough to press his case convincingly before the thoughtless multitude"*
>
> – Woodson, 1933

In any event, in today's Hip-Hop/Rap culture, it is as if all Rap artists must tell their stories of criminality and hyper-sexuality in order to be accepted by the masses. When in reality, the Rap artist must sell the *image* in order to be signed and promoted by the label. (Having been privy to the inside, I can attest that label executives instruct the artist on what the consumer wants.) The detriment is that the artist then presents his criminal experiences—large scale distribution of drugs, pimping and prostitution, substance abuse, assault, and even murder—as his *only* identification of being from "da hood," his only relationship to "da hood." In essence, through Hip-Hop the expressions of criminality and deviance become synonymous with growing up/living in/being from the inner city.

But, it is not enough for artists to express it as "their journey" alone (most of which are made up and/or highly exaggerated journeys), they express it as a universal and homogenous *representation* of everyone's experience in the inner city—one that everyone must directly relate to if they are "real," if they are "truly" from the hood. However, the reality is that most who rap (brag) about the riches that they acquired from their criminal activities in the hood "before they started rapping," did not. They did not have the type of wealth they rap about before they were Rap stars. If anything they were petty criminals, street runners, hand to hand men, or at the highest level, occupying the lowest level of narcotics distribution—inner-city street distribution.

The reality is that they acquire their wealth (or the ability to present a wealthy image) from their role as Hip-Hop artists—by/through their ability to creatively sell the image—get "the consumer" to consume/believe the image. But more importantly, they acquire their wealth by allowing themselves (their creativity and talent) to be controlled and exploited by record labels who pay them to sell their bodies and souls in order to promote images that lend nothing to the progress of a people. "Hate it or love it," that's the true story.

The cars that they present in the videos are not the same cars that they were driving if and/or when they were hustling. The jewelry that they present in the videos is not the same jewelry that they were wearing if and/or when they were hustling. They did not shop at Gucci, or buy Balenciaga, Louboutin, or pop bottles of 500.00 Cristal to the extent that they brag about now, if and/or when they were hustling and/or dating a hustler. Not that it is anything to brag about, and not that the drug trade is being celebrated, but *none* were *ever* —anywhere near the level of "kingpin" status that would be required to command the type of money and material possessions that they rap about having had and/or acquired from "the streets."

Some may have utilized the funds and resources of those who used "drug money" to start independent labels, production companies, or to invest in the careers of those with promise. But, no mainstream rapper was on king pin level—not even Biggie or Jay Z. More importantly, while they are still rapping about it, they *are not* "hustling," murdering, or assaulting people now. The new hustle is that they are getting paid by "selling the new drug—'the story' of criminality" to the masses—the consumer—you. . . .

For even though most mainstream Rap artists "rap" about the drug trade, assault, murder, etc., most are smart enough to understand that real life criminality has consequences—investigation—arrest—loss of resources—civil suits—incarceration—and at worse death—that in their legitimate state they choose not to test. However, there are those—like Shyne, Ghostface Killa, C Murder, Tupac, Lil' Kim, ODB, P Diddy (who lets his henchmen do the work for him) and Snoop Dogg (who was acquitted of charges), and most recently Remy Ma, T.I, Ja Rule, Lil' Wayne, Foxy Brown, and Baby (to name just a few), who get caught up in "*their worlds of make believe,*" and let the fiction or idealism of criminality without consequence make them forget that reality. Consequently, they soon find that in the real world, outside of the studio and from behind the mic, if caught, "real life" possession of any illegal item (guns) or substance (drugs)—"real" assault, "real or even the perception of" rape, and "real" murder—will result in criminal prosecution—conviction (in most cases), real life imprisonment.

Not so differently from male artists are the deviant, if not criminal constructs of the Ho and the Bitch. Each represents either a "feminized" or "masculinized" construction of hyper-sexuality. Artists like Beyonce must adhere to the objectification of their bodies and sexuality and celebrate *that* as the primary source of connection with not only Black men, but national and global audiences.

They often present, even in an elegant and more inconspicuous manner, the image of the prostitute (ho), wherein they must receive money or materials or believe there is a possibility that they will receive money/materials as a requirement for any form of interaction with Black men. In these cases, sex is either the ultimate prize for those who must prove their wealth by giving money or materials, or the tool that is utilized to get those things from those who express conspicuous wealth. . . . Even if the female artist boasts about having her own money/materials, and professes her independence, getting money from the man is still a requirement a la "*Freakum Dress"* (Beyonce).

On the converse is the image of Bitch who attempts to negate the image of the "gold diggin ho" by taking on hegemonic constructions of "Black male gender identity"—which is very common for the more hard core Hip-Hop/Rap artists like Lil' Kim, Trina, Remy Ma, etc. For artists that fit in this category, instead of "playing" the game as in the former example, these women express their rejection of "the game" by assuming the characteristics of the stereotypical construction of Black masculinity—the pimp.

She will have strictly "physical" sex for sport with no emotional attachment—treating a man as he "stereotypically" treats a woman in the interaction and exchange. As the title so adequately suggests, Lil' Kim's *Suck My Dick* is a prime example of this assertion. In this "song," Lil' Kim boisterously asserts her masculinity in this role reversal anthem wherein she illustrates aggressive male sexuality. Or another example is Trina's *Hustlin,'* where, like Lil' Kim, she also makes reference to having a "cock." Once again, in her (Trina's) role of the Bitch, or more significantly, the "Queen Bitch," which represents the ultimate form of masculinity for a female artist, she will objectify and sexualize men and/or even other women, hustle, and murder just as well as a man can. That is her badge.

However, in spite of what has just been presented, most would *still* argue that Hip-Hop *is just* entertainment. And when the debate ensues, supporters will argue that the artist should be able to "tell his/her story," be able to "keep it real" and will question why they are being challenged and/or blamed for the ills of society. Why shouldn't the "icons" be able to express their experiences without repercussion? Why do intellectuals, academicians, conservative politicians, and the Black middle class have to "hate?" Here is the answer.

The first song analyzed, "I'm So Hood," most vividly captures the premise of this work. The song begins with the assertion that the artists who identify themselves as "niggas" are winners. They represent "ghettos" all over. The rest of the song is Khaled's (and guest rappers) interpretations of "what it means" to be from the hood—a vocal manual that illustrates what an individual should wear (jeans and a big white tee, golds up in my mouth), how he should dress (pants below the waist), how he should act when at the club (never dance and be vigilant of "haters"), and what the substance of his life should be about (livin' life like a gangster . . . and don't fight with the fist, murder). But it doesn't stop there because as mentioned above DJ Khaled's song does not only express this as his personal experience—he establishes this as a presentation of "hood life"—as a representation of, not only his 'ghetto' but of "ghettos across the world." And then he issues a call and challenge for the listener to feel him and identify with him, and if the listener cannot it's because he/she is not from the hood.

Although, as stated in the preface, this work is not intended to be a critique of the artist, it must be pointed out that Khaled, is of Palestinian decent, born in America. Although the available literature and biographies about him state that he was born in New Orleans, very little is known about his "upbringing" which is very ironic given the lyrical content of his production. But, again, it is not the voice of DJ Khaled that reigns dominant, it is the voice of T Pain, "my low class ghetto ass". As mentioned above, most derive credibility and popularity from their experiences with criminality, and or their ability to sell the image. In this instance where DJ Khaled has become the author of "the hood anthem" and the authority and representation of "ghettos across the world" the question must be raised, what do you really know about the hood? Whose experiences are you projecting? Is this really a celebration, or is it a mockery of the inner city and those who do, in fact, subscribe to those cultural values?

Further, is the assertion that "we" the artist are winners. Yet the lyrical content and the video do not reflect "winners." In the video itself, it reflects men parading down the streets of impoverished areas, showing off "their rides" to inner city bystanders who look on with envy. And then there are dominant scenes where brothers are lined up against a wall on their knees being searched/harassed by the police. Then the lyrics state things like he will murder "you" (referring to whom?), he does not respect his probation officer or the conditions of his probation or parole (meaning he will return), and is unwilling and or unable to stop using substances in order to maintain his freedom (addiction). Perhaps I have missed the point or do not understand the term, but how does anything about that song and the image of the artist reflect a winner? How are "winners" being defined here?

Does wearing pants below the waist, which is a representation of a "prison" dress code that, according to assertions relates to sexual access in homosexual prison relationships, make one a winner? Does wearing gold fronts, which most often destroys or requires the destruction of one's natural teeth, as a status symbol make one a winner? Does using an AK (high tech automatic weapon) to murder (blew, blew, blew) someone who wants to fight, make one a winner? Does telling the same people who buy the artists album and envy him that he is going to "murder all you niggas" make one a winner? Does one's inability to stop using drugs even when he/is under state control and will face being "stepped back" for a dirty urine, which in my estimation is a true reflection of drug addition (even if it does not emaciate the body like crack) make one a winner? What is the message?

The message is that this is the type of destruction that represents "hood life." This is a reflection of those who reside in the hood. But more specific to the song, is that this is the type of attitude and action that individuals must subscribe to and or carry out if he is truly from the hood. DJ Khaled and the guest artist "represent the hood" and if one is to be accepted he must "subscribe" to that interpretation of "ghetto life." This song clearly encourages the internalization and promotion of deviance and criminality—lyrically and visually.

"Rock Boys" by Jay Z and "Duffle Bag Boy" by Playas Circle featuring "Lil' Wheezy" are both simply hardcore and unadulterated celebrations of street level "dope boys." And each song represents the normalization and respectability of the crack trade. Jay Z begins "Rock Boys" with thanking and giving respect his "connect" and all of the paraphernalia that "hustlers" have symbolically utilized to "hold" their money. Underneath of the thick beat, horns and percussion, and the catchy hook is Jay Z's celebration of the street level hustler, and the women who "hold," carry, and transport drugs across state lines for the hustler and a grand mockery of those who couldn't aim and instead got shot (murdered). But most significantly is the contemptuous homage that is sarcastically paid to the "customer"—whose addiction provides the means by which the "dope boys" can live the life that they celebrate.

To take it one step further, not that I want to psychoanalyze the lyrical content, or the mindset of the writer, (or start anything), but as a social scientist and a poet myself I found Jay Z's metaphoric use of the term 'you' in (giving thanks) to "you" (emphasized) the customer/consumer brilliant. To me it represented a projective/subjective referral to not only the crack addict (customer) which would fit the context of the song, but also to "you" the listener, who, just like the crack addict, buys, and even becomes addicted to a product (crack) that isn't good for you—counterfeit "Hip-Hop," thereby increasing the income and wealth of the artist—(hustler). Hmmmm. . . .

In that same vein is "Duffle Bag Boy" wherein again underneath of the thick beat and almost orchestral track is the message that if he doesn't do anything else he is gonna hustle, make his money, and if something "goes down" he is not going to run. His motto, "Get money."

What more needs to be said? No critique is necessary because each song is clear and self explanatory. If it were a confession, there would be no doubt about the guilt of each rapper. This is especially disheartening in "my assessment of" Jay Z, who, in "real life" is a successful business man, who, whether he sold dope or not, did not derive the wealth and status that he has now from "that life." Instead he was brilliant enough to: (1) negotiate the terms of his contract enough to maximize *his* profit margin, (2) change labels when he believed that he had reached the "glass ceiling" with that company, and (3) wisely and aggressively invest and engage in *many* lucrative business ventures that have moved him to ruling class (although not elite) status, and solidified his wealth even after he truly "retires" from the Rap game. His investments include his record label, clothing line, nightclub, and partial ownership of the New Jersey Nets, and I am confident that his ventures go way beyond just those things.

In 2007, Mr. Carter was listed at number 9 on the Forbes list of highest paid celebrities. And selling drugs does not qualify as "legitimate income" and therefore, does not qualify drug dealers for mention in Forbes. According to Forbes, Mr. Carter's reported earnings from his music career exceeded 80 million dollars—making him the highest paid Rap/Hip-Hop artist, superseding 50 and P. Diddy. Other unconfirmed sources, report his net worth being in excess of 200 million dollars in 2007—even after selling his clothing line to Iconix, and selling his shares of Roca Fella Records. Yet, in Jay Z's presentation, Mr. Carter attributes his wealth and status to his image as a "the number 1 dope boy"—a life that he is far from. So why not more songs like *Thirty Something* where Carter is actually providing a manual that tells the listener how to legitimize him/herself, what it means to really grow up—moving from "street" things to the characteristics that make a successful citizen. Ahhh . . . Lessons.

But, it is not *this* image, *this* lesson that is most heavily promoted by this "mogul," or even given the most predominant promotion/air play, which is a prime example and reflection of the lie—of the deliberateness of the hegemonic presentation. It is so because the *reality* is that Jay Z could arguably, and even more legitimately, "spit rhymes or vocal manuals" about how he really attained the wealth, success, and legitimate status that he now enjoys. How he acquired these things through his *legitimate* business and investment ventures—that far supersedes *any* meager *income*—not wealth—but any income that he may have received "hustling." And now it is *that* lifestyle that allows him to live freely, be globally respected, not have to "watch his back," and maximize his lifespan, not the lifestyle of the hustler and murderer that he raps about. Yet, in spite of this reality, it is through this successful and articulate business man, that "the crack" trade is not only normalized, but celebrated as something that should be more respected and aspired to than his talent and business savvy. So ironically, in his Rap, Jay Z gives "cheers" to his role as a dope boy—only his lyrics are the dope that he sells to his customer—Hov???

Like most Hip-Hop lyrics, the message of Rock Boys is true to form and purpose and proves the point. It is not that there is an absence of positive images or experiences in the lives of the artist, because Sean Carter's life is a positive one. Jay Z—"Hov" "Jigga"—the alter ego, must be present to promote the negative and homogenous image that contradicts his own. So, in this case, it would not be feasible to promote the image or the version of the story or the person (Sean Carter) that teaches the masses how to acquire wealth legitimately, act intelligently, live freely, or even at worse (not that I advocate money laundering, but it is a significant part of the historic economic reality of many of the ruling class families in the U.S.) how to legitimize money.

It has probably even been asserted by A and R's and label management that to do so, to train the masses in a different manner, would be a threat to "the street cred" that the mainstream media has bamboozled Hip-Hop artists into believing they need in order to attract/maintain fans and sell records. When in reality it is the label, not the public or the artist, that *must promote that image.* After all, it is that image that serves the purpose of skewing the mindset of the masses. Consequently, it is that negative and criminal image that the artist must promote in order to "stay off of the shelf"—to stay at the top of the labels promotional priorities, in order to stay on top of the charts, and generate maximum profits. Therefore, one artist cannot alone rebel and make a difference because there are thousands more waiting in the wings, submitting demos praying to take their place if they do not.

Keeping positive presentations of African Americans out of the mainstream media is imperative to the agenda of the ruling class, and essential to the stability of capitalism. Promoting the legitimized version of the Jay Z's and '50s would pose a threat to the ruling class elite in/of the United States because the wealth and development of the country/ruling class was achieved through the physical and mental enslavement of African people. African Americans have been the principle source of collective surplus, cheap, and free labor since their arrival on the shores of America in the 1600s. Equally however, it has been the labor of African-American men and women that has driven production, hence, capital for the elite in this country since its inception.

So, this power/stratification dynamic, the continued suppression of the potential and actualization of the race has continuously been promoted through racial social stratification, discrimination, and exclusion—that is facilitated by diluting the strength of the race through promoting their collective lack of consciousness, hence, their ability to effectively and aggressively question, resist, and rebel against their own oppression. Consequently, it is this collective lack of consciousness that has been integral to the maintenance of the status quo. Therefore, would America not have a vested interest in the continued psychological enslavement of the race? And how can this be promoted without the direct oppression that was once encouraged through local, state, federal, and constitutional laws and by the support of Supremacist organizations such as the KKK?

In order for this power dynamic to be maintained without resistance, African Americans must continue to believe that it is the supremacy of the White race that results in higher levels of achievement and success. They must continue to believe that the "average" Black man will never acquire wealth in this country and the "exceptional" Black man can only acquire wealth through playing sports, entertaining, or hustling. They must believe that the only way that they can acquire the type of wealth that people like Shaquille O'Neal, Michael Jordan, Jay Z, Sean Combs, or 50 Cent have is by selling their labor to the ruling class. They must further believe that it is only through conspicuous consumption, that is proving wealth through high priced materials, that their man/womanhood is validated.

Yet, that relationship, no matter how high the income, does not promote the independence and control that ownership does. Yes, no matter how rich, each artist or athlete derives his wealth through selling his ability to play sports or entertain to the team or label or television or production company owner. Thus, their wealth is still being controlled by the owner.

The athlete must sell his ability to play a sport to the team owner. The artist must sell his ability to sell an image and "spit a verse" to the label owner. Even, the hustler must sell his ability to distribute drugs to the distributor. There is no power or independence in this relationship—what is received, no matter how significant (from a shanty and left over mush to 50 million dollars) is completely dependent on the utilization and/or sale of productive labor power, from picking cotton, playing ball, to rapping. It is still a slave/master relationship.

> That's exactly what he was; in fact, that's what all athletes were: so many pieces of property to be bought, sold, or discarded as their 'owners' saw fit. This was—and still is—allowable in sports because athletes are supposed to be grateful for the opportunity (Rhoden 2006).

And all who exist and operate within the confines of this type of relationship are *completely* dependent on, and at the discretion of, the owner, until they own their own. When Shaq gets too old and becomes a liability, he will be traded or lose his contract. When the label tires of an artist, he will lose his contract. So, they must be grateful for the opportunity to "make such money." And must not challenge the system, go against the grain, resist, rebel, or more importantly, they must not try to take over.

When they (Black men) get money, they must be conditioned to squander—not save or invest so that they might transition to ruling class status, and not be dependent on others for their progress or success. That way they remain enslaved, remain dependent on their physical labor for income—ensuring that owners will continue to be able to use them for maximal profit. For, if Lebron (James) is making 30 million, the owner of the team that he plays for is making 3 billion from him. Therefore, if he were to remove him "self" from the equation he would be removing a significant profit. Think about the implications of that.

Therefore, Jay Z must not deliver the manual in verse because the more Black men aspire to become legitimately successful like Jay Z, or Russell Simmons,' or P. Diddy, or even 50 Cent the greater the threat to the labor relation that drives capitalist wealth. To have the race understand its potential would pose a threat to and/or dilute the exclusivity of a status that is reserved for the ruling class elite. The manual must not be written, the story must not be told.

In the same vain the dreams and wishes presented in Kanye West's *Good Life* must be critiqued. He opens the song expressing the "good life" as being a place where men who sell dope won't even get pulled over by the police while driving a car that is on the "profile list—perhaps a Crown Vic?" Clearly this song equates the good life to an ideal where illegal activities will not be targeted or penalized. But, in the *real* world, of course when one is caught with drugs not only on his/her person, but in his/her car, house, etc., he will be charged with at minimal, possession, at maximum, possession with intent to distribute or even distribution, most of which represent felonies and carry mandatory sentences that will ultimately effect the individuals ability to participate in the social, economic, and political spheres of society—even after he has "paid his debt." But the idealism promotes the acceptance and legitimizes activities that destine the perpetrator to incarceration or death.

The irony is that unlike the "shadow" that exists around DJ Khaled's upbringing, there is no question about Kanye West's. His mother, who was a college professor and Chair, before taking over as West's manager and then CEO of West's charitable organization, sacrificed to succeed and provide a well rounded "middle class" upbringing for her only son. Therefore, if he was ever involved in the trade at all, it would not have been out of need. And his artistry *used* to reflect that. It appears that through his tenure as a up and coming artist, and his own confrontation with death (or even severe disability), Kanye is/was attempting to negotiate and balance his presentation, image, and lyrical content.

Kanye moves through and then away from songs like "Jesus Walks," wherein he asks God for protection because "The devil's tryna break him down," and "Hey Mama" where he pays homage to his "unbreakable, unmistakable, highly capable" mama for struggling to provide a legitimate life for him, providing an opportunity for him to go to college and apparently making that a serious expectation (College Dropout), which gave him a "clean" and "respectable," yet "credible" image—to a more subtle yet negative place.

He deviates from a place that *appears* to be grounded in a spiritual connection—strengthened by reflections of life after his accident. He speaks of being "unbreakable" because upon looking back on his life he realizes that he should have been incarcerated for the mistakes that he made. He hails himself a "champion" who was able to overcome a tragedy that could have resulted in death. And then he quickly moves to a place where 50 appears to have encouraged West to sell his soul—becoming like others who have been paid well to sell murda,' misogyny, and mayhem to the masses.

While the abovementioned songs present the constructs of "the hustler," criminal images that celebrate dope dealing, other notable songs like *Crank Dat* by Souljah Boy, *Hypnotized* by Plies featuring Akon, *Sensual Seduction* by Snoop, which, although not a Hip-Hop song, is mentioned because of Snoop's status as a Hip-Hop artist, *Low* by Flo Rida featuring T Pain—all promote the other side of the spectrum, the pimp. This image represents disdain, hate, disrespect, and/or blatant contempt for the African-American woman as a subjective being. It represents the objectification and exaggerated sexualization of the female body, specifically her "ass," and the fallacy that arousal and eroticism must be the only form of interaction between the two. And sorrowfully, these and other songs such as Jerimih's "Birthday Sex" and Trey Songz "Think I Invented Sex" represent the complete objectification of the sexual and intimate experience. These two variations of the thug—the hustler and the pimp—exist almost exclusively in the Hip-Hop arena.

The continued presentation of these images has been grounded in many rationalizations and justifications that take the focus away from ruling class interest in the presentations. However, as presented, the images do not even truly fit the lives of those who "represent" the image. So, why should they remain "representations" of those in the community?

One of the most common assertions made by label management and A & R's is one of consumers being "stupid" and fickle. They have constructed an image of the public/"fan base" that demands "street credibility" before accepting artists—hence, buying records. They have created an image of what "street credibility" must look like/consist of. And then they have bamboozled artists who do not understand the psychological influence of repetition and its direct relationship to music promotion/airplay and record sales into believing that they are only, or will only, be successful if they "spit" negativity and destruction—"keep it gangsta'," "keep it hood," and "keep it real."

The artist then passes it on "to *you* the customer" who not only supports, but in many instances internalizes the images as real constructions of urban life, manhood and woman hood, and subconsciously aspires to replicate, reproduce, and promote the lie in the community—thereby making it real with real consequences in the urban community.

This arguably brilliant strategy is simple. The psychology of repetition is a theory that identifies how repeating an image, message, etc., will most often lead the individual to connect to/with that image and message, relate to it, internalize it, and ultimately promote it. Not because they truly like it—but it "grows" on the individual. Without understanding the subconscious interplay, individuals are in essence forced to relate—because the repetition is so consistent. "Brainwashing" relies on that principle. Education, as a process, relies on that principle, The military relies on that principle.

This is accomplished through the rotation of songs on radio and video shows. The more airplay a song is given, the more popular it becomes. Think about how many times people have heard a song and hated it. But, it comes on twice an hour on every station, so eventually the individual starts to sing it, even though he/she hated it. And then, "it grows on you" and the person ends up buying the single or getting the ring tone. He/She did not like the song. His/her mind didn't change. It was forced upon the individual, the masses.

This dynamic then lends credibility to the fallacy that this is "what the public wants" when it is only the labels interpretation of what the public wants. And it is not a difficult argument to make when record sales are compared. Look at sales for 50 Cent versus Talib Kweli, where would an artist want to be? But, it is not the fact that the public likes 50 anymore than Kweli. It is the fact that the labels investment in and promotion of 50 far supersedes that of Kweli. As a result, one must be a "die hard" fan of the "underground" to know that one must go to websites such as OKAYPLAYA in order to keep track of Kweli's comings and goings.

In any business, sales are based on promotion because promotion dictates who or how many become exposed to the product. Therefore, if Kweli makes an album that no one knows about, makes a video that the major video stations, such as MTV, VH1, and even BET that is now owned by Viacom, will not put on their rotations, how will the public hear it? How will the public know to know to look for it, much less purchase it? This is why not only understanding but putting the influence of the business of marketing and promotion in its proper perspective is integral to understanding why the counterfeit Hip-Hop is so influential and successful and the real Hip-Hop is no longer fertile, just buried "underground." This is why the internet, as a more unregulated form of promotion becomes so extremely fundamental to the survival of the "underground"—the real Hip-Hop.

The assertion that the counterfeit Rap is what the public wants is contradicted by the Billboard charts themselves. If the argument is that the public wants to hear gangster Rap and "soft" songs will not be accepted, it would be logical to assume that those types of songs would top the sales charts, and those songs that represented the "softer" side of men and women would be rebuked. Yet, as mentioned earlier in the chapter, these songs did not top the charts, not even the R &B/Hip-Hop charts. Therefore, the counterpoint is proven.

This is *not* all that is acceptable to and desired by the Hip-Hop audience. It reflects the reality that consumers are "starving" for and welcome a balanced and "heterogenous" presentation of images, messages—songs.

In January 2008, Alicia Keys topped the charts with the number 1 and 2 songs. "Like You'll Never See Me Again" is a strong testament to a true and spiritual love, connection, relationship and commitment—wherein she encourages her lover to "hold her, touch her, kiss her like you'll never see me again." She underscores the reality that because life is not promised, people must take advantage of the days they have by not being afraid to be "completely" open to expressing love. Number 2—"No One" is another testament to her commitment to not let anyone "get in the way of what I feel for you." At number three was Trey Songz "Cant Help But Wait"—a man's admonishment to a woman for choosing someone that does not love her over 'the good guy'; but, also his expression of patience with her process and his commitment to treating her "better than he can" when she realizes him. This is a very powerful message to the young ladies and young men.

J Holiday was at number 4 with "Suffocate," another very powerful song that shows a real mans ability to express something that is natural and real to the human experience, emotion and deep love that takes his breath away when he talks to her. Again, another intense message to the Brothers and sisters—that it is alright for a man, to not only feel, but to express a spiritual and emotional love and connection to a woman. For women, the song is essential to dispelling the myth that (1) men do not feel, and (2) all (Black) men are dogs because it shows that men can and do love.

The number 5 slot was occupied by Mary J. Blige's "Just Fine," wherein, under the groove of this catchy and upbeat song is a testament to the value of self appreciation that young women need to not only hear but embrace, the message being that it doesn't matter what anyone else says or thinks, she has found comfort in and love for her "self" so everything is "just fine." And Blige, herself, is an example of the transformation that is possible. She is an example of the reality that being from the "hood" does not mean that one must embrace or stay true to the negative characteristics of the "hood." In front of the camera, Mary has actualized into not only a "lady" but a conscious and a beautiful woman who is not afraid to, and has been given permission to share her story in proper context. Her new image is an example of a role model and true Hip-Hop icon that should be respected and can now be emulated.

At number 6 was Justin Timberlake's duet with Beyonce "Until The End of Time," which is not only a beautiful love song, but a social commentary and self analysis as well. In this song Timberlake discusses how the disasters and darkness in the world have made him reflect on his life and embrace the beauty of love. The song is a testament to what a gift his "girl" is "love is" when the world is not alright. Like Alicia Keys, this song is also a testament to appreciating the blessing of love given the crises that exist in the world, with the undertone that, again, life is not promised so we must appreciate love and connection.

Kanye West, was at number 7, with "Good Life," that although critiqued is the most subtle of the Hip-Hop songs on the charts. This position reflects that the fact that more positive and meaningful songs have superseded the negative imagery of "Rap."

At number 8 was Keisha Cole "Shoulda Let You Go," which represents the woman's anthem at this time. It tells the story of a woman who is trying to negotiate being in/getting out of an unfulfilling relationship and a woman seeking to understand why she has fought so hard to try to get someone, who is obviously not willing to love her, to love.

At number 9 was Chris Brown featuring T Pain "Kiss Kiss"—well.... And at number 10 was Snoop's "Sexual Seduction"—which does not represent that the public tired of such songs but represents an underrepresentation of such powerful and positive songs that listeners could purchase.

This list reflects the public's true desire for meaningful lyrics. Yet in evaluating the real, and not reported, airplay of urban radio stations (specifically in Delaware, Philadelphia, New York, New Jersey, and D.C) the songs that were critiqued were played at a 2:1 ratio compared to those that topped the Billboard Charts. Therefore, the labels argument about what the public wants can most certainly be countered. It is thus imaginable to conceive that if the real Hip-Hop was not buried "underground," and thus received the level of promotion as the hegemonic artists, that they would be equally if not more popular and successful and profitable to the label. So again, why the choice?

CHAPTER 6

INTERNALIZING THE LIE: THE PSYCHO-SOCIAL RAMIFICATIONS OF "KEEPING IT REAL"

"They never stopped to worry about the realities in this country that spread poverty and racism and gun violence and hatred of women and drug use and unemployment. People can act like rappers spread these things, but that is not true. Our lives are not rotten or worthless just because that's what people say about the real estate that we were raised on. In fact, our lives may be even more worthy of study because we succeeded despite the promises of failure seeping out from behind the peeling paint on the walls of every apartment in every project."

– Jay Z in Dyson, 2006

A Letter to Jay Z

This passage, written by Jay Z in the Introduction of Michael Eric Dyson's book *Know What I Mean* is a contradiction at best. Initially it reflects the "blame the system" approach that never seems to be utilized to raise the consciousness of the masses; but to instead, justify, in this case, "Hip-Hop's" oppression and exploitation of its own, and excuse it from confronting its contribution to that continued social, political, and economic oppression and exploitation of the race and urban community that it "blames the system" for.

Yes, it is a fact that poverty is the fundamental and unavoidable function and result of capitalism. Yes, it is a fact that unemployment is most often the result of, and directly related to economic and productive shifts that directly influence the way in which a group's labor is being exploited, hence, whether or not they will have a job. And yes, racism, as a socially constructed ideology, action, system, and institution is the means by/through which oppressive relationships, hence, social hierarchies and power dynamics are maintained. These are the inherent results of a functionally oppressive system that cannot and will not be transformed within its confines.

Gun violence (meaning murder), drug use, addiction, and sales (meaning criminality which leads to community mayhem), and hatred of women (misogyny) reflect "a choice." And so the assertion (stated in the passage), just like the destructive sentiments of many who engage in these practices, reflects the choice to use the systematic oppression of the race as a justification for turning the anger inward—toward self (addiction), toward other men and women and toward the urban community (inner-city criminality, murder, and misogynistic and materialistic interactions). So, it also lends to furthering the exploitation and oppression of an already oppressed and struggling group. Consequently then, by making the choice to engage in destructive behaviors and actions, the oppressed oppresses the oppressed by capitalizing on the addiction of the user, murdering a brother or a sister for material or spatial gain, and even spitting lyrics that encourage community members to embrace the very things that promote their own genocide.

It is ironic that Jay Z would then state "People act like rappers spread these things, but that is not true." The very essence of the craft makes it true. When rappers/Hip-Hop artists are telling the consumer to celebrate the "rock boys" (that is the street hustler who peddles crack cocaine), be a rock boy, go and get your money little duffle bag boy, (which, along with shoe boxes, represents where money from the trade is stashed), pour champagne on the ho, give him brain on a plane, (which represents fellatio), shake that ass, pull an AK on a nigga and thank the pastor for giving "your" eulogy, and he/she is selling ten million albums worldwide a piece, he is, in fact, actively promoting the message—hence, "spreading 'these' things!" There *is* no rational defense or justification for this. It just is what it is. No matter how one may attempt to justify or rationalize it to make the ego feel okay for continuing to promote, support, and profit from it, the very essence of "game" makes the assertion that Rap artists spread these things true.

Jay Z furthers, "Our lives are not rotten because of the real estate we were raised on." That is correct, and reflects the total assertion of this work. Where one is raised, should never be a determinant of life success, goal attainment, or worse life expectancy. Yet, as an identification and representation of the "real estate" that *he* was raised on, Jay Z not only presents, but celebrates a "rotten life." No matter how one attempts to rationalize or glorify the brutal lyrics—in them one man's wealth is another man's poverty, one man's life is another man's death, one man's pleasure is another man's pain.

Get mad!!!! But promoting addiction hence, family dysfunction for personal gain is not good. Beating or sexually exploiting a girl or a woman who is looking for love and intimacy and connection is not good. Encouraging a woman to sell her body for money is not good. Murdering someone, who disrespected with a glance or a word, stepped on a shoe, or took over a block, or looked at someone's woman, or didn't pay the total amount for the product, or wanted to fist fight, or held back on twenty dollars, is not good. Smoking weed all day and destroying the quality of sperm (and even ovarian reserves), hence, future son's and daughters is not good. These things *are* rotten. And no matter how one wants to justify it to make the ego feel okay, if one is living this type of life—he is living a rotten one. It is rotten because these things cause spiritual, mental, emotional, and physical anguish, confusion and chaos, despair and destitution, hate and envy, incarceration and death. And all of those things are rotten. And if the argument is the "money is good," it must be noted that the only prosperity that is gained is usually minimal, individual, and short lived. This is not a middle class value judgment, it is a fact.

It is argued that the lives of Rap artists are worthy of study, "Your lives are worthy of study." I agree. Yet unlike the work of Dyson, it must be put in a real—not an ideal context. And it must be analyzed from not only a "biographical perspective" or a perspective that serves to justify a carefully manufactured counterfeit culture that is directing the real one, but as a "total perspective."

Yes, Jay Z, is "successful," but unlike his assertion, he continues to promote his *own* success through the celebration of "promises of failure" that he and his label/distribution company sell to the masses. Per his own assertion, his success was grounded in the crack trade and then through his ability to "tell and sell the stories," however exaggerated, of his "rotten life."

And now, even after he has truly succeeded, he has not yet changed his message. This is promoting "the promise of failure" to "your customers, your consumers" Mr. Carter. How? Because as *all* who are from the inner city have experienced the results of rotten lives and promises of failure—either directly or indirectly. Most, if not all can attest to how the aggressive engagement in the crack trade (that would be necessary to reach the status that you brag about) most often, if not always, ultimately results in death (failure) or incarceration (failure) if one is not able to "get out before it is too late." So, in studying the lives of artists, which may be the next book, the question must be asked. What price must *your* people/*your* community continue to pay for your success? What price are the people paying for the success of the few artists? Or does it matter?

The Influence of the Presentation

The next argument is that the artist should not be, or is not, a role model. Parents must take responsibility for what their children are exposed to. *This* defense—while true—lends support to the industry and the presentation by blaming "the victim" for fulfilling the objective of the music industry—that is getting consumers to respect, envy, love, and even emulate the artist, the image, the icon, so that they will buy the record and paraphernalia and products that are associated with the artist while simultaneously leaving the artist "blameless" for what he presents—hence, how he derives his wealth and fame. That is one reason why it matters.

One cannot present something, say something, do something with "deliberacy" and then fail to take responsibility or even acknowledge the damage that the presentation, words, or actions have caused. It goes from the micro level to the macro level. There is a system of relationships—causative factors to the effect that must be acknowledged. Events do not happen in isolation. So, as a parent, I cannot curse incessantly and then blame my child for cursing without taking responsibility for my role. As a colonial power, Europe cannot usurp the resources of indigenous lands and then blame the people for their conditions without taking responsibility for their role. In the same vain, an artist cannot celebrate and encourage destruction in the inner city, and then blame the community for embracing and reproducing the presentation without taking responsibility for their role. In each case, there must be a level of accountability assigned to the contributor.

Yet, artists fail to understand, acknowledge, or much less take responsibility for the image and the content that he/she represents and promotes to the masses—and instead makes excuses that deviate the focus from the mouth of the messenger. And "the message" would almost be easier to accept if the image and presentation was truly the artists own. But, it is not.

The image that each presents is, most often, not a representation of the subjective being of the individual that the masses relate to. Artists images are most often carefully constructed acts that the label deliberately presents to the consumer. Thus, one cannot truly "love" Beyonce or Mary or Jay Z or 50 Cent because, the consumer does not know them. The consumer knows the image, relates to the image. Consequently, it is not Ms. Knowles, Ms. Blige, Sean or Curtis, as subjects that the individual respects, envies, and desires to emulate—it is the image of each.

Given the nature of the entertainment industry, it is hypocritical to think, much less assert, that he/she should not be viewed as a "role model" because their success depends on the extent to which consumers consider them as such. Jay Z, 50 Cent, Russell Simmons do not make profits from the sale of records, clothes, shoes, and vitamin water because people do not "respect" them, look up to them, hence, view them as role models. Therefore, it cannot be denied that the image is, in fact, integral to the success of the artist and a large contribution to the theoretical fabric of "internalization."

The Impact of Internalization

As a psychosocial concept, "internalization," represents the process of integrating external stimuli into the identification and development of the "self," and hence shapes ones interaction with the environment. Internalization is one of, if not the predominant component of socialization, which is the process by/through which individuals learn their social roles, expectations, norms, and values of society. Socialization is largely accomplished through the individual's interaction with his/her external environment, specifically the family, peers, school, and the media, which sociologists identify as the four "primary agents" of socialization (Macionis, 2007). Through reinforcement (Skinner), imitation (Piaget), conditioning (Pavlov), or mere observation, individuals are taught and conditioned (consciously and unconsciously) to accept and internalize gender, social, and cultural roles and values—that shape his/her identity. Therefore, the external environment, specifically that which he is exposed to, becomes integral to how the individual identifies and relates in/to the world, and ultimately who the individual becomes.

In essence the "you are what you eat" concept of the relationship between nutrition and biological/physiological development and health applies to the concept of images to mental and emotional development and health. What one ingests, through any of the senses, eating, seeing, hearing, breathing, touching, etc., is internalized and will have an effect on one's being. Breathing harmful chemicals whether one smells them or not will impact respiratory functioning, eating unhealthy foods will impact biological functioning. So, in the same vein seeing unhealthy images, hearing unhealthy content will impact ones mental and interactive functioning.

Internalization and socialization can occur on a micro (individual) level or a macro (collective) level, which is why the structure of the community—as the environment in which people are socialized—also plays an integral role. Group conformity is also an extremely important factor in this analysis, because conforming to social norms is one of the predominant aspects of the socialization process. Therefore, as the statement that "one is a product of one's environment" asserts, the norms of the environment become essential to the development and influence of the individual, groups, and ultimately the community—which then has a reciprocal and recurring effect. . This is where, what I have termed, "the culture of abnormality" comes into play.

The Culture of Abnormality

The "culture of abnormality" is a process wherein abnormal/deviant cultural values become the norm in any given environment. It encompasses a transition wherein the gauge for the development and promotion of expectations, values, morals, attitudes, goals—and the barometer of what is "good" and "right," becomes deviant, thereby making that which is normal—abnormal in that environment/culture. As a result, those who exhibit normative behaviors actually become "the deviants." And just as deviants have historically been, those who become deviants are socially ostracized and alienated—not able to find adequate support, and in some instances even violated, abused, and/or eventually encouraged or coerced to affiliate with deviant groups and or behaviors to satisfy a sense of belonging or maintain his/her safety. In such, normative cultural values and behaviors are ultimately suppressed until the abnormal becomes the critical norm and what is normal becomes extinct in a given community.

Examples of the culture of abnormality that have become prevalent in the inner city include the minimization and normalization of the drug trade, the promotion of juvenile delinquency, imprisonment, the use of marijuana, under aged drinking, poor attendance and performance in school, disrespect for elders/authority (without conscious rebellion), promiscuity, detached relationships that are based on sex and objective pregnancies, disregard for "life" and death, and the expectation of a life expectancy that will not surpass the early twenties. In such, the antithesis or opposite of these behaviors which would include not being involved in any form of illegal drug use, possession or distribution, never having been involved with the law or judicial system, getting good grades in school by doing homework, completing assignments and studying, respecting and being reluctant to challenge elders even when they are attempting to impose discipline, being a virgin and making a decision to wait until married, or at least until being in and receiving love before sex or babies, not being willing to use physical violence as a means of conflict resolution, or not being willing to kill/murder have become abnormal—the exception and not the rule.

The sad thing is that reading the latter will probably be funny, corny, too ideal, and/or too unrealistic for many because many have been conditioned—through the internalization of abnormal cultural values—to believe that these things are not possible in the inner city. And, sadly, due to the promotion of this "culture of abnormality," when it comes to dealing with confrontation and violence, in many instances, the assertion that it is "kill or be killed," however sorrowful, becomes true. People who might otherwise be "regular folk" are forced "out of character" in order to, at the lowest level of existence, survive.

In this type of culture then, it is far more palatable to believe assertions that a fifteen year old is a ho, or even a "dyke" rather than believe she is a virgin. It is far more palatable to believe that an eleven-year-old boy who has decent clothes got them because he is a "runner" rather than believe he is a paper boy. It is far more palatable for a student to censure "the smart kid," "the nerd," who is articulate and focused in his studies, than to support, protect, or even nurture his direction or strive to be like him. Because poor performance, being the class clown, or being a thug in the classroom by disrespecting the teacher is more cool and more expected.

Being Black and poor *and* smart has become the greatest contradiction. So consequently, it is far more common to hear assertions that the student who succeeds in school or the Black person who achieves status in society legitimately (without having been involved in anything criminal) is "acting or trying to act or be White" than to accept him as a legitimate member of the African-American community—because many have internalized the fallacy that intelligence and legitimate success are only reserved for White and Asian people. This sentiment *reflects* the internalization of the stereotype of inferiority of the African-American race that was the predominant goal of "the system" when Africans arrived on the shores of America.

It is far more common and palatable for a young man to refer to a young lady as a bitch before addressing her as a queen or to address another man as a nigga (nigger) or a dawg (dog) than address him as a "brother" or "king." And, as even rappers argue, it is more common and palatable to struggle to put money on the books of a prisoner so that he buy cigarettes and even drugs, and then turn around and throw a party for him that everyone attends when "he gets out," than to struggle to get money *for books* for a struggling college student and throw a party for him when he graduates.

And finally, most significant to the struggle is the detriment that it is far more palatable for a friend to hand a friend "the gat" and encourage him to murder his brother to resolve a petty conflict, than to encourage him to walk away from the situation or, worse, forgive. In keeping with that it is far more respectable to "stop or even never start snitching" so that cold-blooded-coward murderers can thrive freely, than to "snitch" on a sociopath that has murdered a love one, so that he can be held accountable for the life/lives that he took, and be removed from his opportunity to freely take more. But, . . . "y'all respect the one who got shot, I respect the shooter."

All of these very real assertions and examples represent how the culture of abnormality manifests itself in the community. The lyrics of the songs presented in the introduction to the last chapter reflects Hip-Hop's promotion of those things. So, whether the egg comes before the chicken or the chicken before the egg, when it comes to the psychosocial ramifications of internalizing the images, both operate as cohorts in the solidification of the "culture of abnormality" and lend to the destruction of the community—and the impending genocide of the race. Thus, all of these values and rituals have very deep connotations and implications.

These constructions of inner-city culture are now at a point wherein it is overwhelming the community. The growth reflects the collective internalization of the stereotypes of "Blackness" that are now becoming very real constructions of the race. The detriment is that as these attributes/practices/beliefs become ingrained as normalized cultural values, they run the risk of becoming not only a part of, but the entire urban culture.

The continued domination of the culture of abnormality poses a great threat to the community because those who might otherwise be positive role models, serve as the antithesis to the negative ones will most often flee. However, in an adversarial environment, those who cannot will ultimately be overshadowed in their own stance or even their influence over their own—yielding the possibility that many will likely, under intense pressure and lack of sustainable alternatives conform or lose their own to conformity. This then leaves the environment void of identifications of cultural normalcy.

The more people buy into abnormal cultural values, the more common the presentation and perpetuation of those values becomes. As abnormal cultural values become dominant in an environment, so do they become "normalized." As they become normalized, an individual's propensity for exhibiting truly "normal" values is suppressed and eventually extinguished. Thus, in the absence of an alternative, people are not given recognizable choices—leaving the abnormal culture as the ONLY identification, and the entire group as a homogenous representation of abnormality, which makes the cultural transmission to the collective's offspring inevitable.

For example, if a young girl watches her mother use her body, and even become pregnant in order to connect with, get, and/or keep a man, and interprets that her mother's connection with her children depends on her relationship with their father(s), she will have that as a dominant identification of how male female relationships are supposed to be. The more people to whom she is exposed who reinforce that relationship by being that or doing so themselves, the more inclusive and normal that identification will become. In the absence of any alternative identification(s), it poses the threat of becoming her only identification and experience, and will most likely result in her engaging in that type of relationship when she begins dating. Or contrarily, if through her mother's relationships, she experiences any psychological or physical trauma or abuse—such as rape or incest, it may also result in a rebellion against heterosexual relationships all together.

If individuals are exposed to negative, dysfunctional, and/or abnormal stimuli and do not have access to alternatives—because family, peers, parental peers, the community at large, and the media all present the same homogenous ideal and image, there is NO WAY the individual could know any different. All are products of the environment. Thus, if abnormality becomes the *only* experience—from the home, to the streets on the way to school, to the school, to the store, to the television and radio—from which perceptions and identifications of self and environment are based, the individual will become "a product" of that experience and environment and will subsequently pass those same norms and values to their offspring. There begins the foundation for the destructive nature of this new legacy—this new cycle.

This "new legacy" represents the ultimate destruction of the race on many levels. As Durkheim asserts, engaging in and promoting criminality as a culture leads to lawlessness/anomie. Without intervention, anomie leads to genocide. For when marijuana (and the use of other drugs) destroys the reproductive capacity (sperm quality and ovarian reserve) of men and women who use it, imprisonment (that is gender segregation and isolation) and (with all due respect for my gay, lesbian, and transgender populations) homosexuality reduces the ability to establish "procreative" relationships, and the murder rate continues to reduce the population, the birth rate will not be able to compensate for the death rate, and the race will diminish and ultimately perish.

Until then, the chaos in the inner city, as is the case today, will continue to justify governmental intervention, i.e. "stop and frisk," "neighborhood crime cameras," "increased police presence," and eventually the implementation of "Gestapo" style policing and serve as the justification for the renewed brutality and murder of community members (Diallo and Bell) and a further increase in the incarceration rate of African Americans without question or resistance because the masses have become desensitized to the cause and purpose of the race. All in all, like the Holocaust, the race will once again, and again without resistance, become "re-enslaved" through the heightened implementation of the new Black codes, the races participation "in the game," and its subsequent relegation to the prison industrial complex—the plantation, labor, or death.

The PsychoSocial Ramifications of "Keeping It Real"

So what role does Hip-Hop play? The media serves a double role as a venue by/through which dominant and stereotypical ideologies are disseminated and a means by/through which people are socialized and conditioned. Therefore, the information that is disseminated through Hip-Hop becomes integral to not only the presentation—hence, the way in which urban communities/African Americans are socialized, but to the way in which others are socialized and informed about urban culture/African Americans.

It becomes not only a means by/through which the message to sell drugs, smoke weed, become involved with the law, not have a connection with brothers or sisters, and to murder for respect is promoted and subsequently internalized as normal practices in the inner city. But it becomes a means by through which Don Imus can learn the term and then flawlessly refer to African-American women as "nappy-headed hoes."

It is through Hip-Hop that all of the things that the struggle sought to undo are being reinstated in and through the voice of the oppressed themselves. Through Hip-Hop, the very stereotypes that the movement sought to deconstruct are being given life and validity. The development and promotion of the "culture of abnormality" are the very reasons why negative images were not allowed to flourish in the homes and urban communities "back in the day when things were cool." No one wanted deviance, criminality, and dysfunction to become commonplace in the neighborhood. That is why community policing and child rearing and familial involvement and intervention, were essential to the movement.

Practices, values, rituals, behaviors, and attitudes that were counterproductive to the well being of the race, hence, the Movement toward social, political, and economic inclusion and equality were simply not acceptable. Consequently, deviants were ostracized, admonished, and controlled by the community because the race did not want to have anyone, much less the masses of the race, present or be presented as anything that even resembled the stereotypes of old that had been and would be used to undermine the subjectivity, humanity, intelligence, potential, and progress of the race.

So, when an artist who is not only presenting, but promoting criminality (Jay Z), hyper sexuality (Souljah boy), idiocy and ignorance (the new Flava Flav), violence, and murder (50 Cent), is given mass airplay that reaches millions of people globally each day, and given credit for being a 'representation' of not only the urban community, but of the race, it directly promotes the internalization of what the representation entails as being an accurate reflection of the race. When artists consistently brag about material possessions, wealth, status, and power that they attribute to the hustle, and then chastise or berate those who do not have the capability to acquire such as "window shoppers"—and "advise" the listener (since they cannot rap) to "Get Rich or Die Tryin," it directly promotes the internalization of crime, deviance, murder, and suicide. When artists, who in that phase, are most often *not* participating in illegal activities promote the notion that they are still committing crimes and murder, are still making millions and not in jail, it promotes the internalization of the extremely fallacious belief that crime has no consequence.

The whole construction of Hip-Hop encourages the consumer to believe that the artist truly represents the hood, that he/she is truly the authority on "hood life," the "hood icon." And it is the concrete objective of the label, to make the public believe that the image is real, or at the least an example of past experiences, so that he/she can be respected among consumers, build a fan base, sell records and products.

Therefore, the promotion of the image encourages the consumer to believe that in order to be legit, to be recognized, to "keep it real" or even worse, to acquire "the artist's status," he/she must utilize the artists fictitious version of reality as a 'real' guide . . . hustle and flow, lil' duffle bag boy, hustle and flow. Not understanding the reality that the very individual behind the image will unlikely do what he raps about/encourages the consumer to do. Why? Because real life criminality, violence, hyper sexuality has consequences—consequences that the individual behind the image would never risk in order to "keep it real."

Jay Z and 50 Cent can rap about murder all day, but neither is going to even slap, much less go out and murder anyone, because neither is going to risk a law suit, much less the continued freedom and ability to acquire wealth—selling that story "to you the customer." Nor is Beyonce going to put her "freakum" dress on, go to the club, go to the middle of the dance floor and "drop it like it's hot." Her image may recreate that scene on the stage or in the video with her dancers surrounding her. But, I can assure that Ms. Knowles would not. Why? Because I would argue that underneath of "the image" of hyper sexuality, Beyonce—who appears to have had a very middle class, structured, pretty much functional, and apparently sheltered upbringing—is a lady. She is not the artist who in "real life" is running around acting like Sharon Stone, getting out of cars, legs open, cameras flashing, with no panties on.

Yet, because the artist depends on these presentations to sell and profit from the image, it is unlikely that he/she will stop. Most would rather present the image and "blame the parents/consumers" for either listening or allowing their children to listen and watch or for internalizing and replicating the image. The same artist that will rap about bustin' an AK and thanking the pastor for rappin' at your eulogy, is the same artist that will stand alongside Bill Cosby, sit on Oprah, march, or do a spot for the stop the violence campaign. Therefore, the consciousness of the masses, the consumers, must be checked.

The image is a lie that is completely counterproductive and detrimental to the Black community. Yet, supporting and subsequently internalizing the lie is a choice. Giving the lie breath, life, off of the stage and outside of the studio is a choice. Just as the artist is a puppet for the ruling class, so are those who believe that they are "keeping it gangsta" by selling drugs to their mothers, fathers, sisters, and brothers—by using the supply to create a demand or "murdering" mothers, fathers, sons, daughters, brothers and sisters, kings and queens for twenty dollars or preserving a reputation. Yes, Rap artist are responsible for promoting the image—"spreading these things in verse," but the masses are responsible for giving them life, not "keeping them real" but "making them real" in the community

The culture of abnormality wherein individuals take on and become characters that cannot connect, love, stay free, forgive, be good and present fathers and mothers, stay away from the sale and use of the drugs that were placed into the community to destroy the mind, body, and spirit of the user and seller, commit to monogamous relationships, use bodies as subjects and not objects, and value the lives of their brothers and sisters as something that will never be returned once taken, is a conscious choice. So, the consciousness or conscience of the masses has to be reached.

The escalating adverse condition of the race is reflective. The fact that there is not ONE day when someone is not murdered in at least 10 urban areas in the United States is reflective. The fact that all of these murders are murders committed upon the bodies of one brother or sister by another is reflective. The fact that the news media are now keeping body counts across the nation is reflective of the war that the race has waged upon and against its own. When the images are confused, accepted, internalized and then promoted as a real identification of what men and women in the inner city are supposed to be, supposed to do—death is the end.

CHAPTER 7

WHAT DOES HIP-HOP HAVE TO DO WITH AMADOU DIALLO AND SEAN BELL?

Affect Control Theory and Hip-Hop

February 4, 1999, Amadou Diallo, a 23 year old West African immigrant, who like countless numbers of other immigrants—who will never have to fathom the type of confrontation that Diallo did because of their different racial/ethnic affiliations—came to the United States to get an education—a better life. Instead, he was shot "to death" by 4 plainclothes officers attempting to question him for a series of rapes, for which he was not responsible or involved—41 times—blang . . .

According to the officers' testimonies, Diallo "matched" the description of a rape suspect. When they attempted to apprehend him, he ran. They summoned him to "stop," and he did not, instead, attempting to open the door to his apartment building. According to the officers, while attempting to enter his building "He reached in his jacket as if he were reaching for a gun." One officer yelled, "gun"—and they commenced to firing—41 times. There was no gun! On February 25, 2000, *all* officers were acquitted—on all charges.

On November 25, 2006, Sean Bell, like many other grooms to be, left his Bachelor's party at a local gentlemen's club with a group of friends, on his way to get a few hours rest before his wedding some hours later. According to his family, he was looking forward to starting his new life with his wife and daughter. Instead, the 23 year old African American "husband-to-be" and father was shot "to death" by 4 plainclothes officers who were allegedly investigating the club that Bell had exited—50 times—blang blang

blang blang blang blang blang blang blang blang blang blang blang blang blang blang . . .

According to the officers' grand jury testimonies, Bell and his friends had been "flirting" with a dancer, after being summoned to "stop," Bell got in his car and attempted to drive away. As he attempted to drive away, he and another victim "reached" as if reaching for a gun. The officer yelled "gun" and the officers commenced to firing—51 times. There was no gun! On April 25, 2008, *all* officers were acquitted—on all charges.

While the Diallo Decision was shocking in 2000, the Bell Decision, today in 2008, as heart crushing as it may have been, was not. As a matter of fact, any other decision would have been far more shocking than *this* full acquittal. Why? Because by *not* convicting the officers of *any* of the charges, the Judge in this case not only "ruled" the officers' use of force (firing 51 shots) against this group of unarmed "men of color" justifiable, but more significantly, the Judge's decision reflected his own sentiment, belief, and agreement that the officers actions were grounded in their perception and judgment that the men, who they *assumed/perceived* to be "armed and dangerous," indeed posed a threat.

For even as Detective Isnora's own testimony reflected, "In my mind, I knew, Guzman, had a gun" (Hays 2008). And even as Hays (Reuters 2008) reported, the defense even "painted a picture of the victims as being a group of drunken 'thugs' whom they believed were armed and dangerous." And as was reported, Judge Cooperman believed, as he stated, "The officers testimony to be more credible than that of the witnesses."

So while it is appalling, the rationale behind the detectives perceptions and the judges ruling is understandable. It is highly believable and conceivable that today, more than at any point in the past, the detectives *perceived* the men to be a threat to their lives. And it is the threat, that produces fear—and fear that produces the action that is grounded in a level of contempt and hatred of/for the object or the subject of the fear. So, in such it is understandable why they were acquitted. This relationship poses the most significant and dangerous issue.

In the Bell case, in order to convict the officers, the Judge had to be made to believe that the detectives use of force, and the extent of the force, was not justified. In such, he would have had to be convinced that, either Bell and his companions "did not" pose a threat to the officers safety, or he would have had to believe that the officers excessive response was not justified by their "belief" (or perception) that the men posed a threat to their safety. So, just as in the Diallo case, where there was proven to be absolutely *no* threat to any of the officer's lives and safety, because there were no "guns"—what is left is assessing two key factors in each case, perception and judgment.

These two factors become critical—especially when it involves the perception and judgment of those (officers) who are charged with enforcing the law, have the deadly means to do so, and are protected by the state when they do.

Perception and judgement are critical for those who must utilize that perception and judgment in determining how to react/respond to the members of the communities that they are supposed to "protect and serve," and those men and women (judges) who must attempt to neutralize or negate their own subjective experiences (that ultimately shape their perception and influence their judgment) to keep the blindfold on lady justice.

This *must* lead all to question how, and what factors influence and shape social perception and judgment—specifically about African-American males, especially for those who have either had limited or no contact with "men of color" in urban areas, or those who have been forced/programmed to abandon their subjective experience in order to embrace the dominant ideologies that allow them to be accepted in mainstream society? Moreover, how does this perception affect judgment and/or influence individual and collective interaction with the same?

To bring the point back, in cases such as Diallo and Bell, the question has to be asked, what would make Detective Isnora, so sure that Guzman had a gun? What would make any of these officers so sure that "a sudden movement," or a "reach" or the appearance of "a reach" meant that the individual was "reaching" for a "gun?!" And what would make the judges and juries believe and rule that shooting an unarmed man 41 or 50 times was justifiable?

Now, introducing the race card, let us all take a moment to do an internal examination when we ask ourselves this question without becoming defensive. If the victims had been "White women" in the exact same situations, would the officers' perceptions hence responses differed? Or if the officers had responded in the same manner shooting 2 innocent unarmed White women—one a European immigrant coming to the United States to study biochemistry, another a White American mother of an infant daughter and a wife to be—on her wedding day—who may have been fearful of/or even resistant of several unidentifiable plainclothes police officers attempting to apprehend them "on a hunch," 41 and 50 times, how would the judge and jury's responses and rulings have been, and how different would mainstream public opinion have been and why?

It cannot be argued, as it is stated in the testimony of all officers involved in each case, that the perception that shaped the officers judgments and reactions to both Diallo and Bell is—fear—Fear of the Black Man. And the fear cannot be denied because that same fear has been engrained in our American culture for centuries. It has been promoted in American society since the first African set his first foot down on these soils.

Stereotypes about the aggressive, hypersexual, and violent nature of African—and then African-American men—were developed by the European to justify the enslavement of African people and promote acceptance for the brutality, exploitation, and oppression that Africans in America would endure for hundreds of years. Those very stereotypes were specifically developed and designed to discourage bonds and interactions with, sympathy or empathy for the race.

That way they could be enslaved, deprived, raped, bred, beaten, whipped, lashed, punched, kicked, burned, cut, castrated, amputated, dragged, hanged, and shot 50 times with minimal, if any, social question, resistance, or outrage. That is the reason why the Civil Rights and Black Power Movements struggled so vehemently, simultaneously, to restore the subjectivity of the African American by deconstructing the stereotypes that had been utilized to justify racial oppression, exploitation, and assassination. That is why deconstructing the myth of the angry Black man and the hypersexual Black woman was so critical. They fought so that the world would gain respect for the freedom, bodies, and lives of African-American people. Remember?

So Diallo and Bell are not new. Unfortunately, their situations are not isolated, but are regurgitations of a history that many have forgotten. Their murders are identifications of the most sorrowful and detrimental end to the countless numbers inter racial officer/African-American male interactions that are dominated by mutual fear, and hence teeter on that very fine line between life and death.

Unfortunately for the African-American male, as a citizen and a human being, he is often at the receiving end of a power dynamic that renders him completely defenseless to the perception and actions of the officers whose badges often erase any empathy for/identity with the African-American race. This dynamic most often, if not always, leaves him unable to command/demand his rights as an American citizen at that moment, to protect himself against unfair/unconstitutional treatment, assault, or brutality at that moment, or to even move or "reach" the wrong way for fear that any such movements could very likely and easily result in his death at that moment. And during this exchange, that threat continues until the officer(s), who in his/her fear often becomes an unwitting or deliberate aggressor, perpetrator, or assailant, has gained control "over" the individual and has assured him/herself that the individual no longer poses a threat—which most often does not occur until the individual has been "subdued" regardless of the situation. In essence, the African-American male must be subjected to this breach of his rights just to survive—not because he really poses a threat, but because he is perceived as such by others.

The Bell Decision needs to give rise to the essentiality of revisiting how the images of African Americans, that are unilaterally and homogenously presented in all mediums, shape the social perception of the race and influence interactions and beliefs about African-American men—especially. The race cannot continue to deny how relevant these presentations are to reinforcing and promoting the same historic stereotypes, of the innate violent tendency of the Black man, that drive and promote support for the real fear that leads to tragedies such as this. One cannot continue to holler about the White mans fear of the Black man when the race is simultaneously promoting the "angry, violent, thug" image in every video, song, lyric, interview, movie, and photograph. How are people supposed to perceive any thing other than that when *that* is all society absorbs as the rule of the race—rather than the exception?

Visit how everything about urban music, videos, movies, culture presents this homogenous image of the criminal, violent, aggressive, murdering thug who has no respect for the law—tear drops, blunts, rock boys, guns, angry faces. Then understand that there are many who have had limited contact with "real" Black folk from the neighborhood, and only have the media as their frame of reference for, most, if not all, African-American people. Then there are others who have had the experiences but still choose to allow their perceptions to be shaped by what mainstream media heavily promotes on every medium—the images that African Americans, themselves, voluntarily represent as being accurate and real reflections and identifications of "hood life" and "hood mentality" with no variations.

To revisit the question, the reason why it is highly unlikely that officers would have responded in the same manner to a 23 year old White woman is simply because society does not view a 23 year old White woman, or any White woman for that matter, as being a threat to the safety and lives of others. White women are rarely ever viewed and/or presented as murderers or thugs. That is why it is so shocking to the world when a White woman kills. That is why, even when they are proven to be murders or thugs, there is always much discourse that attempts to provide an explanation for the actions, which often results in a level of social sympathy, empathy, or understanding to why or "what went wrong." Or, when it is "cold-blooded" a conscious media effort is most often made to ensure that she is acknowledged as the unique exception to the rule.

But this is not so for African-American men. The media presentations have replaced and superseded the subjectivity of African-American men, just as the stereotypical accounts did in the past. Yet in this era of technology, the stereotypical constructs that are presented are more easily accepted and internalized as real because there is a visual attached to the stereotype and he is not in Black face, he is Black face.

Today, real life African-American men are viewed as being a threat, and therefore a collective that should be feared. There is no separation between fact and fiction—that is the fact that the majority of African-American men, like the majority of other races, are NOT criminal or dangerous—whether they are disproportionately represented in the prison system or not. The fictitious version of the Black man that is represented in urban mediums has replaced that reality. Therefore, it is the fictitious version that shapes public perception and influences the fear that lends to the contempt that results in tragedies such as the deaths of Diallo and Bell and the decisions that follow.

The race can no longer remain blameless in the deaths of Diallo and Bell. The race can no longer blame society and the system for its continued injustices without visiting its own accountability. The race can no longer holler about "the White man!" without visiting the races influence on how the White man shapes his perceptions. And the artists, stars, and entertainers that present and promote the same images that foster the real life fear and beliefs about the Black man that contributed to the deaths of Diallo and Bell need not speak hypocritically on these cases.

The reality of this situation is that the African-American community—who has not only failed to hold accountable, but has continued to support the return of the race to Post Emancipation Jim Crow America, through embracing a form of "entertainment" that has become detrimental to a people and community—has just as much to do with, and are just as much to blame, for the vicious murders of Amadou Diallo and Sean Bell—as the police officers who pulled the triggers and the Justice system that supported their perception and judgment. The community cannot continue to be hypocritical in its projection of anger, because much of that perception has been shaped by what the race promotes and presents about itself.

The State has successfully conned a people into promoting and readily consuming the exploitation and oppression of its own people—in the name of entertainment. It has conned a people into failing to hold its race accountable, on many levels, for its aggression against itself. It has conned a people into believing that it has no control over its own justice and must continue to rely on those outside to give justice to it. And in such it has conned a people into giving others a seemingly legitimate excuse to restore the blatant disregard for African-American life that is reminiscent of the antebellum and Post emancipation period.

A 23 year old middle class bride to be and mother of a beautiful daughter was gunned down in a hail of 50 shots while leaving a local club after her bachelorette party with her college friends and bridesmaids. A 23 year old college student was shot by police 19 times in a hail of 41 bullets when police attempted to question her for a crime in which she was not involved. After failing to respond to several plainclothes officers, and reaching, the police believed they were armed and dangerous. The response would be outrage. The "perception" of fear would have been absurd. And the question of the excessiveness of the force used given each situation would have been undeniable. The verdict—guilty. And for the abuse of power and public trust, the sentence—maximum.

The deaths of Diallo and Bell reflect the reality that "the fear of the Black man" has re-solidified as a very real construction of the relationship between African-American men and American society. The manner in which they were murdered reflects the hatred and disregard that the power structure has for the lives, subjectivity, and citizenry of African-American men.

The verdicts in the Diallo and Bell cases are signs of the time. They are signs of the regression that the race is undergoing in its relationship to larger society on a multitude of levels. The fact that the justice system was unable to view these cases as the blatant misuse of power and exertion of excessive force that they were is a testament to the deeply ingrained internalizations of the criminal Black man that has penetrated all layers of society. The fact that the Judge and jury failed to support the rights of the innocent citizen, father, and husband or the business owner and student over the misguided perceptions of officers is a testament to the lack of understanding, sympathy, or empathy or even the ability to be truly objective in matters involving the lives of African-American men.

The racial divide in public response to the verdict is reminiscent of times past, Emmit Till. The fact that African Americans seem to be the only ones that see the injustice reflects the result of the successful manipulation of social perception about African-American men that African-American men have voluntarily allowed themselves to be used to perpetuate. It is clear that because of the presentation of the images of 50 Cent and Ghostface Killa, real men like Diallo and Bell cannot walk the streets without being feared.

The deaths of Diallo and Bell must bring life to the reality of the entertainment that we support and defend—for it is that very entertainment that will continue to give rise to more and more deaths, incarcerations, and subjective verdicts if we do not commit to make a change. These murders must be testaments to the dangers of the perceptions that we currently promote and embrace. They must be a call for us to buy our souls back and stop selling our images so that they can be utilized to promote a greater agenda. If we do not, the deaths of Amadou Diallo and Sean Bell will remain in vain—not by the hands of the system, but by "our" own.

CHAPTER 8

THE ROOTS:
BURIED UNDERGROUND AND NEO-SOUL

My chocolate covered paradise
I see the pain in children's eyes
They searchin' for that ghetto pride
Sullen promise, crooked vibe, broken dreams
But they keep askin why they cryin
Like they don't know the reasons why
Society keep sellin' lies
Broken promises, sullen dreams
And I can see em standin' by
As they watch our babies mothers die
Crack cocaine suicide
Sullen promise, broken dreams
And you know my passion aint a lie
If you ever seen a brotha die
Those Siren sounding homicides
Sullen promises, broken dreams
Oweoo
I didn't think that you would do
The evil that the devils do
To—another human being like you, you, you
And who-we-ooo do you think created you
But you never give the props that's due-oops
I'm gonna have to take it
Take the time and rearrange what you created
Oweoo
I didn't think that you could do
The evil that the devils do
To—another human being like you, you, you

And who-we-oo do you think created you
Why don't you tell the world the truth—Fools
Or we gonna have to take it
Take the time to recreate what you created

Black river with cobalt grains of sand
Pass through this dirty land
Like blood shed by your brothers hand
But still we don't understand
The need for a firm stance
Conquer our own circumstance
As soon as we get the chance
To rise! To rise!
And still we rise
In spite of the—sullen promise, crooked vibe, broken dreams
– Zoe Spencer, *Sullen Promises* 2005

What is underground and neo-Soul? Underground—beneath the surface of the Place that secures/concretizes our existence, "in concealment or secrecy; existing, situated, operating beneath the surface; an underground space or passage; a movement or group existing outside the establishment and usually reflecting unorthodox, avante garde, or radical views" (Dictionary.com). Radical—"of or going to the root of origin; Root—the fundamental or essential part; the source or origin of a thing; a persons original or true home, environment, and culture" (Dictionary.com).

Neo-near Earth, object; recent new. Soul—the principle of life, feeling, thought, and action in humans, regarded as a distinct entity separate from the body, the spiritual part of humans as distinct from the physical part; of, characteristic of, or for Black Americans or their culture. (Dictionary.com)

Neo-Soul: New life, new feeling thoughts and actions that nurtures or uplifts the spiritual part of one's being. Underground music: Avante garde music that must operate beneath the surface because of its expression of conscious views.

The definition of the terms provided, in something as simple as an online dictionary, speaks volumes about the terms alone. Woven together, the terms and meanings provide an intricate and beautiful answer to—what is underground and neo-soul? Underground is where the original Hip-Hop has been buried, concealed, hidden. It is where the genre, the craft, the art that was true to the experiences and struggle of a people is being kept out of the view and grasp of the masses.

Just like the Black Power Movement and the Civil Rights Movement were dismantled so that they would not contradict or interfere with, hence, pose a threat to the agenda of the United States government/ruling class, so has Hip-Hop been taken from the forefront. The messages that challenged the system and promoted the consciousness of the people, once again, had to be suppressed in order to reduce or counter the likelihood of the resistance that was developing in the late '80s.

During that time, Hip-Hop represented the development of the New Movement that was camouflaged as entertainment—just as the new Hip-Hop is camouflaging the promotion of genocide today. However, unlike this counterfeit Hip-Hop, under the beat of the real Hip-Hop was a strong message promoted by the voice of the artists like Chuck D and KRS One that was designed to promote the consciousness, activism, and movement, not the destruction, of an oppressed and exploited people. Again think about the lyrics to *Fight the Power* or even *Fuck the Police*. And if you don't remember, pull out the insert to the cassette tape and read them. The comparison of the two represents an "oppositional sameness" that proves the point that not even entertainment is without purpose or foundation. Therefore, for the same reason some music is promoted other music must be suppressed. Given the assertion being made herein then, how could the powers that be allow *this* type of message to be promoted and internalized by the masses?

Yet, unlike the movements were dismantled, deconstructed, leaders assassinated, Hip-Hop has not yet been. The term (underground) represents where the root and foundation is being suppressed, kept secret. It exists beneath the surface because it cannot be given light (commercialization/promotion) because underground is not just music. It is a collective movement of conscious artist who understand the "nature of the beast" and use verse and rhythm to promote the consciousness of the masses—just like the ancestors did, just like the true "O.G.s" did. Therefore, being underground serves a mutual purpose. It must be suppressed, hidden by the industry and power structure because it contradicts the ideology and agenda of the ruling class—that is to allow the race to self destruct. It contradicts, and would be the alternative that gives choice to the messages that are now being promoted by the "counterfeit Hip-Hop artists." It tells truths that the masses must not embrace and must not antagonize the counterfeit Hip-Hop in this manner. Mos Def says it most poignantly in his underground classic, "The Rape Over," where he critically dissects the relationship between the artist and the label—asserting that corporations that are headed by White men are "running" Rap music and therefore controlling the lyrical messages that promote murder, misogyny, and mayhem. But more importantly, he also places the blame for its promotion on the artist and the consumers who have become "confused" by what Hip-Hop or Rap is supposed to be.

Contrarily, for the people, underground must exist outside of "the establishment" because it cannot be monitored, controlled, dictated, or destroyed by the ruling class. It must serve as the "passage to freedom" by providing a safe space to create, organize, and move toward freedom and liberation—just like "The Underground Railroad" did. So if the masses desire to seek consciousness, they must dig to find it, just as they must dig to find the truth in literature, libraries, pyramids, tombs, and the earth of the Motherland. All truths are "underground."

The Root of the movement and a people exists underground. There it is protected, and more greatly allowed to provide the foundation and nourishment for that which, or those whom, exist on the surface. It is, therefore, essential to/for that which, those whom, exist above the surface to be cognizant and protective of the root—to protect that which provides its nourishment and ensures its survival. Without the root, the life of the organism cannot/will not survive and no new organisms of the same can be reborn.

In this instance then, it appears that the root does not yet present a threat to the "establishment" because the masses give more credence to that which the ruling class perpetuates. Yet to survive the race must ensure that the culture of abnormality, the new cultural values do not become the root, *our* root. For if it does, all that emerges from it—will be *of it*. If the roots are consciousness, it will produce and then reproduce consciousness. If the roots are destruction, it will produce and then reproduce destruction. To understand this reality, to embrace this simple truth without rationalization is to begin to make change. The Roots speak to this in their underground classic *"Nuttin New"* where they celebrate the consciousness raising that is possible through true Rap/Hip-Hop music, while shedding light on the reality that the "hijacked Hip-Hop" artist who promote the negativity "ain't sayin' nuthin' new."

In concert, neo-Soul reflects the principle of life that emerges from a place that is greater than the physical. It is grounded in a spirituality that encourages the acknowledgement and reverence of and for something greater than the self. It is embodied in a people—hence, a culture, carried forth from generation to generation—yet, slowly diluted. Soul is not new, it has been a part of a collective experience that allowed a race to survive in spite of the harsh conditions that it has *always been* subjected to. And now in its rebirthing process it manifests in the voices of those who represent this struggle, this genre. So as Lauryn Hill sings in "I Find It Hard To Say" (Rebel), in order to stop the social and psychological infiltration of these negative messages and images, we must see through the lies, understand the consequences, stop allowing others to define the valued of Black life, and "Rebel."

CHAPTER 9

BLACK CONSCIOUSNESS, BLACK POWER

"Almost always, during the initial stage of the struggle, the oppressed, instead of striving for liberation, tend themselves to become oppressors, or 'sub-oppressors.' The very structure of their thought has been conditioned by the contradictions of the concrete, existential situation by which they were shaped. Their ideal is to be men; but for them, to be men is to be oppressors. This is their model of humanity. This phenomenon derives from the fact that the oppressed, at a certain moment of their existential experience, adopt an attitude of 'adhesion' to the oppressor. Under these circumstances they cannot 'consider' him sufficiently clearly to objectivize him—to discover him 'outside' themselves. . . . Their perception of themselves as oppressed is impaired by their submersion in the reality of oppression. At this level, their perception of themselves as opposites of the oppressor does not yet signify engagement in a struggle to overcome the contradiction; . . . but to identification with the opposite pole. . . . Even revolution, which transforms a concrete situation must confront this phenomenon. The oppressed, having internalized the image of the oppressor and adopted his guidelines, are fearful of freedom. Freedom would require them to eject this image and replace it with autonomy and responsibility. Freedom is acquired by conquest, not by gift. It must be pursued constantly and responsibly. . . . This, then, is the great humanistic and historical task of the oppressed: to liberate themselves and their oppressors as well."

– Freire in Pedagogy of the Oppressed, 1972

If "money (as a social construct) is the root of all evil," capitalism (as a political and economic construct) is its seed. It has promoted the development and growth of systems, nationally and globally, that have promoted wealth accumulation and established it as the means by/through which power, control, dominance, and status are achieved. It is the quest for wealth, beyond all else, beyond any ideology—beyond any desire to promote an indigenous humanity—that has led Europe, France, Spain, Portugal, and then the United States to conquer and exploit (rape) indigenous lands, resources, and people.

It is the very nature of global capitalism, beyond any assertions of the cultural inferiority, savagery and/or barbaricism, or even the tyranny of the indigenous systems or rulers, that may have provided the rational for colonial and imperial expansion, that creates the First World/Third World wealth and power dynamic. For it is through the maximal exploitation of the lands, resources, and labor power of *others* that the extreme disparity in the wealth/power margin between the colonizer and the colonized has been sustained. Contrary to any assertions of the innateness of the biological and/or cultural dominance of the European, it is the system of global capitalism that creates and maintains the power dynamic and economic relationship that ensures Colonial dominance and third world dependence and impoverishment.

Africa, being the richest continent on this Earth, is not a third world and impoverished continent because of the lack or resources, the inferiority of the people, or the primitiveness of the culture. It is so because all of the resources in Africa, from diamonds to quartz, are being extracted and exported as a part of the European and European corporate, not African, trade economy. Therefore, the profits from the export of *all* of the natural resources that are extracted from colonized lands go to the colonizer. Not only that, under this system, the African government is also taxed and held responsible for paying for the infrastructural development that is necessary in order to extract the resources that Europe capitalizes on. This relationship ensures the continued indebtedness of the continent, hence, its dependence on Europe.

The people are not starving because there is a lack of food or a means to produce it. The continent also produces agricultural resources for extraction as well; therefore, they could certainly produce their own food in abundance. It is the most fertile continent in the world, and its people have been producing for thousands of years. However, wealth accumulation requires "harnessing" and exploiting the collective labor power of the masses to maximally extract resources for trade. The transition for producing for subsistence to producing for trade, and the transition into a wage labor relationship with the colonizer again promotes a dependence. In this relationship, the people are no longer able to produce their own food, because they do not have the time and upon giving the land to the colonizers, they do not have the space. Therefore, while they produce exports for Europe they must import the necessities, such as food, and use the wage that is earned from working for the colonizers to in many instances purchase what they produce.

It is the quest for wealth (capital) accumulation—greed—that propels men to believe in the infinite potential of it—desire to seek the infinite potential of it. It is that freedom to seek wealth accumulation that becomes a "subjective right" under the Western construction of democracy, that leads to the mass and extreme exploitation, violation, and social, political, and economic oppression of the masses globally. And it is the ideology of democracy that clouds the consciousness men, and disturbs his connection to anything outside of that capitalist purpose—and justifies the condition of the oppressed. Expansion, war, exploitation, oppression, and genocide become functional casualties of the capitalist endeavor.

The colonization of the United States of America is the direct result of capitalist expansion. Slavery was the direct result of capitalist expansion. The construction of race is the direct result of capitalist expansion. Globalization is the direct result of capitalist expansion. Imperialism is the direct result of capitalist expansion. The Prison Industrial Complex is even the direct result of capitalist expansion. And no ideological assertion could be a replacement for this truth, this reality.

The United States was colonized in order to provide resources for European trade. And the American Revolution was "fought" so that the U.S. (British colonizers) could profit from the export of "its own" resources (lesson to Africa). It is clear that knowing the political and economic nature of capitalism, the British who colonized America did not want to exist under that rule, but instead wanted to be its own independent "nation" so that it, like Europe, could colonize other countries and people. Hence, it became its own capitalist country.

The construction of race, especially that of the European (White) and the African (Black), was designed as an ideology, hence, is a social construct, that serves as the justification for why one group can be exploited while others are not. Predominantly it serves as a justification for why Africans, could be considered non-humans—and thus used to promote the agricultural—hence, capitalist development of the United States.

The brainwashing/breaking of the African was a necessary practice. The African had to be forced to negate his origin and root, his memory of his ancestry, his identification of his culture and being—in order to promote his conformity to, acceptance of, and even the promotion of his own oppression so that he would not only be physically dependent but psychologically, mentally, and emotionally dependent on him as well. Seeking the acceptance of the European, identifying with the European, self-hate, acting as a "sub-oppressor," and assuming the characteristics associated with European stereotypes of the race are all results that lead to the collective's failure to seek true liberation. The history of breaking and other oppressive practices, the promotion of fear, and the cultural transmission of survival mechanisms that promoted the current state of passivity and apathy toward and/or adhesion to the oppressor.

As Akbar (1996) and Asante (2007) both argue, while many may criticize the constant revisiting of slavery in order to understand contemporary issues, it *is* necessary. It is necessary because, unfortunately, the 400 years of oppression, exploitation, discrimination, racism, and the physical, mental, emotional, and intellectual colonization of a people has not yet been undone.

"In order to fully grasp the magnitude of our current problems, we must reopen the books on the events of slavery. Our objective should not be to cry stale tears for the past, nor to rekindle old hatreds for past injustices. Instead, we should seek to enlighten our path of today by better understanding where and how the lights were turned out yesterday" (Akbar, 1996).

Neither the signing of the Emancipation Proclamation, nor the passage of Brown or the Civil Rights Act removed, negated, minimized or liberated the race from the identification of the collective "self" that exists within the confines of the dominant social construction of the race. It is only through seeking and reaching true consciousness (about not only who we are and where we are from, but about the tools that have historically and unchangingly been utilized to ensure our conformity to our own oppression) and then accepting *that* "truth" that true liberation will be achieved.

Consciousness yields the power that is necessary to secure liberation. It is the root and foundation of true liberation. Without consciousness, enlightenment, understanding the conditions, the race will not be able to see or understand the nature of the oppression, much less understand the need for change—transformation. History has proven that movement without consciousness reaps superficial reforms at best, or at worse transitions/shifts in power dynamics that allow the oppressed to become an oppressor.

Consciousness requires an awakening of the mind, a willingness to go through the process of deconstructing centuries of mental manipulation, mental colonialism so that one can see the realities that exist behind the presentation. This concept is likened to *The Matrix* wherein there is a choice to take the red pill or the blue pill. The red pill represents "consciousness" the ability to remove oneself, elevate above ones current condition so that all can be witnessed, so that all can be viewed outside of ones subjective immersion. The blue pill, allows the individual to continue to exist in that system without awareness, realization, or acceptance of its purpose or effect.

Admittedly, which is why severe oppression is not being promoted as it was during the Post Emancipation era of Southern White supremacist terror, it is most often easier to just take the "blue pill" so that one can exist in his condition without challenge or cause. In such, one is not forced with consciously confronting the crossroads of taking a stand or accepting his condition—knowing. It is evident that history's lessons have been learned and incorporated in new "covert" systems of oppression. Under conditions of severe oppression the detriments of the oppression are undeniable, usually threatening the basic drive to survive, which forces one to confront the condition and seek transformation/change in order to avoid extinction. History has proven that severe oppression inevitably leads to violent resistance and/or revolution, which is why ideology over force, coercion, and violence has been most successful means of promoting the masses conformity to and acceptance of his own oppression.

> Most always, during the initial stage of the struggle, the oppressed, instead of striving for liberation, tend themselves to become oppressors or 'sub-oppressors.' The very structure of their thought has been conditioned by the contradictions of the concrete, existential situation by which they were shaped (Freire 1972:30).

Because the African experience in America has been borne out of (1) the removal of a people from their true roots and origin, (2) conditioning them to accept a fictitious identification and construction of not only themselves but their ancestors (3) forcing them to believe in the ideology of White supremacy (European dominance) that negates their own subjectivity and potential, and (4) systematically disenfranchising them from the social, political, and economic spheres of the nation, "the self-hate" and collective inferiority complex has become almost inevitable. In such, as was mentioned in the previous chapter, one cannot embrace a reality that he does not know, embrace an experience that he has not had, see a reality that he has not seen. All people are products of their experiences, what has been taught/learned, observed, etc. As a collective, the sum of their shared experiences shape and "condition" their thoughts and perceptions—who they become, hence, shape the culture of the people.

> Their ideal is to be men; but for them, to be men is to be oppressors. This is their model of humanity. This phenomenon derives from the fact that they oppressed, at a certain moment of their existential experience, adopt and attitude of 'adhesion' to the oppressor (Freire 1972:30).

For generations, and under the institution of slavery, African men and women were removed from not only their subjective being, but from their own indigenous cultural identifications of "manhood" and "womanhood." In such and absent any alternative cultural constructions and identifications with such, they were forced to accept European ideals of manhood and womanhood. These ideals took two forms—the "dominant ideal" which represented the gender constructs and characteristics of the European and only applied to the European, and the "stereotypical ideal" which represented the stereotypical constructions of the gender characteristics of the African that were designed to promote their exploitation and oppression. Consequently for the race, in the absence of any indigenous identifications, the movement naturally sought to promote the races acceptance and conformity to the dominant ideals of men and women. Not understanding that both forms represented the oppression of African people.

> Under these circumstances they cannot 'consider' him sufficiently clearly to objectivize him—to discover him 'outside' of themselves. This does not necessarily mean that the oppressed are unaware that they are downtrodden. But their perception of themselves as oppressed is impaired by their submersion in the reality of that oppression (Freire 1972:30).

Today, after centuries of being under the control and influence of the ruling class, being "submerged" and "absorbed" in the ideology that European/White represents all that is good and right, all races have been lulled into believing that equality can truly exist in a system that is naturally and inherently oppressive. Consequently in the individual and collective quests of the race to achieve what has been deemed "success" or "the American dream" each from the middle class who adapt dominant cultural values, ideologies, and practices and promote the oppression of their own to the inner-city youth who sell drugs in the neighborhood, or spit lyrics promoting such—actively engages in not only their own oppression but the oppression of their own. Each profits from his own exploitation and the exploitation of their own.

> At this level, their perception of themselves as opposites of the oppressor does not yet signify engagement in a struggle to overcome the contradiction; . . . but to identification with the opposite pole . . . (Freire 1972:30)

Although African Americans recognize, as Collins terms the "binary construction" of their racial identification—that is being opposite to what is defined as superior, because the race is immersed in the system itself, and views it as being all inclusive and unchangeable, many within the race do not recognize the struggle. Because the race is no longer being actively targeted by the power structure or supremacist organizations, because the race has been given a 'temporary pass' to the façade of equality, because the conditions of other people who face starvation, war, disease, and death daily—appear to be worse conditions than their own, the race has been conditioned to negate or disbelieve that a struggle even exists today.

That is one of the main reasons why revisiting slavery becomes essential to reaching consciousness. Without viewing "today" within its historical cradle, this generation is able to forget about the struggle that was driven by hate, oppression, exploitation, and exclusion, and allowed to believe that it is far removed from the conditions of slavery and legal exclusion, and therefore far removed from oppression and struggle. In such, consciousness becomes irrelevant/unnecessary because current conditions become a non-changeable reality. Subsequently then, either the people believe that there is no need for liberation because they are already "free" or they seek "their identification of liberation" through, legitimately or illegitimately gaining the material and power privileges of the dominant class. Ultimately though it is his envy of/for the position of the oppressor that forces an allegiance to and identification with, if not the oppressor than the privileges that the racial and class status affords.

> Even revolution, which transforms a concrete situation must confront this phenomenon. The oppressed, having internalized the image of the oppressor and adopted his guidelines, are fearful of freedom. Freedom would require them to eject this image and replace it with autonomy and responsibility (Freire 1972:31).

For most who do not have consciousness, even their identification and definition of liberation is skewed. If one forms an allegiance with the dominant class, his definition of liberation will be to have the freedom to assume the status of the oppressor—which means that he would only be free to oppress others for his own personal gain.

This reflects the confusion and condition of the new Hip-Hop collective. In their quest to gain the status of the oppressor, they actively engage in their roles as sub-oppressors. They are not themselves oppressors because they too are being exploited and oppressed by the ruling class. They sell their talent and image to the label/ruling class where it is exploited for the maximal profit of the label and the fulfillment of a ruling class agenda.

Without understanding the nature of the relationship, the artist believes that he is being given an opportunity that he would not otherwise have. The wage that the artist commands allows a level of economic power and social status that enables him to not only purchase the materials that make him to feel more aligned to the ruling class, but to minimize the stigma attached to his race by using class as a superseding factor. This is why purchasing "freed slave badges" such as: "the biggest diamond" (harvested in the European diamond mines in Africa), the fanciest car produced in Europe (as defined by the European), smoking the fanciest cigar (as defined by the European), drinking the fanciest champagne (as defined by the European), vacationing in the fanciest spot (as defined by the European), and buying the fanciest and most expensive home that he can afford—regardless of need (in predominantly White suburban neighborhoods)—becomes the primary goal of unconscious Rap artists. Even more significantly is the ultimate badge of receiving awards such as the American Music Awards, MTV Awards, and most importantly the Grammy Award that shows that his "work" is validated and accepted by the European.

It is the unconscious identification with the oppressor that makes seeking the acceptance of the dominant class through various means the principal goal of most African Americans who find wealth. Even in his own success, he defines and measures it not by his own cultural standard—those in which the music he promotes is supposed to be reflective of, but by the acceptance and validation of those outside of his race, ethnicity, and culture. This is the dominant idea of freedom and liberation from their own collective condition.

Nevertheless, individual (or even small collective) material success that is achieved within the confines of an inherently oppressive system, is not freedom. It does not represent true liberation because *true liberation* rests in the transformation of a system that promotes oppression. *True liberation* is where all, not just a miniscule few are free.

However, if it is the goal of the ruling class, who have in their unconsciousness state become oppressors, to maintain the status quo, to ensure the survival of a system that has yielded vast accumulations of wealth by the few—to continue to promote stereotypes that have historically been utilized to justify the oppression and enslavement of a people, then it is not plausible to conceive that the oppressor will ever change the conditions that he thrives upon. Therefore, it is up to those who are being exploited and oppressed to promote transformation—first from within.

Those who have been conditioned to accept their conditions are often fearful of transformation because they have been conditioned to be so. Again, they have not been given alternative frames of reference. They have been convinced of the consistency and finality of their own oppression. Consequently, just as slaves were convinced of their dependence on the slave master, conditioned that the repercussion for resistance, fleeing, or rebellion would be severe and unwanted, and were thus afraid to seek freedom, so are men afraid to seek liberation now.

> Freedom is acquired by conquest, not by gift. It must be pursued constantly and responsibly. . . . This, then, is the great humanistic and historical task of the oppressed: to liberate themselves and their oppressors as well. (Friere 1972:31)

Consciousness is essential to the acquisition of freedom. Liberating the mind must be the first step. But, consciousness does not ensure freedom. One can achieve consciousness and then consciously decide to continue to act as sub oppressors or oppressors by justifying their role. One can achieve consciousness and still consciously decide to remain apathetic to, passive participants in, and/or perpetuators or promoters of their own oppression by rationalizing their apathy. Ultimately, as stated, consciousness must act in concert with movement/action in order for liberation and freedom of the collective to be achieved. It will most certainly *not* be given by the ruling class.

Thus, the success of the few does not signify or represent freedom and liberation. The middle class (Black) and the few ruling class Blacks, as was argued by Frazier (1935) are not free. As long as the masses of the race remain in the bondage of exploitation and oppression, so is the entire race. That is the reality that is lost when few achieve. There simply are no exceptions or justifications to/for that. And whatever contributes to that oppression, whoever contributes to that oppression, must be held accountable. It does not matter if the contribution comes from outside of or from within the race, none can be given more or less weight or accountability—because in concert they ensure the destruction of the race. All contributors must be held accountable, this includes "Hip-Hop."

Those within the race should take responsibility for change. The artists should take responsibility for change because the message cannot be transmitted if there is no messenger. And if they cannot or will not sacrifice their individual identification of wealth and/or success, the masses must not support them at the peril of its own culture and stability. If change is to occur, if true freedom is to be achieved, the race cannot minimize the detrimental effects that it imposes on itself. It must evaluate the collective condition and understand what factors contribute to that condition. If it were to do so, the race would most likely find that if it removes itself—collectively—from the equation the destruction of the community would not be so imminent.

If artists did not rap about promoting the destruction of brothers and sisters, if those within the community did not purchase songs that glorify and promote its own destruction, if those in "da hood" did not sell drugs period, if those in "da hood" did not use the drugs that are distributed in our community, if all took education seriously, if the race went back to educating (truths to) our own, if there was not a mass acceptance of the stereotypes that have been assigned us, if the race did not participate in its own exploitation and oppression, if it would build its own economy and exercise the economic power that it has on the mainstream economy, if it did not hate itself, if it could establish meaningful relationships and not murder its own, genocide and racial cleansing would not be so imminent. Consciousness equals power.

CHAPTER 10

CONCLUSION

As I reach this place, I am lightened and burdened at the same time. This book has been one of my most difficult journeys. I have been "full" trying to cover all of the aspects that I believe contribute to and influence this relationship. I can admit that it has been a labor of love to address the limitations and potential arguments and criticisms, be as thorough and theoretical as possible without making it a difficult read, and to balance "my own gangsta" with my professionalism. Even more, it has been very difficult to try to maintain balance between the sentiments and emotions that I experienced during the different phases of this book—which included the shootings and deaths of people that I both know and love, volunteering at the Richmond City Jail where I am overwhelmed by the misguided brilliance and the vast numbers of my soldiers that reside there—with the purpose of this work. Sometimes it just "makes me wanna holla!" As I stated in the Introduction which was truly the alpha—the beginning of this process, this has most definitely been a "labor of love."

As I continued to write, I realized more and more that while this work may have been borne out of my sentiments about Hip-Hop this work is not about me and that is what helped me to complete it. It has taken nearly three years to complete, where in the middle of the third chapter, I stopped and did not look at it for months. I had also stopped listening to the radio and watching music videos, urban television stations, and the news as well. And in hindsight, I realized that that was my way of hiding from the reality that fueled my emotion and the purpose of this work—taking the "blue pill."

It was not until I was forced to listen to the radio as I rode from the outskirts of Philadelphia to my home in DC, that I was reminded of the purpose of this work, and it was profound. Just listening for the two hours that it took to get there reinforced the need to complete this work by reminding me of what people were consistently being force-fed and how truly detrimental the messages are. It was as if the spirit of the ancestors and my higher power forced me to *Juslissen*. By the time I arrived to my Mom's, I could not wait to open my laptop and revisit this work, and I did not stop until it was finished.

As I re-read the book, I realized that I have placed a heavy burden on the shoulders of the counterfeit Hip-Hop artists. So, I have to reiterate that by no means is this work intended to place all blame for the destruction of the community and people, on "Hip-Hop." Instead, it is designed to illustrate how truly relevant Hip-Hop has become to the deteriorating condition of a people and culture with hopes that like Dave Chappelle did, some will buy their souls back.

This work represents the "red pill." It has examined one of the principle means by/through which, even 143 years after slavery, the oppression, exploitation, subsequent destruction of the race is being carried forth—voluntarily. Still sadly, I know that the contents will be met with contradiction, criticism, and even hate—and is sure to be controversial for a variety of reasons. But what is burdensome is the possibility that those who should be nourished by this work, who should be enlightened and reach higher levels of consciousness through taking this "red pill," will either stay away from it all together or regurgitate it after it has been taken in, so that they do not have to "move."

I must say that I am prayerful that this work will truly promote the change that is essential to social transformation because I am tired of seeing my brothers and sisters die—daily, and I want to ensure "life" for my grandchildren. I am tired of going to the penitentiary and seeing nothing but my beautiful brothers who will never know freedom, or be too late to procreate. I am tired of seeing the black lips and broken out faces of adolescent and young adult chronic "weed heads" that do not believe that just like the crack head, they too are addicts. Tired of seeing the blank faces of those who do not realize how their habit/addictions destroy sperm quantity and quality and the quality of ovarian reserves—hence, diminishing their ability to reproduce. I am tired of seeing broken hearted women complaining about "no good men" and cold hearted men complaining about "gold digging" women as if that is the totality of our experiences. And I am tired of turning on the radio and hearing brothers and sisters celebrating and profiting from the promotion of all that I am tired of.

So, in spite of it all, I am firm in my stance and theory because I see the results of the influence and internalization of what I have herein deemed the "counterfeit" Hip-Hop as real constructions of a people everyday. With each body count, personal or communal, I see the results. With each promise to resolve conflict with a gun or violence, I see the results. With each student I lose to incarceration, I see the results. With each student I see get high, I see the results. Every time I hear a man call another man a nigga, or a woman a bitch, I see the results. In my Sociology of Marriage and the Family class where students cannot even fathom the concept of love and having healthy relationships, I see the result. When I walk into the cafeteria or the student lounge or at halftime at a game, and hear the music that is designed to promote all of these things blaring and the kids boppin' their heads and singing the hook with a committed passion, or staring at the television screen as if studying the video, I see the results.

Each time I go to the mall in my jeans and HBCU T-shirt and people follow me like I am a thief I see the results. With the escalation of racial tension, violence, and hate crimes in the United States, I see the results. Each time I attend a basketball game or a football game in the Pennsylvania State Athletic Conference and either get called a nigger or hear them refer to our team as "those niggers" not "niggaz"—"niggers," I see the results. With each acquittal of agents of the state who murder unarmed and unthreatening Black men because of a fear they feel justified to have, I see the result. In the growing lack of sympathy and empathy that mainstream society has for the condition of our community, and the quality and value of the lives of my people, with the tolerance and minimization of every lynching, monkey, thug, and assassination of the President of the United States story, I see the results.

But, again, it is not that I am completely blaming Hip-Hop because I am a social scientist who knows that there are a whole host of variables that work together to promote this beast. But, a part of changing the conditions requires that we not only look at the system, but that we also look at, analyze, and correct self. We must not let the 1960s blame the "the White man" or the most popular blame "the system" be our scapegoat or justification for our own contribution to our own oppression. Be it a direct or indirect function, oppression has now found a way to encourage us to destroy ourselves by funneling itself through music that we create, promote, consume, and identify with.

We must not allow ourselves to be used as puppets in our own destruction in our blatant ignorance, or failure to seek consciousness, or our failure to acknowledge and change what we do see. We must not let our envy of capitalist (material wealth) make us sell the stock that we have in our own spirits and souls. And we cannot wait and expect for those who profit from our exploitation to truly give us our freedom.

> We must also take self affirmative steps to transform our own world. We must carefully monitor the images to which we expose ourselves that perpetuate this destructive influence. . . . We must begin to develop . . . artistic productions . . . which deny the implication of our inferiority (Akbar 2006).

As mentioned in the previous chapter and as materialist theorists would argue, it is foolish to expect any entity who may be profiting from a system to stand up and acknowledge the truths in this book—to say "yeah this music is destructive so let's do something more positive." For even I will admit, that while I hope my spiritual and actualized connection to something greater than myself would force me to evaluate or even reevaluate if I were in their position, I know that it would be difficult to do as my hero, Dave Chappelle, did and give up the 50 million dollars to get my soul back. Therefore, we must stop waiting for those who profit from the oppression to save us and save ourselves by understanding the forces that are operating. This is just one of the many forces, but it is a dominant and prevalent one.

Some would argue that truths and realities are subjective. I argue that it is *not* the truth or the reality that is subjective, it is one's interpretation of the truth or reality that is subjective. The truth will always be the truth whether it is accepted or rejected, distorted, minimized, or denied. The truth will always remain nothing less than—the truth. The same can be said for reality. Herein lies the truth, the reality of a variable that strongly influences the condition of a people. The interpretation of this truth is up to you. My sentiments are most profoundly reflected in one of my favorite movies, The Matrix. The movie was so profound because through that one scene where Morpheus explains the matrix, it promoted the "inner-standing" that when we have existed and accepted "the matrix" (that is the elites ideology and control of world-views) as our reality for so long, truth, vision, and consciousness-as a choice, can sometimes be a hard pill to swallow. So, I'll wait right here, while, as you close the cover of this book, you run and get that cup of water.

BIBLIOGRAPHY

Akbar, N. (1996). *Breaking the Chains of Psychological Slavery*. Mind Productions. Tallahassee, Fl.
Anderson, C. (1994). *Black Labor, White Wealth: The Search for Power and Economic Justice*. Edgewood, MD. Duncan and Duncan.
Asante, M. (2000). *The Egyptian Philosophers: Ancient American Voices from Imhotep to Akhenaten*. Images. Chicago IL.
Asante, M. (2007). *The History of Africa: The Quest For Eternal Harmony*. Routledge. N.Y., NY.
Asante. M. (2005). *Race, Rhetoric & Identity: The Architecton of Soul*. Humanity Books. Amherst, NY.
Baca–Zinn, M., Eitzen, D. (2002). *Diversity in Families, 6th ed*. Boston, MA. Allyn and Bacon Press
Berberoglu, B. (1998). *An Introduction to Classical and Contemporary Social Theory: A Critical Perspective 2nd ed*. General Hall. Dix Hills NY.
Bogle, T. *Toms, Coons, Mulattoes, Mammies and Bucks*.
Broad, R. (2002). *Global Backlash: Citizen Initiatives for A Just World Economy*. Lanham, MD. Rowman and Littlefield Publishers.
Carrington, S. (2003). *The Sugar Industry and the Abolition of Slave Trade 1775–1810*. Gainsville, FL. University of Florida Press.
Clark–Hine, D. (1997) *A Shining Thread of Hope*. N.Y., NY. Broadway Books.
Collins, P. (2001). *Black Feminism and Black Feminist Thought*. N.Y., NY. Routledge
Collins, P. (2004). *Black Sexual Politics*. N.Y., NY. Routledge.
Cowan. R. (2003). *Cornel West: The Politics of Redemption*. Malden, MA. Blackwell Publishers.
Davis, A. (1999). *The Prison Industrial Complex*. AK Press. Oakland, CA.
Diawara, M. (1993). *Black American Cinema*. N.Y., NY. Routledge.
Disch, E. (1997). *Reconstructing Gender: A Multicultural Anthology*. Mountainview, CA. Mayfield.
Environmental Protection Agency, Report on Greenhouse Gasses, 2004

Feagin, J. (2001). *Racist America: Roots, Current Realities and Future Reparations.* Routledge Press, N.Y., NY.

Frazier, E. F. (1962). *Black Bourgeoisie.* London. MacMillan Press.

Gibson, J. (1987). *The Montgomery Bus Boycott and the Women Who Started It.* Knoxville, TN. University of Tennessee Press.

Gomes, R., Williams, L. (1995). *From Exclusion to Inclusion: The Long Struggle for African American Political Power.* Connecticut. Praeger Press.

Gunther, L. (1982). *Black Image: European Eyewitness Accounts of Afro-American Life.* Port Washington, NY. National University Press.

Hasaan, T. (2001). *Gendered Visions.* New Jersey. Africa World Press.

Hooks, B. (1994). *Outlaw Culture: Resisting Representations.* N.Y., NY. Routledge.

James, J., Sharpley–Whiting, T. (2001) *Black Feminist Reader.* Massachusetts. Blackwell Publishers.

Katz–Fishman, W., Scott, J. (2003). *The Globalization Toolkit.* Washington D.C.

Katz–Fishman, W. *Lecture Notes Handouts*

Kelly, R. 2003. *Freedom Dreams.* Boston, MA. Beacon Press.

Kuumba, M. (2001). Gender and Social Movements. Lanham, MD. Rowman and Littlefield Publishers.

Liska, G. (2003). *Twilight of a Hegemony: The Late Career of Imperial America.* NY, NY. University Press of America.

Macionis, J. (2001). *Sociology, 8th ed.* Upper Saddle River, NJ. Prentice Hall.

Mapp, E. (1972). *Blacks in American Films: Today and Yesterday.* Metuchen, N.J. Scarecrow Press.

Marx, K. (2001). *Wage-Labor and Capital Value, Price and Profit.* International Publishers. USA.

Massey, D. and Denton, N. (1993). *American Apartheid.* Harvard Press. Cambridge MA

Massood, P. (2003). *Black City Cinema: African American Urban Experiences in Film.* Philadelphia, PA. Temple University Press.

McGuire, P., McQuarie, D. (1994). *From the Left Bank to the Mainstream: Historical Debates and Contemporary Research in Marxist Sociology.* Dix Hills, NY. General Hall.

Mengara, D. (2001). *Images of Africa: Stereotypes and Realities.* Trenton, NJ. Africa World Press

Mies, Maria. (1996). *Patriarchy and Accumulation on A World Scale.* N.Y., NY. Zed Books.

Miller, D., Salkind, N.(1991) Handbook of Research Design and Social Movement 6th ed. CA. Sage Publications

Morris, M. (1975). The Politics of Black America. N.Y., NY. Harper and Row.

Murray, J. (1973). *To Find An Image: Black Films From Uncle Tom to Superfly.* NY, NY. Bobbs Merrill Company Inc.

Nahal, A. (2003). *Lecture Notes and Handouts.*

Nesby, J. (1982). *Black Images in American Films, 1896–1954.* Lanham, MD. University Press.

Rhoden, W. (2006). *Forty Million Dollar Slaves*. Crown Publishers. N.Y., NY.
Ritzer, George. (2000). *Modern Sociological Theory*. McGraw Hill. Boston, MA.
Roberts, D. (1999). *Killing The Black Body*. Vintage Books. N.Y., NY.
Schacht, R. (1971). *Alienation*. Garden City, NY. Anchor Books.
Schlosser, E. (1998). *The Prison Industrial Complex*. The Atlantic Monthly.
Somerville, P. (2000). *Social Relations and Social Exclusion: Rethinking Political Economy*. N.Y., NY. Routledge.
Staples, R. (1973). *The Black Woman in America: Sex Marriage and the Family*. Chicago, IL. Nelson Hall Publishers.
Staples, R. (1999). *The Black Family: Essays and Studies*. Belmont, CA. Wadsworth Publishing Company.
Strong, B., DeVault, C., Sayad, B., Cohen, T. (2001). *The Marriage and Family Experience*. Australia. Wadsworth.
Wallace, M. (1978). *Black Macho and the Myth of the Superwoman*. N.Y., NY. Dial Press.
Wallace–Sanders, K. (2002). *Naked, Neutered, or Noble: Extremes of the Black Female Body and the Problem of Photographic History*. Ann Arbor, Michigan. University of Michigan Press.
Williams, L. (2003). *The Constraint of Race: Legacies of White Skin Privilege in America*. Pennsylvania. PSU Press.
Willis, R.E. (1984). *The Black Woman, 2nd Ed.* Flint, MI.
Yanow, D. (2003). *Constructing Race and Ethnicity in America*. Armonk, NY. Sharpe
Zald, M., McCarthy, J. (1979). *The Dynamics of Social Movement*. Cambridge, MA. Winthrop Publishers.
Zeitlin, E. (1997). Ideology and the Development of Sociological Theory, 6th Ed. Theoretical Perspectives in Sociology. N.Y., NY. Prentice Hall.

www.ingramcontent.com/pod-product-compliance
Lightning Source LLC
Chambersburg PA
CBHW052048300426
44117CB00012B/2028